The Bible Speaks Today

Series editors: J. A. Motyer (OT)
John Stott (NT)
Derek Tidball (Bible Themes)

The Message of the Person of Christ

The Bible Speaks Today: Bible Themes series

The Message of the Person of Christ

The Word made flesh

Robert Letham

*Director of Research and senior lecturer
in Systematic and Historical Theology,
Wales Evangelical School of Theology, Bridgend*

Inter-Varsity Press

InterVarsity Press
P.O. Box 1400, Downers Grove, IL 60515-1426
Internet: www.ivpress.com
Email: email@ivpress.com

ISBN 978-0-8308-2416-8 (print)

ISBN 978-0-8308-8447-6 (digital)

Printed in the United States of America ∞

Library of Congress Cataloging-in-Publication Data
A catalog record for this book is available from the Library of Congress.

P   22   21   20   19   18   17   16   15   14   13   12   11   10   9   8   7   6   5   4   3   2   1
Y   31   30   29   28   27   26   25   24   23   22   21   20   19   18   17   16   15   14   13

Contents

Part 4: Christ risen

Part 5: Christ ascended

GENERAL PREFACE

THE BIBLE SPEAKS TODAY describes three series of expositions, based on the books of the Old and New Testaments, and on Bible themes that run through the whole of Scripture. Each series is characterized by a threefold ideal:

- to expound the biblical text with accuracy
- to relate it to contemporary life, and
- to be readable.

These books are, therefore, not 'commentaries', for the commentary seeks rather to elucidate the text than to apply it, and tends to be a work rather of reference than of literature. Nor, on the other hand, do they contain the kinds of 'sermons' that attempt to be contemporary and readable without taking Scripture seriously enough. The contributors to *The Bible Speaks Today* series are all united in their convictions that God still speaks through what he has spoken, and that nothing is more necessary for the life, health and growth of Christians than that they should hear what the Spirit is saying to them through his ancient – yet ever modern – Word.

ALEC MOTYER
JOHN STOTT
DEREK TIDBALL
Series editors

Author's preface

It has been a great privilege to write this book. No greater theme could be imagined. I am extremely grateful to the series editor, the Rev. Dr Derek Tidball, and senior commissioning editor (theological books) at Inter-Varsity Press, Dr Philip Duce, for inviting me to make a contribution to the series.

Over the years I have received a variety of influences too great and numerous to mention. If you have ever had the dubious pleasure of interacting with me at any length I am sure you have left your imprint upon my thinking in some way or other, as I am keen to learn from any intelligent and informed source. Any errors here are all my own.

Once again, my thanks are due to Derek Tidball and Philip Duce for their kind and highly efficient attention to detail, to the anonymous external reader for his or her generous comments, and to Alison Walley for her perceptive copy-editing. The faculty, students and staff of Wales Evangelical School of Theology (WEST) have provided a pleasant environment in which to work. Above all, I give thanks to God for my wife, Joan, for her constant love, care and encouragement, and to our children and grandchildren, scattered across the globe but connected via email, Skype, and increasingly costly air travel.

Robert Letham
Tuesday in Easter Week, 2013

Abbreviations

AB	Anchor Bible
ANF	*The Ante-Nicene Fathers*, ed. A. Roberts and J. Donaldson, rev. A. C. Coxe (repr., Grand Rapids: Eerdmans, 1969–73)
BDB	*A Hebrew and English Lexicon of the Old Testament*, ed. Francis Brown, S. R. Driver and Charles A. Briggs (2nd ed., Oxford: Clarendon Press, 1977)
CD	Karl Barth, *Church Dogmatics*, 14 vols., ed. G. W. Bromiley and T. F. Torrance (Edinburgh: T&T Clark, 1965–77)
DJG	*Dictionary of Jesus and the Gospels*, ed. Joel B. Green, Scot McKnight and I. Howard Marshall (Downers Grove and Leicester: IVP, 1992)
DPL	*Dictionary of Paul and His Letters*, ed. Gerald F. Hawthorne, Ralph P. Martin, Daniel G. Reid (Downers Grove and Leicester: IVP, 1993)
DLNTD	*Dictionary of the Later New Testament and Its Development*, ed. Ralph P. Martin and Peter H. Davids (Downers Grove and Leicester: IVP, 1997)
GCS	*Die griechische christliche Schriftsteller der ersten drei Jahrhunderte* (Berlin: 1897–)
HTR	*Harvard Theological Review*
ICC	International Critical Commentary
Institutes	John Calvin, *Institutes of the Christian Religion*, 2 vols., trans. Ford Lewis Battles, ed. John T. McNeill (Philadelphia: Westminster Press, 1960)
JBL	*Journal of Biblical Literature*
JTS	*Journal of Theological Studies*
LXX	Septuagint
NCBC	New Century Bible Commentary
NIBC	New International Biblical Commentary

9

NICNT	New International Commentary on the New Testament
NICOT	New International Commentary on the Old Testament
NIGTC	New International Greek Testament Commentary
NPNF[1]	*A Select Library of the Nicene and Post-Nicene Fathers of the Christian Church*, First Series, ed. P. Schaff (repr., Grand Rapids: Eerdmans, 1979)
NPNF[2]	*A Select Library of the Nicene and Post-Nicene Fathers of the Christian Church*, Second Series, ed. P. Schaff and H. Wace (repr., Grand Rapids: Eerdmans, 1979)
NT	New Testament
OT	Old Testament
PG	J. P. Migne *et al.* (eds.), *Patrologia Cursus Completus: Series Graeca* (Paris, 1857–66)
SJT	*Scottish Journal of Theology*
SWJT	*Southwestern Journal of Theology*
TNTC	Tyndale New Testament Commentary
WBC	Word Biblical Commentary
WTJ	*The Westminster Theological Journal*

Select bibliography

Achtemeier, E., *Minor Prophets I*, NIBC (Peabody: Hendrikson, 1996).

Allen, L. C., *The Books of Joel, Obadiah, Jonah and Micah* (Grand Rapids: Eerdmans, 1976).

Anderson, A. A., *2 Samuel*, WBC 11 (Dallas: Word Books, 1989).

Athanasius, *On the Incarnation*, *NPNF²*, vol. 4.

——, *Of Synods*, *NPNF²*, vol. 4.

——, *On the Decrees of the Synod of Nicaea*, *NPNF²*, vol. 4.

——, *Orations Against the Arians*, *NPNF²*, vol. 4.

Augustine, *De Spiritu et Littera*, *NPNF¹*, vol. 5.

Ayres, L., *Nicaea and Its Legacy: An Approach to Fourth-Century Trinitarian Theology* (Oxford: Clarendon Press, 2004).

Baillie, D. M., *God Was in Christ: An Essay on Incarnation and Atonement* (New York: Charles Scribner's Sons, 1948).

Barnes, M. R., 'Introduction', in M. R. Barnes (ed.), *Arianism After Arius: Essays on the Development of the Fourth Century Trinitarian Conflicts* (Edinburgh: T&T Clark, 1993), pp. xiii–xvii.

Barr, J., *The Garden of Eden and the Hope of Immortality* (Minneapolis: Fortress Press, 1992).

Barrett, C. K., *The Gospel According to St John: An Introduction with Commentary and Notes on the Greek Text* (2nd ed., London: SPCK, 1978).

Barth, K., *CD*.

Basil of Caesarea, *On the Holy Spirit*, *NPNF²*, vol. 8.

Bauer, D. R., 'Son of God', in *DJG*, pp. 769–775.

Bavinck, H., *Reformed Dogmatics: Volume 2: God and Creation* (Grand Rapids: Baker Academic, 2004).

Beale, G. K., *The Book of Revelation: A Commentary on the Greek Text*, NIGTC (Grand Rapids: Eerdmans, 1999).

Bratt, J. D. (ed.), *Abraham Kuyper: A Centennial Reader* (Grand Rapids: Eerdmans, 1988).

Brown, R. E., *The Gospel According to John (I-XII)*, AB (Garden City, New York: Doubleday, 1966).

Bobrinskoy, B., *The Mystery of the Trinity: Trinitarian Experience and Vision in the Biblical and Patristic Tradition*, trans. A. P. Gythiel (Crestwood: St Vladimir's Seminary Press, 1999).

Bruce, F. F., *Commentary on the Epistle to the Hebrews: The English Text with Introduction, Exposition and Notes* (London: Marshall, Morgan & Scott, 1964).

——, *The Epistles to the Colossians, to Philemon, and to the Ephesians*, NICNT (Grand Rapids: Eerdmans, 1984).

Calvin, J., *Sermons on Isaiah's Prophecy of the Death and Passion of Christ*, trans. and ed. T. H. L. Parker (London: James Clarke, 1956).

——, *Institutes*.

——, *Calvin's Commentaries: The First Epistle of Paul the Apostle to the Corinthians*, trans. D. W. Torrance and J. W. Fraser (Grand Rapids: Eerdmans, 1960).

Carlson, R. A., *David, the Chosen King: A Traditio-Historical Approach to the Second Book of Samuel* (Stockholm: Almquist & Wiksell, 1964).

Carson, D. A., *The Gospel According to John* (Leicester: IVP, 1991).

Collins, C. J., *Genesis 1–4: A Linguistic, Literary, and Theological Commentary* (Phillipsburg: Presbyterian & Reformed, 2006).

Colwell, E. C., 'A Definite Rule for the Use of the Article in the Greek New Testament', *JBL* 52 (1933), pp. 12–21.

Cyril of Alexandria, *On the Unity of Christ*, trans. J. A. McGuckin (Crestwood: St Vladimir's Seminary Press, 1995).

Daley, B., 'Leontius of Byzantium: A Critical Edition of His Works, with Prolegomena', D.Phil. dissertation, Oxford University, 1978.

Davies, W. D. and Allison, D. C., *A Critical and Exegetical Commentary on The Gospel According to Saint Matthew: Volume I*, ICC (Edinburgh: T&T Clark, 1988).

——, *A Critical and Exegetical Commentary on the Gospel According to Saint Matthew: Volume III*, ICC (Edinburgh: T&T Clark, 1997).

Davis, D. R., *2 Samuel: Out of Every Adversity* (Fearn: Christian Focus, 1999).

Davis, L. D., *The First Seven Ecumenical Councils (325–787)* (Collegeville: The Liturgical Press, 1990).

Dawson, G. S., *Jesus Ascended: the Meaning of Christ's Continuing Incarnation* (Edinburgh: T&T Clark, 2004).

de Margerie, B., *The Christian Trinity in History*, trans. E. J. Fortman and S. J. Petersham (Petersham: St Bede's Publications, 1982).

Di Berardino, A. (ed.), *Encyclopedia of the Early Church* (New York: Oxford University Press, 1992).

Driver, S. R., *The Book of Genesis: With Introduction and Notes* (London: Methuen, 1926).

Dunn, J. D. G., *Christology in the Making: A New Testament Inquiry Into the Origins of the Doctrine of the Incarnation* (2nd ed., London: SCM, 1989).

——, *The Epistles to the Colossians and Philemon: A Commentary on the Greek Text*, NIGTC (Grand Rapids: Eerdmans, 1996).

Ellingworth, P., *The Epistle to the Hebrews: A Commentary on the Greek Text*, NIGTC (Grand Rapids: Eerdmans, 1993).

Epiphanius, *The Panarion of Epiphanius of Salamis*, trans. F. Williams (Leiden: Brill, 2009).

Eusebius of Caesarea, *Against Marcellus*, GCS, 14.

Farrow, D., *Ascension and Ecclesia: On the Significance of the Doctrine of the Ascension for Ecclesiology and Christian Cosmology* (Edinburgh: T&T Clark, 1999).

Fee, G. D., *The First Epistle to the Corinthians*, NICNT (Grand Rapids: Eerdmans, 1987).

——, *Paul's Letter to the Philippians,* NICNT (Grand Rapids: Eerdmans, 1995).

Fesko, J. V., *Last Things First* (Fearn: Mentor, 2007).

Fitzmyer, J. A., *The Gospel According to Luke (I–IX)*, AB (New York: Doubleday, 1970).

——, *First Corinthians: A New Translation with Introduction and Commentary* (New Haven: Yale University Press, 2008).

France, R. T., *The Gospel According to Matthew: An Introduction and Commentary*, TNTC (Leicester: IVP, 1985).

Frend, W., *The Rise of the Monophysite Movement* (Cambridge: Cambridge University Press, 1972).

Gaffin Jr, R. B., *The Centrality of the Resurrection: A Study in Paul's Soteriology* (Grand Rapids: Baker, 1978).

Green, J. B., *The Gospel of Luke*, NICNT (Grand Rapids: Eerdmans, 1997).

Gregg, R. C. and Groh, E., *Early Arianism: A Way of Salvation* (Philadelphia: Fortress Press, 1981).

Grillmeier, A., *Christ in Christian Tradition: Volume One: From the Apostolic Age to Chalcedon (451)*, trans. J. Bowden (rev. 2nd ed., Atlanta: John Knox Press, 1975).

——, *Christ in Christian Tradition: Volume Two: From the Council of Chalcedon (451) to Gregory the Great (590–604): Part Two: The Church of Constantinople in the Sixth Century*, trans. T. Hainthaler and J. Cawte (London: Mowbray, 1995).

13

Grosseteste, R., *Robert Grosseteste: On the Six Days of Creation: A Translation of the Hexaëmeron by C. F. J. Martin*, Auctores Britannici Medii Aevi (Oxford University Press for the British Academy, 1996).

Gunton, C., 'Two Dogmas Revisited: Edward Irving's Christology', *SJT* 41 (1988), pp. 359–376.

Guthrie, D., *New Testament Theology* (Leicester and Downers Grove: IVP, 1981).

——, *The Letter to the Hebrews: An Introduction and Commentary*, TNTC (Leicester: IVP, 1983).

Gwatkin, H. M., *The Arian Controversy* (London: Longmans, Green and Co., 1914).

Hagner, D. A., *Matthew 1–13*, WBC 33A (Dallas: Word Books, 1993).

——, *Matthew 14–28*, WBC 33B (Dallas: Word Books, 1995).

Hanson, R. P. C., *The Search for the Christian Doctrine of God: The Arian Controversy 318-381* (Edinburgh: T&T Clark, 1988).

Hardy, E. R. (ed.), *Christology of the Later Fathers*, The Library of Christian Classics (Philadelphia: Westminster Press, 1954).

Harris, M. J., *Colossians & Philemon* (Grand Rapids: Eerdmans, 1991).

Hertzberg, H. W., *I & II Samuel: A Commentary* (London: SCM, 1964).

Hill, D., *The Gospel of Matthew* (London: Marshall, Morgan & Scott, 1972).

Holland, T., *Contours of Pauline Theology: A Radical New Survey of the Influences on Paul's Biblical Writings* (Fearn: Mentor, 2004).

Hoover, R. W., 'The Harpagmos Enigma: A Philological Solution', *HTR* 64 (1971), pp. 95–119.

Hughes, P. E., *A Commentary on the Epistle to the Hebrews* (Grand Rapids: Eerdmans, 1977).

——, *The True Image: The Origin and Destiny of Man in Christ* (Grand Rapids: Eerdmans, 1989).

——, *The Book of the Revelation: A Commentary* (Leicester: IVP, 1990).

Hurtado, L. W., 'Christology', in *DLNTD*, pp. 178–179.

——, 'Lord', in *DPL*, pp. 560–569.

——, 'Pre-Existence', in *DPL*, pp. 743–746.

Irenaeus, *Against Heresies*, *ANF*, vol. 1.

Kannengiesser, C., *Arius and Athanasius: Two Alexandrian Theologians* (Aldershot: Variorum, 1991).

Keener, C. S., *A Commentary on the Gospel of Matthew* (Grand Rapids: Eerdmans, 1999).

Kelly, J. N. D., *Early Christian Doctrines* (London: Adam & Charles Black, 1968).

Kim, S., *The Origin of Paul's Gospel* (Grand Rapids: Eerdmans, 1982).

——, *Paul and the New Perspective: Second Thoughts on the Origin of Paul's Gospel* (Grand Rapids: Eerdmans, 2002).

Kopecek, T. A., *A History of Neo-Arianism*, 2 vols. (Cambridge, MA: The Philadelphia Patristic Foundation Ltd., 1979).

Lane, A. N. S., *Justification by Faith in Catholic-Protestant Dialogue: An Evangelical Assessment* (London: T&T Clark, 2002).

Lane, W. L., *Hebrews 1–8*, WBC 47A (Dallas: Word Books, 1991).

Lebreton, J., *History of the Dogma of the Trinity: From Its Origins to the Council of Nicea*, trans. A. Thorold (8th ed., London: Burns Oates and Washbourne, 1939).

Letham, R., 'The Man-Woman Debate: Theological Comment', *WTJ* 52 (1990), pp. 65–78.

——, *The Work of Christ* (Leicester: IVP, 1993).

——, *The Holy Trinity: In Scripture, History, Theology, and Worship* (Phillipsburg: Presbyterian & Reformed, 2004).

Lightfoot, J. B., *Saint Paul's Epistle to the Philippians: A Revised Text with Introduction, Notes, and Dissertations* (London: Macmillan, 1881).

——, *Saint Paul's Epistle to the Galatians* (London: Macmillan, 1900).

Lindars, B., *The Gospel of John*, NCBC (Grand Rapids: Eerdmans, 1972).

Lloyd-Jones, D. M., *Studies in the Sermon on the Mount: Volume One* (London: Inter-Varsity Fellowship, 1959).

Lorenz, R., *Arius Judaizans? Untersuchungen Zur Dogmengeschichtlichen Einordnung Des Arius* (Göttingen: Vandenhoeck und Ruprecht, 1979).

McGrath, A. E., *Thomas F. Torrance: An Intellectual Biography* (Edinburgh: T&T Clark, 1999).

McGuckin, J. A., *St Cyril of Alexandria and the Christological Controversy: Its History, Theology, and Texts* (Crestwood: St Vladimir's Seminary Press, 2004).

McKane, W., *The Book of Micah: Introduction and Commentary* (Edinburgh: T&T Clark, 1998).

MacLeod, D., *The Person of Christ* (Leicester: IVP, 1998).

Marcellus of Ancyra, *Die Fragmente Marcellis*, GCS, 14.

____?, *Expositio Fidei*, PG, 25:199–208.

Marshall, I. H., *The Gospel of Luke: A Commentary on the Greek Text*, NICTC (Exeter: Paternoster Press, 1978).

Martin, R. P., *Philippians*, NCBC (Grand Rapids: Eerdmans, 1980).

——, *Carmen Christi: Philippians ii.5–11 in Recent Interpretation and in the Settting of Early Christian Worship* (Grand Rapids: Eerdmans, 1983).

Mascall, E. L., *Christ, the Christian and the Church* (London: Longmans, Green and Co., 1946).

Metzger, Bruce M. 'The Jehovah's Witnesses and Jesus Christ', *Theology Today* 10/1 (April 1953), pp. 65–85.

Meyendorff, J., *Christ in Eastern Christian Thought* (Crestwood: St Vladimir's Seminary Press, 1975).

Milligan, W., *The Ascension and Heavenly Priesthood of our Lord* (London: Macmillan, 1892).

Morris, L., *The Revelation of St John: An Introduction and Commentary*, TNTC (Grand Rapids: Eerdmans, 1969).

——, *The Gospel According to John: The English Text with Introduction, Exposition and Notes* (London: Marshall, Morgan & Scott, 1971).

——, *The Gospel According to Matthew* (Grand Rapids: Eerdmans, 1992).

——, *Luke: An Introduction and Commentary*, TNTC (Leicester: IVP, 1997).

Motyer, A., *Isaiah: An Introduction and Commentary*, Tyndale OT Commentary (Leicester: IVP, 1999).

Moulton, J. H., *A Grammar of New Testament Greek: Vol. I: Prolegomena* (3rd ed., Edinburgh: T&T Clark, 1908).

Nolland, J., *Luke 1–9:20*, WBC 35A (Dallas: Word Books, 1989).

——, *Luke 18:35–24:53*, WBC 35C (Dallas: Word Books, 1993).

——, *The Gospel of Matthew: A Commentary on the Greek Text*, NIGTC (Grand Rapids: Eerdmans, 2005).

Norris Jr, R. A., *The Christological Controversy* (Philadelphia: Fortress Press, 1980).

O'Brien, P. T., *Colossians, Philemon*, WBC 44 (Waco: Word Publishing, 1982).

——, *The Epistle to the Philippians*, NICTC (Grand Rapids: Eerdmans, 1991).

O'Collins, G., *The Tripersonal God: Understanding and Interpreting the Trinity* (London: Geoffrey Chapman, 1999).

Oswalt, J. N., *The Book of Isaiah: Chapters 1–39*, NICOT (Grand Rapids: Eerdmans, 1986).

——, *The Book of Isaiah: Chapters 40–66*, NICOT (Grand Rapids: Eerdmans, 1998).

Owen, J., 'A Discourse Concerning the Holy Spirit', in *The Works of John Owen*, vol. 3, ed. W. H. Goold (London: Banner of Truth, 1966).

Pelikan, J., *The Christian Tradition 1: The Emergence of the Catholic Tradition (100–600)* (Chicago: University of Chicago Press, 1971).

——, *The Christian Tradition 2: The Spirit of Eastern Christendom* (Chicago: University of Chicago Press, 1974).

Percival, H. R. (ed.), *The Seven Ecumenical Councils of the Undivided Church: Their Canons and Dogmatic Decrees, NPNF*[2] (Edinburgh: T&T Clark, 1997 reprint).

Person, R. E., *The Mode of Decision Making at the Early Ecumenical Councils: An Inquiry Into the Function of Scripture and Tradition at the Councils of Nicea and Ephesus* (Basel: Friedrich Reinhardt Kommissionsverlag, 1978).

Plummer, A., *A Critical and Exegetical Commentary on the Gospel According to S. Luke*, ICC (Edinburgh: T&T Clark, 1896).

Polanyi, M., *The Tacit Dimension* (Chicago: University of Chicago Press, 1958).

Prestige, G. L., *Fathers and Heretics* (London: SPCK, 1940).

——, *God in Patristic Thought* (London: SPCK, 1952).

Relton, H. M., *A Study in Christology: The Problem of the Relation of the Two Natures in the Person of Christ* (London: SPCK, 1917).

Richardson, A., 'Satan', in *Dictionary of Christian Theology*, ed. A. Richardson (Philadelphia: Westminster Press, 1969), p. 304.

Ridderbos, H. M., *The Epistle of Paul to the Churches of Galatia* (London: Marshall, Morgan & Scott, 1961).

——, *Paul: An Outline of His Theology* (Grand Rapids: Eerdmans, 1975).

Robertson, A., *A Critical and Exegetical Commentary on The First Epistle of St Paul to the Corinthians* (Edinburgh: T&T Clark, 1999).

Russell, N., *Cyril of Alexandria* (London: Routledge, 2000).

Satterthwaite, P. E., Hess, R. S. and Wenham, G. J. (eds.), *The Lord's Anointed: Interpretation of Old Testament Messianic Texts* (Carlisle: Paternoster, 1995).

Schaff, P., *The Creeds of Christendom*, 3 vols. (Grand Rapids: Baker, 1966).

Schilder, K., *Christ Crucified*, trans. H. Zylstra (Grand Rapids: Eerdmans, 1944).

——, *Christ on Trial*, trans. H. Zylstra (Grand Rapids: Eerdmans, 1950).

Schnackenburg, R., *The Gospel According to St John: Volume One: Introduction and Commentary on Chapters 1–4* (Tunbridge Wells: Burns & Oates, 1968).

Sellers, R. D., *The Council of Chalcedon: A Historical and Doctrinal Survey* (London: SPCK, 1953).

Simonetti, M., *La Crisi Ariana Nel IV Secolo* (Rome: Institutum Patristicum Augustinianum, 1975).

Smith, H. P., *A Critical and Exegetical Commentary on the Books of Samuel*, ICC (Edinburgh: T&T Clark, 1912).

Smith, J. M. P., *A Critical and Exegetical Commentary on Micah, Zephaniah, Nahum, Habakkuk, Obadiah and Joel*, ICC (Edinburgh: T&T Clark, 1912).

Smith, R. L., *Micah-Malachi*, WBC 32 (Waco: Word Books, 1984).

Stead, C., *Divine Substance* (Oxford: Clarendon Press, 1977).

Stibbs, A. M., *The Meaning of the Word 'Blood' in Scripture* (London: Tyndale Press, 1948).

Studer, B., *Trinity and Incarnation: The Faith of the Early Church*, trans. M. Westerhoff, ed. A. Louth (Collegeville: Liturgical Press, 1993).

Swete, H. B., *The Ascended Christ: a Study in the Earliest Christian Teaching* (London: Macmillan, 1910).

——, *The Apocalypse of St John: The Greek Text with Introduction, Notes and Indices* (London: Macmillan, 1906).

Thiselton, A. C., *The First Epistle to the Corinthians: A Commentary on the Greek Text*, NIGTC (Grand Rapids: Eerdmans, 2000).

Torrance, T. F., *Space, Time and Resurrection* (Grand Rapids: Eerdmans, 1976).

——, *Incarnation: The Person and Life of Christ* (Milton Keynes: Paternoster, 2008).

Von Rad, G., *Genesis: A Commentary* (rev. ed., Philadelphia: Westminster Press, 1961).

Vos, G., *The Teaching of the Epistle to the Hebrews* (Nutley: Presbyterian & Reformed, 1975).

Wainwright, A, *The Trinity in the New Testament* (London: SPCK, 1963).

Wallace-Hadrill, D., *Christian Antioch: A Study of Early Christian Thought in the East* (Cambridge: Cambridge University Press, 1982).

Waltke, B. K., *Genesis: A Commentary* (Grand Rapids: Zondervan, 2001).

Ware, T., *The Orthodox Church* (London: Penguin Books, 1969).

Watts, J. D. W., *Isaiah 1–33*, WBC 24 (Waco: Word Books, 1985).

——, *Isaiah 34–66*, WBC 25 (Waco: Word Books, 1987).

Weinandy, T. G., 'Cyril and the Mystery of the Incarnation', in T. G. Weinandy, *The Theology of St Cyril of Alexandria: A Critical Appreciation* (London: T&T Clark, 2003), pp. 23–54.

Wenham, G., *Genesis 1–15*, WBC 1 (Waco: Word, 1987).

Wesche, K. P. (ed.), *On the Person of Christ: The Christology of Emperor Justinian* (Crestwood: St Vladimir's Seminary Press, 1991).

Westcott, B. F., *The Gospel According to St John: The Greek Text with Introduction and Notes*, 2 vols. (London: John Murray, 1908).

Westermann, C., *Isaiah 40–66: A Commentary* (London: SCM, 1966).

——, *Genesis 1–11: A Commentary* (Minneapolis: Augsburg Publishing House, 1984).

——, *Genesis 12–36: A Commentary* (Minneapolis: Augsburg Publishing House, 1985).

Whybray, R. N., *Isaiah 40–66*, NCBC (Grand Rapids: Eerdmans, 1975).

Wildberger, H., *Isaiah 1–12: A Commentary* (Minneapolis: Fortress Press, 1991).

Wiles, M., 'Attitudes to Arius in the Arian Controversy', in M. R. Barnes (ed.), *Arianism After Arius: Essays on the Development of the Fourth Century Trinitarian Conflicts* (Edinburgh: T&T Clark, 1993), pp. 31–43.

Williams, R., 'The Logic of Arianism', *JTS* 34 (1983), pp. 56–81.

——, *Arius: Heresy and Tradition* (London: Darton, Longman, and Todd, 1987).

Witherington III, B., 'Lord', in *DLNTD*.

Wittgenstein, L., *Philosophical Investigations*, trans. G. E. M. Anscombe (3rd ed., Oxford: BasilBlackwell, 1989).

Wright, N. T., *The Epistles of Paul to the Colossians and to Philemon* (Leicester: IVP, 1986).

——, 'Harpagmos and the Meaning of Philippians ii.5–11', *JTS* 37 (October 1986), pp. 321–352.

——, *Jesus and the Victory of God* (London: SPCK, 1996).

Introduction

The purpose of this book is to show how the Bible, progressively and in ever greater detail, speaks to us of its central figure, Jesus Christ. In this, Scripture is rather like a detective novel, in which at first reading the plot may seem puzzling, the central figure a mystery, and the ultimate resolution obscure. However, cumulatively a case may be built up and the culprit eventually disclosed. Then, on second and subsequent readings, events that originally appeared tangential now come to possess much greater significance than first thought. So, as we read the OT, and allow its overall plan to emerge, we can find evidence accumulating that directs us to the one whom God promises, who will deliver humanity from sin, misery, and death. At first oblique, as time passes the picture comes into ever greater focus until eventually we are given to see that the deliverer and saviour foretold and promised throughout is this one person, Jesus Christ.

The requirements of the series mean that this is neither a biblical commentary nor a theological treatise, although at times it may seem like it is one or the other, or both. Some might want a more detailed discussion of the theological issues, a full-blown Christology dealing with questions raised in the modern era. We have considered some in passing, for example the kenosis theory, particularly in connection to Philippians 2. However this is the intention neither of the series nor of this volume. I expect to discuss these questions in detail in a forthcoming systematic theology. Nor does the book deal in detail with critical exegetical matters, except incidentally or where they are particularly relevant. Its purpose is to trace the development and fulfilment of the theme of the promised saviour. Involvement in intricate theological or exegetical questions would simply divert us from this central purpose. There are plenty of resources elsewhere that consider such questions in detail and do it far better than I could.

Although I have added a chapter on the historical development of the church's understanding of the person of Christ, this is not an exercise in historical theology either. The historical appendix is intended to demonstrate the continuity of the pronouncements of the early church councils with the teaching of the Bible. It stops at the second Council of Constantinople (AD 553). Conceivably I could have taken the story on to the third Council of Constantinople (680-81) in its assertion that Christ has two wills, a human and divine, for if Christ did not have a human will and so make human choices he could not have been man, and so we could not be saved. However, we stop at Constantinople II since the main issues in Christology were brought to a head at that time and resolved, and our purpose in this book is to present the case that this is in congruity with the teaching of both OT and NT.

My procedure in the following chapters is to investigate the main themes that Scripture develops, in the order in which they appear in the biblical account. I aim to focus on the main narrative that traces the emergence and unfolding of God's plan to glorify himself in the salvation of the human race. Here I stand with the church down the ages in affirming that this is the key to understanding what the Bible is all about.

This plan centres on his Son, Jesus Christ. From the earliest pages of the OT, Christ is the key. At first in vague and indistinct ways, the plot gathers pace and thickens. The OT, read appropriately, narrows the clues until all point in vivid clarity to this one person, identified by angels, by John the Baptist, by the apostles and – above all – by his life and works, his death, resurrection and ascension.

It shows us that the Bible is a concerted whole, a unity throughout. The notion that we can discard the OT as no longer relevant today is grossly mistaken. Jesus explained that the whole of OT Scripture referred to himself. One can travel to London from all parts of Great Britain, from some more directly than others. In turn, all parts of the Bible lead to Christ, some indirectly, others clearly and plainly.

In recent years, many scholars have supposed that each biblical book is to be considered as a separate and distinct entity. As a result, they miss any idea of an ongoing and developing plan. Underlying this mindset is the notion that Scripture is a purely human product, that predictive prophecy is effectively a myth, and that a meta-narrative – an overarching theme that transcends the particulars of the biblical documents – is to be ruled out of court. However, this is to regard the Bible in a radically different way than its own claims would suggest. This is hardly a scientific approach; rather it is an imposition on the text by the mind of the interpreter.

To my mind, it is tragic that so many see it this way. God gave the Bible to the church, not to universities – which did not exist at the time – nor to disinterested observers. Certainly, it is a collection of books open to academic inquiry. However, in the last three hundred years an increasing portion of the time of believing biblical scholars has been consumed in dealing with critical, technical questions, often posed by those with little or no personal stake in the salvation found in Christ. It is right and proper that these attacks be answered. Nevertheless, in the course of these considerations, concentration has come to be on critical minutiae, with the result that all too often scholars are unable to see the wood for the trees.

Consequently, writing this book has been simultaneously the best of times and the worst of times. On the one hand, it is a supremely enjoyable task to write about the Lord and Saviour of the church, the one who gave his life for us and our salvation, and who now – risen from the dead – rules the universe. I know of no greater subject and I am aware of no greater privilege. On the other hand, it has been a depressing exercise to see so much energy expended by so many biblical commentators with so little in the way of positive comment to show for it. I have been reminded of a tale my father told about one of his schoolteachers, when he was at school around the time of the First World War. This man, a favourite teacher of many as he was once goalkeeper for Bolton Wanderers, taught mathematics. Faced with incomprehension by students, he would sometimes grab them by the scruff of their neck, march them to the blackboard, and rub their faces in the chalk, yelling 'do you see it now, you duffer?'! Sadly, this obtuse refusal to see how the Bible speaks of Christ includes some who are known as evangelical. I have come to sympathize with David Steinmetz's suggestion that, in general and apart from technical matters, medieval and early modern exegesis is superior to that of the post-Enlightenment period.

The tale starts in the book of Genesis. There we read of the sad event of Adam's fall into sin. Notwithstanding, there is hope. God promises a reversal of the effects of the fall. At first the promise is generalized. The first intimation is God's declaration that the offspring of the woman will crush the serpent; one of the human race will deal a mortal blow to the enemy that brought the temptation. Later, the identity of the deliverer is disclosed as being one of Abraham's descendants, who is to be the means of worldwide blessing. Subsequently, Abraham learns that this person will be in the line of Isaac, not Ishmael, and in due course Isaac is informed that the line of Jacob, not Esau, is the chosen one. And so the focus narrows as we proceed. Once the whole biblical revelation is complete, and we have the NT as well as the OT, we can then look back and see these early pointers more clearly.

Without more ado, let's begin at the beginning.

Genesis 1:26–28; 3:1–13
Prologue

1. Adam as the image of God (Gen. 1:26–28)

a. The uniqueness of humanity's creation

In order to see the setting in which Christ is first foretold, we should recall the original situation in which the human race was placed. Then it will also be necessary to grasp what happened, the plight into which the race was plunged, so bringing about the need for a deliverer.

First of all, we note how the first chapter of Genesis presents the creation of human beings as distinctive. With the creation of humanity there is the unique deliberation *let us make man in our image*, expressing a plurality in God (26–27). Von Rad comments that this signifies the high point and goal to which all God's creative activity is directed. But what does it mean? A variety of interpretations have been advanced to explain it. Some suggest God is addressing the angels and placing himself in the heavenly court, so that humanity is made like the angels.[1] However, the beings he addresses are invited to share in creating humanity. The Bible elsewhere never attributes creation to the angels. Driver is one of those who suggest a plural of majesty, a figure of speech underlining God's dignity and greatness.[2] However, this view is no longer as favoured as once it was. Among other things, plurals of majesty are rarely if ever used with verbs. Westermann and many recent interpreters favour a plural of self-deliberation or self-encouragement. Yet few parallels support it. Wenham puts forward a variant on the theme of the heavenly court, only in his case he argues for God inviting the angels to witness the creation of humanity rather than

---

[1] Gerhard Von Rad, *Genesis: A Commentary* (rev. ed., Philadelphia: Westminster Press, 1961), pp. 57–59.

[2] S. R. Driver, *The Book of Genesis* (London: Methuen, 1926), p. 14.

to participate in it. He points to Job 38:4–7 where at creation the morning stars are said to sing together and all the sons of God (angels?) shout for joy.[3] This is closer to the mark.

However, Scripture has a fullness that goes beyond the horizons of the original authors. Many of the Fathers saw this statement as a reference to the Trinity. The original readers and the OT saints as a whole could hardly have understood it this way, since they lacked the knowledge that came later in the course of time, but the Fathers had a good eye for the trajectory of the text. Rabbinical commentators were often perplexed by this passage and other similar ones referring to a plurality in God (Gen. 3:22; 11:7; Isa. 6:8). Philo thought they referred to subordinate powers assisting God in the creation of humanity. Puzzling over these passages, Jewish interpreters tried to see them as somehow expressing the unity of God.[4] It is true that the NT never refers to Genesis 1:26 in connection with God, but that does not mean it is wrong to see here a forward-looking reference to the Trinity. The NT does not refer to *everything* but it does give us the principle that the OT contains in seed form what is more fully made known in the New. That is why we may look back to the earlier writings much as at the end of a detective mystery we reread the plot seeing clues that we missed the first time which now are given fresh meaning by our knowledge of the whole. In other words, in terms of the *sensus plenior* (the fuller sense or meaning) of Scripture, God's words here attest a plurality in God, a plurality later expressed in the doctrine of the Trinity. The original readers would not have grasped this but we, with the full plot disclosed, can revisit the passage and see there the clues.

In tandem with this I have suggested elsewhere, commenting on Genesis 1:26–27, that

> man exists as a duality, the one in relation to the other . . . As for God himself . . . the context points to his own intrinsic relationality. The plural occurs on three occasions in v. 26, yet God is also singular in v. 27. God is placed in parallel with man, made in his image as male and female, who is described both in the singular and plural. Behind it all is the distinction God/Spirit of God/ speech of God in vv. 1–3 . . . this relationality will in the development of biblical revelation eventually be disclosed as taking the form of a triunity.[5]

[3] Gordon J. Wenham, *Genesis 1–15*, WBC 1 (Waco: Word, 1987), p. 28.
[4] Arthur Wainwright, *The Trinity in the New Testament* (London: SPCK, 1963), pp. 23–26.
[5] Robert Letham, 'The Man-Woman Debate: Theological Comment', *WTJ* 52 (1990), p. 71.

I refer there to similar comments by Karl Barth.[6] The relational God made humanity in his own image, also as a relational being.

b. Poetic parallelism highlights humanity's importance

Much debate has surrounded the nature of Genesis 1. Its account of creation is presented in prose; the repeated use of the *waw-*consecutive plus the imperfect tense is the customary form of historical narrative in the OT. However, the unusual use of words and the unique nature of the subject matter have led scholars like Jack Collins to describe the chapter as 'exalted prose narrative'.[7] It is a description of an ordered process by which God created, formed and adorned the world. It does not include everything; the creation of the angels is omitted. It does not explain everything that it includes either. Yet Christ and the apostles teach that Adam was an historical person and, moreover, the first human being; the parallel and contrast between Adam and Christ are crucial to Paul's understanding of salvation.

What stands out from the rest of the chapter is the creation of man, male and female. It is signalled by the sudden and unexpected emergence of poetry. Hebrew poetry is marked by parallelism, in which a line is repeated or contrasted by a mirroring line. It is present in verse 27:

> So God created man in his own image,
> in the image of God he created him;
> male and female he created them.

This poetic insertion into a narrative that, however unusual, is essentially prose, is as if Moses is highlighting this point in fluorescent yellow, drawing our attention to it, and affirming that this above all is the centrepiece of the whole picture. The goal towards which creation moved has now been reached. Humanity is the crown of creation. The world, the universe, was brought into existence by God for the very purpose that humans might live there and govern it. The world which at first was empty, dark, formless and wet – unfit for human habitation – is now formed, dry, lit by sun and moon, populated by vegetation and creatures, a place now suitable for the prize specimen of creation to take his place at its head.

---

[6] Karl Barth, *CD*, III/1, p. 196.

[7] C. John Collins, *Genesis 1-4: A Linguistic, Literary, and Theological Commentary* (Phillipsburg: Presbyterian & Reformed, 2006), pp. 36, 44, 71, 83, 229.

c. The image of God

What does it mean that humans were created in the image of God? What *is* the image of God? Since this is the focus of Genesis 1, the goal to which it is moving, what does it mean? In the NT, Paul says that believers are being renewed in the image of God in knowledge, righteousness and holiness (Eph. 4:24; Col. 3:10). The question of whether fallen humanity is still the image of God and, if so, in what sense this is true, has been debated at great length through the years. Some statements in the Bible suggest that this is true of all people, regardless of their relationship to God,[8] whereas these Pauline passages imply that it is true only for those renewed by the Holy Spirit. Theologians have understood this dilemma in terms of a twofold aspect to humanity as the image of God, speaking of the image in the broader sense, in which all people participate, and in the narrower sense, which relates only to Christian believers. This has appeared unsatisfactory in a range of ways. The resolution is to be found in terms of redemptive history. In doing so, we are retrieving what the Greek fathers had taught centuries earlier.[9]

d. Humans were created in Christ the image of God

The text of Genesis states that Adam and his wife were created *in* the image of God. The image of God in which they were created is identified for us in the NT. Paul points out that it is Christ who *is* the image of God (2 Cor. 4:4; Col. 1:15). In discussing the resurrection of the body, he compares Adam with the risen Christ. From Adam we inherit the image of the earthly, in weakness and mortality, whereas in the risen Christ we receive the image of the heavenly, powerful and immortal, under the direction and domination of the Holy Spirit (1 Cor. 15:45–49).[10] Paul is saying that Christ as the second Adam *is* the image of God. Adam was created *in* Christ, then fell from that condition, but now, in grace, we are being renewed in the image of God, *in Christ the second Adam*, and thus in knowledge, righteousness and holiness. The author of Hebrews says much the same thing. In the first paragraph, the letter states that the Son, by whom God has spoken his final and ultimate word, is 'the brightness of his [God's] glory and the express image of his being'.[11]

---

[8] See 1 Cor. 11:7; Jas 3:9.

[9] Philip Edgcumbe Hughes, *The True Image: The Origin and Destiny of Man in Christ* (Grand Rapids: Eerdmans, 1989), pp. 281–286.

[10] Richard B. Gaffin Jr, *The Centrality of the Resurrection: A Study in Paul's Soteriology* (Grand Rapids: Baker, 1978).

[11] Heb. 1:3.

In each of these passages in the NT, the author has the first chapter of Genesis at the back of his mind. In 2 Corinthians 4:4–6 Paul compares God's speech at creation when he said 'Let there be light!' to his shining in our hearts to give the light of the knowledge of his glory in the face of Jesus Christ. In Colossians 1, as soon as Paul has declared that the Son is 'the image of the invisible God' he adds that he is 'the first-born of all creation. For by him all things were created'.[12] In turn, the writer of Hebrews, in stating that the Son is the express image of God's being has in the immediately preceding context affirmed that he is the one through whom all things were made (Heb. 1:2–3).

Therefore from the very first God's ultimate purpose was foundational to all that he did – all things were moving under his direction to the goal he had set for them, to be headed up under the lordship of Christ. The incarnation was planned from eternity as an integral part of the whole work of salvation in Christ.[13]

e. Christ the creator

Flowing from the biblical presentation of creation as a work of the whole Trinity comes the NT assertion of the creation mediatorship of Jesus Christ. This is a theme I have discussed elsewhere.[14] It is found in John 1, where the Logos is described as existing 'in the beginning', a phrase strongly reminiscent of Genesis 1:1. This Logos, who was with God and who was God, who became flesh and lived among us, is also described as the creator of all things (John 1:3). This follows from his being life itself; he is not merely the author of life, as if life were something independent and autonomous, but he himself *is* life (John 1:4). His creating is free but it is also an expression of who he is.

Paul expounds a similar theme in Colossians 1:16–17, where he affirms that 'all things were created in him, things in heaven and on earth, things visible and invisible, whether thrones and dominions, rulers and authorities, all things were created through him and to him. And he is before all things, and in him all things hold together.' In this Paul argues that Christ as the pre-existent Son (cf. Col. 1:13) is the creator of the universe. 'All things' is comprehensive, excluding

---

[12] Col. 1:15–16.

[13] This is quite different from the speculative claim that Christ would have become incarnate if Adam had not sinned; if the incarnation and atonement were determined eternally, as the Bible testifies, so too was the fall of Adam. For a fascinating discussion of the relationship between Genesis 1 – 2 and the final purposes of God see John V. Fesko, *Last Things First* (Fearn: Mentor, 2007).

[14] Robert Letham, *The Work of Christ* (Leicester: IVP, 1993), pp. 197–209.

nothing. Personal and impersonal, angelic and human, animal and plant – all owe their existence to the Son. Moreover, not only did he create them all but he did so in such a way that he is their head. Creation was made *in Christ*. In turn, the cosmos has a purpose. It is held together by the Son. He sustains it at every moment and directs it towards the end he intends for it. That end is himself. All things were created and are sustained *for Christ*. The reason the universe exists is for the glory of Christ, the Son of God. The goal towards which it is heading is conformity to him. As Paul wrote to the Ephesians, all things will be under the headship of Christ for eternity (Eph. 1:10).[15]

The author of Hebrews describes the Son in whom God's final word has been given as the one who created the ages (Heb. 1:2) and who continues to uphold all things by his powerful word, directing them to the end he has eternally intended (Heb. 1:3). As has been widely noted, the imagery is not static, as if he was carrying the world as a dead weight, but dynamic, directing it purposefully to its destined goal. There is more than a hint here that the author is identifying Christ, the Son, with the word spoken at creation (cf. Gen. 1:5).

Furthermore, in the great vision in Revelation 5, John sees that the Lamb alone is both able and worthy to open the seals and so to govern world affairs. He is sovereign over all that happens in the world and to his church. The rest of the book spells this out in terms of judgment on the world and ultimate victory for the persecuted church.[16]

2. The fall: unity disrupted (Gen. 3:1–13)

a. God and humanity: distinct yet compatible

Since Adam was created in the image of God, he was made for communion with God, to rule God's creation on his behalf. This is clear from Genesis 1, where the man and his wife were given dominion over the earth, over all that God had created. Psalm 8:3–8 reflects on this poetically.

> When I look at your heavens, the work of your fingers,
>   the moon and the stars, which you have set in place,
> what is man that you are mindful of him,
>   and the son of man that you care for him?

[15] Letham, *Work of Christ*, pp. 198–202.
[16] See, *inter alia*, G. K. Beale, *The Book of Revelation: A Commentary on the Greek Text*, NIGTC (Grand Rapids: Eerdmans, 1999).

> Yet you have made him a little lower than the
>   heavenly beings
>   and crowned him with glory and honour.
> You have given him dominion over the works
>   of your hands;
>   you have put all things under his feet,
> all sheep and oxen,
>   and also the beasts of the field,
> the birds of the heavens, and the fish of the sea,
>   whatever passes along the paths of the seas.

Humans are therefore creatures made by God, not eternal or intrinsically immortal but the highest creatures, to whom and for whom the world was made. As a finite creature the human being has been given the great privilege of governing the earth on behalf of his creator. At the same time he was also connected to God, made in his image and living in communion with him. The implication of Genesis 2 is that there was regular communication between God and Adam before the fall. God charged the man and the woman verbally to multiply and have dominion (Gen. 1:28–30), instructed Adam to abstain from the tree of the knowledge of good and evil, while being free to eat of all other trees in the garden (Gen. 2:16–17), and brought to him the woman he had made for him (Gen. 2:21–22). In rather different circumstances, after the fall, he addressed the errant pair (Gen. 3:8–9).

b. Adam's task and God's covenant

Adam was taken from the earth. His name means both man and earth. His task was to till the ground in pursuance of the mandate given by God at creation (Gen. 2:15). At the same time, God breathed life into him directly (Gen. 2:7). So Adam was both earthly and material, while simultaneously related to God. His task was mainly agricultural, although as Fesko indicates, it had both priestly and kingly foci.[17] Many theologians have taken this to represent a covenant, called variously a covenant of nature or creation, a covenant of life or a covenant of works. Each of these terms highlights a distinct aspect of Adam's state in creation. Of course, the word covenant is not there in the text of Genesis. However, all the ingredients of later covenants are present. There are two parties – God and Adam. Paul argues that Adam represented the entire human race and so the parties are effectively God and the whole gamut of

[17] Fesko, *Last Things.*

humanity in solidarity with him. God's grace to Adam and the race is superabundantly evident – a vast profusion of food, beauty in abundance, fellowship with God, and the provision for Adam of a wife. Moreover, God gives Adam a law, prohibiting him from eating the fruit of the tree of knowledge of good and evil. There is a clear warning of the consequences of disobedience. In the Bible where a warning or a promise is given by God we are usually to understand a corresponding promise or warning is implied. In this case, the implication is that whereas death would certainly follow disobedience, since Adam would be cutting himself off from his creator, who is life itself, continued faithfulness would lead Adam into the fullness of life in union and communion with God. There was also a sacrament – the tree of life. This tree is connected with eternal life. After the fall, Adam and Eve are prevented from returning to the garden in case they should eat of this tree and so live forever. In Revelation, the tree of life is seen as present for the healing of the nations (Rev. 22:1–2).

c. Sin enters: all is changed

Sin entered; Genesis 3 tells the sorry tale.[18] Adam and his wife disobeyed God's law and reaped the consequences, ultimately found in death. An immediate result of human sin was a disrupted relationship with the created order. Adam was placed in the garden to till the ground, to bring it into subjection.[19] Now that sin entered, Adam's work, intended as a blessing, became a curse, the land yielding thorns and thistles. Work became hard labour, the fruits of human toil paltry in comparison with what they would and could have been (17–19).

Hebrews 2:5–9 reflects on the poetic account of the place of the human race in creation found in Psalm 8. God put everything under its feet. However, this goal is not yet realized; we do not yet see everything subject to human beings. It is all too evident in the world around us. The environment is in a precarious position. Unwise governmental policies, unchecked exploitation of natural resources, disruptive and destructive wars, the repression of human enterprise by totalitarian dictatorships and meddlesome, domineering bureaucracies, have all contributed to severe problems that affect the quality of life, the food chain, and much more. Above all, the human race

---

[18] The absence of terms for sin, guilt or rebellion need not imply that Genesis 3 cannot be read as a record of disobedience. The presence or absence of a concept is not determined by the vocabulary alone (Collins, *Genesis 1–4*, p. 155).

[19] This was an agricultural task, although there is good evidence that it was not limited to that but was primarily a function of a priest-king. See Fesko, *Last Things*.

cannot exercise self-control. Constant strife, unchecked self-interest, societal breakdown, and violent religious fanaticism run rampant. Since we cannot even exercise discipline over our own inclinations, how can we bring the cosmos into godly subjection? Thankfully this is not the whole story. The rest of this book will show how this dire problem is overcome.

Part One
Christ promised

Genesis 3:15
1. The offspring of the woman

The Lord God said to the serpent,

> 'Because you have done this,
>> cursed are you above all livestock
> and above all the beasts of the field;
>> on your belly you shall go,
> and dust you shall eat
>> all the days of your life.
> *I will put enmity between you and the woman,*
>> *and between your offspring and her offspring;*
> *he shall bruise your head,*
>> *and you shall bruise his heel.'* (14–15)

1. Warfare foreshadowed but victory promised

Against the bitter background of the fall of the human race into sin, with the introduction of death and misery into a world hitherto blissfully pleasant, there comes a ray of hope. The OT unfolds a contrasting picture of deliverance by the God against whom Adam had so inexplicably rebelled. No sooner had he and the woman been cast out of the garden than God springs into action. He launches a narrative to trump the destructive misery of sin.

a. Perpetual conflict between Satan and the human race

The serpent, the agent of the temptation, is hardly to be understood as simply a literal serpent acting on its own behalf, with the ability to speak biblical Hebrew. Serpents do not eat dust, as the penalty on this creature in part contained. Rather, eating dust signifies defeat and utter humiliation.[1] The implication is that the serpent represents a greater force ranged against humanity.[2] The traditional interpretation of the church, reflecting earlier Jewish understandings, that behind all this is Satan is well founded.[3] Satan is a fallen angel, cast out of heaven due to overweening pride.[4] God's central purposes for the universe are not centred in angels but in the human race, with angels in a subordinate role. The incarnation is proof of that. As the author of Hebrews states, it is not to angels that the coming world, the eternal kingdom, has been subjected, but to mankind (Heb. 2:5–9). Hence, Satan's jealousy is directed against humanity: *I will put enmity between you and the woman, and between your offspring and her offspring*. It is seen in the temptation of Adam and Eve. It will surface again, time after time, throughout the pages of the Bible and through the course of human history. Constant warfare is to occur.

b. Satan will cause significant damage to the human race

You shall bruise his heel. The name 'Satan' means adversary, opponent.[5] Satan opposes the human race largely by promoting discord and conflict. Daniel 10 – 11 provides a glimpse behind the scenes of world history, vast angelic powers in constant combat impacting the course of international politics, the rise and fall of kingdoms and empires. Strife and disorder is the business of the fallen angels, stirred up in an attempt to overthrow God's purposes but opposed by Michael and other mighty spirits ranged on the side of God and his people. Humankind will be severely battered or damaged by the malignant vindictiveness and jealousy of the serpent.[6] The verb denotes striking, resulting in wounds. This

---

[1] C. J. Collins, *Genesis 1–4: A Linguistic, Literary, and Theological Commentary* (Phillipsburg: Presbyterian & Reformed, 2006), p. 163; Bruce K. Waltke, *Genesis: A Commentary* (Grand Rapids: Zondervan, 2001), p. 93.

[2] S. R. Driver, *The Book of Genesis: With Introduction and Notes* (London: Methuen, 1926), p. 48.

[3] G. J. Wenham, *Genesis 1–15*, WBC 1 (Waco: Word, 1987), p. 80; Waltke, *Genesis*, p. 90.

[4] Rev. 12:7–9. See A. Richardson, 'Satan', in A. Richardson and John Bowden (eds.), *Dictionary of Christian Theology* (Philadelphia: Westminster Press, 1969), p. 304; Waltke, *Genesis*, p. 90. Besides this passage, Genesis shows significant interest in interaction between angels and the human race; see Gen. 16:7–14; 18:1 – 19:22; 28:10–12, besides Gen. 6:1–4, one of the main interpretations of which is of sexual union between angels and human women.

[5] *BDB*, p. 966.

[6] See G. Von Rad, *Genesis: A Commentary* (rev. ed., Philadelphia: Westminster Press, 1961), p. 92.

opposition was to be repeated over and over again[7] and would reach its pinnacle when Christ came. Apparently, it triumphed when he was nailed to the cross, died and was buried in the tomb.

c. Satan will be dealt a mortal blow by a descendant of the woman

He shall bruise (crush) your head. The singular is significant here, as Collins indicates, for in biblical Hebrew where singular pronouns are present a singular reference is meant rather than a collective one. So in this instance the reference is to a particular individual rather than to the human race in general.[8] This is reinforced by the singular pronoun for the woman's offspring in the previous clause. In short, a member of the human race was to inflict a decisive and deathly blow to the serpent. This offspring of the woman would overcome and annul the damage caused by the serpent, the consequences of the fall and its aftermath.[9] Lack of productivity, sorrow and toil, bodily decay and death intruded themselves upon Adam and his descendants as a consequence of God's just judgment on the race for sin (3:17–19). Greatly increased pain in childbirth accrued for the woman (3:16). However, at some future stage, this person was to retrieve the situation and vanquish the serpent. This is an oracle of judgment on the serpent and all who operate within its circle. By the same token, because it speaks of the serpent's overthrow it is a message of hope and expectation for the human race, against which the serpent had set itself.[10] If a nation is at war with a malicious opponent, news of that opponent's defeat signals the nation's triumph.

2. The promised victory fulfilled

This promise was to be fulfilled when Jesus, born of a woman, took Adam's place, overcame temptation, cast out the demons, healed the sick, died on the cross to atone for human sin, and finally defeated death by his resurrection to life everlasting. Whereas Adam was tempted in a beautiful garden and succumbed, the woman's offspring was tempted in a barren desert and remained faithful throughout. The consequences of sin were all routed by his public conquest of the demons, his binding of Satan, and his triumph over death and

[7] Wenham, *Genesis 1–15*, p. 80.

[8] Collins, *Genesis 1–4*, p. 156, *contra* C. Westermann, *Genesis 1–11: A Commentary* (Minneapolis: Augsburg Publishing House, 1984), p. 260–261. Waltke favours both singular and collective senses (*Genesis*, p. 93).

[9] *Contra* Von Rad, *Genesis*, p. 93, who provides no convincing reason for his scepticism, nor considers other instances of 'seed' (offspring) in Genesis.

[10] Driver, *Genesis*, p. 48.

sin. Laborious toil was transformed into fruitful work, with increases thirtyfold, sixtyfold, a hundredfold (Matt. 13:1–23). The pains of childbirth (3:16) were to be the means through which final deliverance came, through his covenant with Abraham and his offspring, through the birth of the incarnate Son by the blessed virgin, and through the faithful raising of covenant children (1 Tim. 2:12–15). Death would be swallowed up by life.

So much was as yet hidden from Adam and his successors, for it was unveiled only gradually, bit by bit over the course of a tortuous history in which human sin was shown to be still very much alive and well.[11] Just as in personal circumstances God often leaves us in suspense, calling us to exercise faith in him while living to an extent in the dark, so here the full identity of his plan of deliverance appears like a distant light at the end of a long and murky tunnel. The point to note at this stage is that God's declaration of final victory states that it is by a member of the human race that this was to be attained – the offspring of the woman. Yet humans were all under the just judgment of God for their sin. How could this be? This is the story of the unfolding saga of God's mighty salvation.

---

[11] See T. Desmond Alexander, 'Messianic Ideology in the Book of Genesis', in P. E. Satterthwaite, R. E. Hess and Gordon J. Wenham (eds.), *The Lord's Anointed: Interpretation of Old Testament Messianic Texts* (Carlisle: Paternoster, 1995), pp. 19–39, cited in Collins, *Genesis 1–4*, p. 157; Wenham, *Genesis 1–15*, pp. 80–81.

Genesis 12:1–3
2. The seed of Abraham

1. A call to discipleship (1)

World history has marched on for an indefinite period. Generation after generation has passed by. Cataclysmic events have thrown the world into turmoil (Gen. 6:11 – 9:17; 11:1–9). One thing has remained constant. The penalty of sin has been meted out down the years; death has been the constant companion of the race. The genealogies of the early chapters of Genesis proclaim it loud and clear – 'and he died' is the continual refrain. Then suddenly and, we must surely believe, totally unexpectedly, a man called Abram receives a command from the Lord. It is an imperative. It comes out of the blue. No-one has prayed for it. It is entirely from the side of God. He takes the initiative, he makes promises, he effects the outcome.

Abram had lived in Ur of the Chaldees, a thriving, stable city with a developed culture and a literate population. According to Joshua, his family were idolaters (Josh. 24:2). We know that moon worship was common in Ur; it may well have been that Abram was raised to worship the moon. Into this context, so different from what he later came to know, God called him to leave and go to a far off land which he would show him at a later date. According to Stephen, in his final speech before his martyrdom, when the call came Abram's father and the entire entourage had left for Canaan already (Acts 7:2–4). However, they never got there. On the way they stopped off in Haran, to the northwest, on the route that curved around the north of the vast desert area and there they stayed.

We cannot be sure whether the call reached Abram when he was in Haran or at an earlier time.[1] It is conceivable that it refers to an

[1] S. R. Driver thought it came in Haran (S. R. Driver, *The Book of Genesis: With Introduction and Notes* [London: Methuen, 1926], p. 144). So do Westermann (Claus Westermann, *Genesis 12–36: A Commentary* [Minneapolis: Augsburg Publishing

event that had occurred when the family was in Ur. What it contained was the summons to Abram to leave his country, the familiar surroundings and the comfortable culture to which he and the clan were accustomed. This was inevitably a huge wrench and it was to remain so for the rest of his life, for he never was able to settle. As the author of Hebrews puts it, he went out not knowing where he was going, his focus on the promises God gave him, seeking a city that has foundations, whose reality would only appear at some time in the indeterminate future (Heb. 11:8–16). If you have ever left your homeland and emigrated you will sense something of the disturbance of such a change. Sometimes even moving from one area of the country to another can dislocate us for a while; the commonplace everyday features are no longer there.

Moreover, Abram was to abandon his clan and his father's house. Even those social units that provide the closest and firmest cohesion were not to get in the way of God's calling. After leaving Ur this was the one human entity that exerted the greatest gravitational pull on Abram's life, yet he was to leave it. Later, Jesus required his disciples to forsake all and follow him (Matt. 9:9; 16:24; John 10:4; 12:26).

Did Abram wait until his father died before moving on from Haran? Stephen seems to think so (Acts 7:2–4), although the chronology of the Massoretic text indicates that Terah was alive for another seventy-five years. However, there is no evidence that he was still living when, later, Abraham sent his servant to obtain a wife for Isaac from his own clan in Haran (Gen. 24:1–61).

2. Covenant promises (2–3)

The focus, however, is not on Abram but on the covenant promises of the Lord. In particular, his sovereignty is in the foreground. Not only does the Lord call Abram but his initiative and power are clearly displayed in everything that happens. Note the repeated 'I will . . .' *Go . . . to the land that I will show you. And I will make of you a great nation, and I will bless you and make your name great . . . I will bless those who bless you, and him who dishonours you I will curse.* These future actions are not due to Abram's initiative; they are free and sovereignly effected by the Lord. From first to last, he is in charge. As Von Rad commented,

> Why God's choice did not fall upon Ham or Japheth, but rather upon Shem, and within Shem, upon Arpachshad, and within the

House, 1985], p. 147) and Wenham (Gordon J. Wenham, *Genesis 1–15*, WBC 1 [Waco, Texas: Word, 1987], p. 274). Waltke thinks the call came when Abram was still in Ur (Bruce K. Waltke, *Genesis: A Commentary* [Grand Rapids: Zondervan, 2001]), p. 204.

descendants of Arpachshad upon Abraham, the narrator does not explain. Yahweh is the subject of the first verb at the beginning of the first statement and thus the subject of the entire subsequent sacred history.[2]

These promises all relate to the future. They required faith on Abram's part and action stemming from that faith. None of these blessings were to reach fruition just yet; long centuries will pass before the land will belong to Abram's descendants. Moreover, they will be frequently at loggerheads with their neighbours in the rest of Genesis. Indeed, the book – from one angle – is a record of protracted family feuding.

The promises consist, first, that *God will make Abram a great nation*. Later on we find the Lord deliberating with himself on the point that he will not hide from Abram his intentions regarding Sodom, since he was to make of him a great nation (Gen. 18:18). In this promise, the penalty of the fall is ameliorated. Whereas death resulted from sin and painful childbirth was the lot of the woman, in God's covenant with Abram there is an abundance of life, so much so that from this one man will emerge a vast multitude of people. The promise is for life in full measure, a plenitude.

Second, *the Lord was also to make of Abram a great name*. Since only Yahweh possessed a great name this, together with the later similar promise to David (2 Sam. 7:9) could only come in the context of his covenant, in which he binds himself to his people in grace. Naming in the ancient world denoted that authority belonged to the one who gave the name. Adam named the animals, parents named their children, only God names himself. Abram and the nation that stemmed from him would clearly be living under the authority of Yahweh.

Third, *Abram was to be the source of blessing to the world*. There is a universal reach to this call and the promises God gave. Blessing is at the heart of the Lord's covenant with Abram, as recorded in Genesis 17:7–8, for 'blessing' occurs five times in these two verses. In turn, Abram would be a blessing to the world. The favour, well-being and prosperity entailed in God's covenant personally were to overflow in superabundance to the rest of the human race. The linguistic and ethnic confusion that arose in connection with Babel (Gen. 11:1–9) will be reversed. Those who take a favourable attitude towards Abram and do good to him will in turn be blessed by the Lord. On the other hand, he who regards him lightly or disdains

[2] Gerhard Von Rad, *Genesis: A Commentary* (rev. ed., Philadelphia: Westminster Press, 1961), p. 159.

him[3] will suffer judicial sanctions, just retribution, the curse of God. The overwhelming balance here is favour of blessing. *Those* (plural) who bless Abram, the Lord in turn will bless, while *he* (singular) who disdains him will be cursed. Most will bless him.

Indeed, all the families of the earth will be blessed in conjunction with Abram. The books of the OT in general, and Genesis in particular, do not regard the human race as a sum total of individuals but see it in terms of corporate entities. Hence, *the families of the earth* are in view. This does not mean that each and every individual person will be blessed. Rather, the blessing of God's covenant with Abram will extend beyond his own family and tribe and ultimately spread throughout the world. Abraham is a mediator of God's saving blessing to the world. That he is not the real and ultimate mediator is evident in the following chapters, where he finds himself frequently at odds with family members (Gen. 13:1–13) and leaders of other tribes (Gen. 12:10–20; 20:1–18).[4]

3. The focus of the promises

a. God's covenant promises were given to Abraham and those in his household

In the first instance, the Lord promises these great blessings to Abram. The declaration is intensely personal. The Lord speaks directly to Abram and promises that he himself will receive these benefits. However, they extend to all those who are in union with Abram, for whom Abram is their leader, head and representative, to the family and its extended entourage. As Genesis unfolds, these commitments are reiterated to his son Isaac, and to Isaac's son, Jacob. Even Ishmael, although he is not in the line of God's specific covenantal grace, is nevertheless promised by the Lord that his descendants will themselves become a great nation (Gen.17:20; 21:18). Thus the covenant is made with Abraham and his seed throughout their generations for an everlasting covenant (Gen. 17:7–8). Abraham's seed or

---

[3] Wenham, *Genesis 1–15*, pp. 276–277.

[4] There has been a longstanding debate on whether the *niphal* of *brk* should be passive (be blessed) or take the reflexive meaning of the *hithpael*, which is more common (bless themselves), with advocates on both sides. Von Rad thought the reflexive did not fit the universal saving message of the pericope, while others such as Driver and Delitzsch took the contrary position. Westermann and Waltke think both senses boil down to the same result, since if the families of the earth bless themselves, their receiving the blessing is entailed. See Driver, *Genesis*, p. 145; Von Rad, *Genesis*, pp. 158–161; Westermann, *Genesis 12–36*, pp. 151–152; Waltke, *Genesis*, p. 206. However, Wenham, who favours a middle position (find blessing), argues that a reflexive sense is possible but not required: Wenham, *Genesis 1–15*, pp. 277–278.

offspring, those descended from him in the line of Isaac and Jacob and all under their patronage, are to be the source of worldwide blessing (Gen. 22:18).

b. Ultimately this seed or offspring is Christ

In Christ all the families of the earth will be blessed, is Paul's argument in Galatians 3. He uses the fact that Genesis refers to the singular, 'your offspring', rather than employing a plural. Hence, the promises are refracted or focused, rather like a magnifying glass held over grass concentrates the rays of the sun into one spot. Their refracted light focuses on Christ.

Paul is able to say this for two very good reasons. First, the NT writers saw that throughout the OT certain events, people or entities mirrored events, people or corresponding entities in the NT. In particular, the OT analogies tended to point to Christ as their fulfilment. This became a commonplace theme in the writings of the church fathers. Typology, for that is what it is called, is evident in the NT in books like Hebrews and Revelation. Second, there is an especially close relationship between Christ and the church, such that Paul can call the church Christ's bride, or the body in relation to which Christ is the head. Christ and his church are in union. This fulfils the promise of the Abrahamic covenant 'I will be your God and you shall be my people'.[5] As such, Christ was to embody many aspects of Israel, the people of God, in his priestly work and as the leader who was a second Moses but greater than Moses. Matthew saw the infant Jesus' brief spell in Egypt as the fulfilment of the exodus, due to his union with his people (Matt. 2:15; cf., Hos. 11:1).

Therefore, Paul's assertion that the promise of the Abrahamic covenant refers to Christ, the seed or offspring of Abraham (Gal. 3:16), is grounded not on a pedantic view of Hebrew grammar but on his understanding of the deep-seated connections underlying the history of redemption and the covenantal grace of God.[6] As Herman Ridderbos states 'The promises right from the start were intended for and directed to those who are in Christ or of him'.[7] From the first, God intended to refer not to all Abraham's descendants but to *the* descendant, Jesus Christ.

This tells us that we should read the OT in the light of the ongoing history of God's purposes of salvation. All aspects of the OT, to

[5] Exod. 6:7; Lev. 26:12; Jer. 30:22.

[6] J. B. Lightfoot, *Saint Paul's Epistle to the Galatians* (London: Macmillan, 1900), pp. 142–143.

[7] Herman M. Ridderbos, *The Epistle of Paul to the Churches of Galatia* (London: Marshall, Morgan & Scott, 1961), p. 132.

some degree or other, lead eventually to Christ. These books were not given as mere historical curiosities, nor primarily as ammunition for private individual meditation, but to record and present the mighty deeds of God in unfolding his plans to deliver the human race from sin and death.

c. Abraham's offspring reverses the curse on Adam

We saw how the sin of Adam put the human race under divine judgment. Yet, immediately afterwards, God promised that another member of the human race would eventually deal a mortal blow to the serpent, the devil. He did not let Adam wallow in despair but promised eventual release. He has not abandoned us. He brings hope and deliverance out of decay and death. Now the light burns brighter. Now this plan is reinforced and its focus is sharpened. This human conqueror will be descended from Abraham. He will bring worldwide blessing, extending beyond Abraham's own family and even further than the great nation that will descend from him and be in covenant with him. He will annul the curse and bring blessing. He will restore life in place of death. Not only will he destroy the serpent but he will lead the human race into untold favour and well-being. He will be of the lineage of Abraham.

2 Samuel 7; Psalm 110
3. The son of David

1. David's plan (2 Samuel 1–3)

David, after a long and tortuous path, was now firmly established by Yahweh as king of Israel, and had entered a new stage of his rule. Secure both militarily and politically, with the construction of his palace now complete, and the ark of the covenant safely in Jerusalem (2 Sam. 6:1–23), his thoughts turned to building a temple to house the ark. This, with the establishment of his kingdom now secure, would be the crowning point of his rule. As Hertzberg observes, although David's own palace was well built, a house of cedar being the epitome of a well-constructed building for the time, one befitting a king,[1] the ark was still in tents or curtain-tents (2 Sam. 6:17), the dwellings of nomads, who were the lowest rank on the social scale, structures weak and easily destroyed. What an insult to Yahweh! Nathan the prophet agrees.[2] The priorities are wrong. As Haggai was to proclaim after the exile, the house of Yahweh must come first (Hag. 1:2–5).

2. Yahweh's promise (2 Samuel 4–17)

Yahweh replies to Nathan that he had never asked for a permanent house (4–7). His customary manner of dwelling with Israel from the time of the exodus had been in a tent. He had revealed himself in a temporary mode. He had never required a temple. He is omnipresent, not bound to one place. His revelation of himself was the yardstick of what he required of his people. While the ark had been

[1] It is possible that it was constructed of stone, with cedar panelling, by Phoenician craftsmen (2 Sam. 5:11). See A. A. Anderson, *2 Samuel*, WBC 11 (Dallas: Word Books, 1989), p. 117.
[2] H. W. Hertzberg, *I & II Samuel: A Commentary* (London: SCM, 1964), p. 284.

housed in a building at Shiloh, it seems that this may have been regarded as a temporary expedient.[3]

This oracle from Yahweh should not imply that Nathan's original comment was in any way defective. At first Nathan agreed fully with David's proposal, on the grounds David himself presented, on a matter of general principle. The word of the Lord does not contradict David or Nathan; it affirms their general sentiments but sets them in a larger context, both of time and orientation.[4] It is simply that David was not to be the person to build the temple; his son would do so at a later date (12–13). Instead, Yahweh was to build a house for David (11–16)! He was to give further security to David's kingdom and to Israel. We can look at the oracle in three sections:

First, *past benefits* (8–9a). In the past God had taken David from humble origins as a shepherd and made him king, protecting him from danger and granting him victory over all obstacles. Shepherds were lowly in status yet Yahweh had anointed him as king over all Israel. He was raised from the lowest place and exalted to the seat of highest honour. Moreover, says Yahweh, *I have been with you wherever you went*; he had protected David from the continual persecution from Saul, established his kingdom and enabled him to conquer his enemies. Throughout, the action of Yahweh is in the forefront.

Second, *future blessings* (9b–11a). There is uncertainty as to whether these statements refer to the past or the future.[5] The context suggests strongly that it is a promise of future prosperity and security for Israel, consisting of relief from their enemies and safety, *that they may dwell in their own place and be disturbed no more*. In the midst of this happy scene is the assurance that Yahweh will make for David *a great name* (9b).

Third, *an everlasting house* (11b–16). Instead of David constructing a house for Yahweh, Yahweh will build *a house* for David. Furthermore, the house that Yahweh will build will be of far greater permanence than the one David intended to erect. David's offspring will be confirmed in the kingship and he will be the one to build the temple. This refers to Solomon, David's future son (12; he was not

---

[3] Hertzberg, *I & II Samuel*, p. 285.

[4] *Contra* Dale Ralph Davis, *2 Samuel: Out of Every Adversity* (Fearn: Christian Focus, 1999), pp. 69–71.

[5] See, *inter alia*, Henry Preserved Smith, *A Critical and Exegetical Commentary on The Books of Samuel*, ICC (Edinburgh: T&T Clark, 1912), p. 299; Hertzberg, *I & II Samuel*, pp. 285–286; Anderson, *2 Samuel*, p. 120; R. A. Carlson, *David, the Chosen King: A Traditio-Historical Approach to the Second Book of Samuel* (Stockholm: Almquist & Wiksell, 1964), pp. 106–107.

yet born), for he was the one who would build the temple (13). He would sin; Yahweh would discipline him but would not cast him off (14–15). His relationship to Yahweh was to be as a *son* to a *father*; the theme of adoption comes strongly into view here. A succession of kings was to follow in David's line. His kingdom would last *for ever* (16). This phrase *for ever* is repeated (13, 16). Self-evidently, it extends the reach of this prophecy beyond David and Solomon. It was hardly realized in those that followed either, for their sins and failures are paraded before the reader in graphic detail throughout 1 and 2 Kings.[6] The kingdom would eventually divide, the northern tribes be sent into exile, to vanish into the mists of history, while Judah was to be cast out into Babylon. The line of Davidic kings was at that point to go into abeyance, while the ten northern tribes would largely disappear. While terms for 'covenant' are not present here, nevertheless the theme underlies these promises. *Steadfast love* (15) is synonymous with the loyalty expressed by Yahweh in his covenant, and it is with his covenant people that he makes this commitment. Despite the terrible ordeals that lay ahead, the expectation would remain that Yahweh would revive the Davidic kingdom again and one day install a ruler who would be in the line of David. This intense anticipation is powerfully evident at the time of Jesus, whose opponents recognized that he was of the lineage of David. Indeed, ultimately, Yahweh was to make a house for himself in and among his people, the Word becoming flesh and making his tabernacle among us (John 1:14).

This episode further narrows the focus of God's promise of deliverance. The conqueror of Satan was to be a member of the human race, the offspring of the woman. Worldwide blessing was to come from a descendant of Abraham, and more specifically of Isaac and Jacob. Now attention is refracted even further to the family of David. From humanity, to Abraham, to Isaac and now to David the trail narrows. Moreover, it declares vividly that God keeps his promises, is true to his word, and will implement his plans. It was a huge assurance to David; it is an equally great encouragement to us.

3. A further elaboration (Psalm 110)

The Davidic psalm, Psalm 110, has a close connection with this great promise of 2 Samuel 7. David, as king, was forbidden to be priest in Israel. The priesthood was taken from the tribe of Levi, and, within

---

[6] 3 and 4 Reigns in the LXX, 1 and 2 Samuel being the first two of a four-volume book.

that tribe, the high priest was of the line of Aaron; David belonged to Judah. It is possible that he reflected on this strict separation of powers in Israel after conquering Jerusalem. Jerusalem was the ancient seat of Melchizedek, who had combined the two offices in his own person, as king of Salem and priest of God Most High (Gen. 14:17–20). In this sense, Melchizedek was a greater figure than David. What he did David could not do.

However, here in this psalm appears a king who is also a *priest*, who sits at the *right hand* of Yahweh and is a priest for ever (1, 4). It is obvious that David cannot refer to himself or to any king or priest in Israel. Moreover, David likens the priesthood of this figure to Melchizedek's, as an everlasting priesthood: *you are a priest for ever according to the order of Melchizedek* (4). The notable thing about the record of Melchizedek in Genesis is that there is no mention of his father or mother, in stark contrast to the Levitical priests of Israel who were required to be from the tribe of Levi and so to be able to establish their ancestry. It is as if he emerges independently of human origins or generational succession, from outside the web of time and space.

Not only that, as king, the dignitary in Psalm 110 is installed by Yahweh in the position of supreme authority at his *right hand* (1). Moreover, David describes him as *Adonai*, his *Lord*, a word used to vocalize the unpronounceable covenant name Yahweh. He is distinguished from Yahweh, yet identified with him. As king, he rules over his enemies (2), commanding ready allegiance from his people (3), being an everlasting priest (4), achieving a crushing triumph over the nations (5–7), and subjugating all his enemies (1). No one figure from the entire OT met all these specifications. The scope of future kingship and deliverance is broadening to vast and mysterious proportions, and somewhere David and his dynasty has the crucial part to play.

> The Lord said to my Lord:
> 'Sit here at my right hand,
> Until I make your foes a stool
> on which your feet may stand.'
>
> The Lord will make your reign
> extend from Zion's hill;
> with royal power you'll rule among
> those who oppose your will.
>
> When you display your power,
> your people flock to you;

at dawn, arrayed in holiness
your youth will come like dew.

Unchangeably the Lord
with solemn purpose swore;
'Just like Melchizedek you are
a priest for evermore.'[7]

[7] *Sing Psalms: New Metrical Versions of the Book of Psalms* (Edinburgh: The Psalmody Committee of the Free Church of Scotland, 2003), pp. 149–150. Used by permission.

Isaiah 7:14–17; 9:6–7; 11:1–5; Micah 5:2–5
4. The great king

Our main passage is Isaiah 9:6–7, which we will consider in the light of the wider message of Isaiah and as it is taken up and developed in other parts of the Old Testament. First, we will take a brief look at what Isaiah has to say a little earlier. Afterwards, we will see something of how he develops this theme and how it is sharpened elsewhere.

1. The virgin shall conceive (Isa. 7:14–17)

> Again the Lord spoke to Ahaz, . . . *Therefore the Lord himself will give you a sign. Behold, the virgin shall conceive and bear a son, and shall call his name Immanuel. He shall eat curds and honey when he knows how to refuse the evil and choose the good. For before the boy knows how to refuse the evil and choose the good, the land whose two kings you dread will be deserted* (14–16).

At the time Isaiah made this prophecy Judah was under attack from Syria, whose king was Rezin, and from Israel, led by Pekah the son of Remeliah. Despite Judah's own problems with idolatry, in breach of the covenant Yahweh made at Sinai, he assures them they will not be overcome.

a. The sign

Here Yahweh offers King Ahaz a sign, a pledge of assurance to show that he will do what he says he would do.[1] Ahaz refuses to accept

---

[1] '. . . so that someone may know that God is fulfilling the promises he had made', John D. W. Watts, *Isaiah 1–33*, WBC 24 (Waco: Word Books, 1985), p. 96.

the offer, under the seemingly pious reason that he did not want to put Yahweh to the test (Isa. 7:10–12). In reality, as Oswalt agrees, it was Ahaz who was being tested.[2] He was refusing the word of Yahweh, hardening himself against his offers of grace to his people. Meanwhile, Ahaz was negotiating an alliance with Assyria. He knew full well that this was unacceptable to Yahweh. In reality he wanted God to keep out of his life and the life of Judah. Ironically, in only a few years the very Assyrians Ahaz was counting on for help were to turn against Judah and demand that Jerusalem surrender (Isa. 36 – 37). Isaiah's reference to 'my God' may be intended to imply that the connection with the house of David has been broken and that he, rather than the king, represents the faithful remnant.[3]

Instead Yahweh offers the sign himself, to prove his grace would break through to his people's deliverance. This, despite Ahaz's unbelief and the eventual termination of the line of Davidic kings at the Babylonian exile.[4] The sign concerns a future pregnancy and birth. The tense is future. The clause starts with *hinnēh* (look, see, behold), regularly used by Isaiah concerning future events. For that reason, it does not relate to the prophecy about Isaiah's own son, Maher-shalal-hasbaz, mentioned in 8:1–4. The word *'iššâ* (wife) is absent. Nor is there evidence that Isaiah had a son called *Immanuel*; if he had, it would clearly have been noteworthy. Recent opinion has often favoured a reference to a son of King Ahaz but this is by no means clear.[5]

b. The mother and child

So the question arises: who is to be pregnant with this child? The word *'almâ* means a young woman of marriageable age. It does not demand virginity, although a virgin could qualify. Apart from Proverbs 30:19, it is never used of a married woman in the Old Testament[6] nor at all outside.[7] There was another word, *bĕtûlâ*, which meant a maiden living in her father's house, some way from marriage, that Isaiah could have used if the intention was to refer to a virgin without ambiguity, it has been widely supposed. However,

---

[2] John N. Oswalt, *The Book of Isaiah: Chapters 1–39*, NICOT (Grand Rapids: Eerdmans, 1986), p. 203.

[3] Hans Wildberger, *Isaiah 1–12: A Commentary* (Minneapolis: Fortress Press, 1991), p. 306; Alec Motyer, *Isaiah: An Introduction and Commentary* (Leicester: IVP, 1999), p. 77.

[4] See Oswalt, *Isaiah 1–39*, pp. 206–207.

[5] For a substantial discussion of competing proposals, see Wildberger, *Isaiah 1–12*, pp. 306–312.

[6] Wildberger, *Isaiah 1–12*, p. 308.

[7] Motyer, *Isaiah*, p. 78.

a young woman of marriageable age in Israel would be assumed to be a virgin.[8] The LXX translates with *parthenos*, which can mean virgin or young woman depending on the context. Lexicography leaves the identity of the child-bearer unclear.[9] However, it would hardly be a sign if a young woman gave birth to a child in an ordinary manner; these things happen all the time. Moreover, the lexicography by no means excludes a reference to virginity.

Not only is the identity of the child and the mother left to some extent unanswered but the timing of this sign is also left open. The context refers to the defeat of the opposing armies happening before the child is grown, followed by the threat from Assyria (16–17). However, there is no child who apparently meets this description in this time frame. Nor are there candidates in the middle term.[10] Again, we are left with the statement that at some indeterminate time a young woman will give birth to a child; that this is to be a sign points to something distinctive about this birth and also something not readily apparent to the original hearers or readers of the prophecy.

The unusual nature of this event is highlighted by the point that the child will be named by his mother. Normally in Israel the father named the child. Naming denoted a certain authority exercised by the one who named over the one who was named, and this fitted best into the task of the father of the family. In exceptional circumstances, such as the father's death or absence, the mother would take over that function (1 Sam. 4:19–22). That the mother here names the son highlights the distinctive and unusual nature of this child. While this practice may have been more common in extended royal households, the significant point is that the father does not enter the picture at all. Indeed, it is the child who is the sign, for he is to be named *Im-anu-el* (God-with-us). By naming the child with this name, the mother will declare that Yahweh is faithful to his covenant. The child will be a living demonstration of this great, all-important reality. Yet the timing of the sign, and the identity of mother and child, was to remain a mystery not only for Isaiah but for succeeding generations. What is clear from verses 15–17 is that before this was to happen the threat of Syria and Israel would cease and be replaced by that of Assyria. Moreover, at the time the child is born Judah would be in straitened circumstances, for *curds and honey*, used to feed very young children, would still be the child's food when he reached an age of moral responsibility.

[8] Oswalt, *Isaiah 1–39*, p. 210.
[9] See Watts, *Isaiah 1–33*, pp. 98–99.
[10] See Oswalt, *Isaiah 1–39*, pp. 212–213, who suggests an identity between Immanuel and Maher-shalal-hashbaz in Isa. 8:1–4.

This sign is not one of dramatic conquest of enemies. Rather, it points to severe weakness, and deliverance coming from a child. Yahweh's faithfulness to his covenant and the deliverance he had long promised was to be effected in very different conditions than a human scriptwriter would have proposed. This is the context for the dramatic oracle in chapter 9.

2. To us a child is born (Isa. 9:6–7)

a. Judah and its deliverance

This weakness of Israel is emphasized again with stark clarity. The northern extremity of Israel was a land subject to almost constant invasion. It was the first part of the land to be overrun by the Assyrians. Yet, when this great deliverance was to come, it would be the first to see it (9:1–2). As we know, Jesus lived in Nazareth, in Galilee, and Capernaum was in effect his home town. Israel was to become utterly dark before the great day dawned. Yet when it came Yahweh would bring light, and give intense joy and victory. Throughout the OT God's presence is described as light, and nothing can prevent it shining.[11] Hostile forces were to be annihilated (9:3–5). The people will be filled with joy in the Lord, since he has freed them from the oppressor.[12] The warfare that caused the bondage will cease (5). It will cease because a ruler will emerge who will govern with *justice and truth* for ever (6–7). A son was to be born, a human child, who would rule.

> *For to us a child is born,*
> *to us a son is given;*
> *and the government shall be upon his shoulder,*
> *and his name shall be called*
> *Wonderful Counsellor, Mighty God,*
> *Everlasting Father, Prince of Peace.*
> *Of the increase of his government and of peace*
> *there will be no end,*
> *on the throne of David and over his kingdom,*
> *to establish it and to uphold it*
> *with justice and with righteousness*
> *from this time forth and forevermore.*
> *The zeal of the LORD of hosts will do this.*

[11] Oswalt, *Isaiah 1–39*, p. 242; Wildberger, *Isaiah 1–12*, pp. 395–396.
[12] These are most likely prophetic perfects: Oswalt, *Isaiah 1–39*, pp. 242–243.

b. The child and his names

Probably, Isaiah saw the son described here as identical to the child foretold in 7:14–17. Ever since the promise to David of a son who would reign over his throne forever, an expectation was in the air. Here Isaiah gives substance to this promise. The person in view is a mere child. Yet this child was to be a great king, although he himself is not called a king. No king in the line of David remotely comes near these descriptions. No human king could compete. The OT stressed the distinction between God and his creatures; the kings of Israel were never accorded divine status, unlike Egyptian rulers.[13] This is a birth announcement, not a coronation hymn, as Oswalt remarks.[14]

This child's name was to be *Wonderful Counsellor*. The word *wonderful* (*pele'*) is reminiscent of the self-naming of the angel of the Lord in Judges 13:18–20, in reply to Manoah. The angel asked why Manoah wanted to know his name, seeing it was 'wonderful', whereupon he went up into heaven in the flame of the offering. Manoah was terror-struck, since he had 'seen God'.[15] That event was connected also with the impeding birth of a son. The name points to the divine nature of the son who Isaiah foretells. His name, nature and character are beyond comprehension, beyond human access. He himself is a wonder.

The child is also described as *counsellor*. In chapter 11 Isaiah says of the Messiah that 'the spirit of counsel will rest upon him'.[16] He will be endowed with the Holy Spirit. He will be able to give counsel to his people, leading them for their good. He himself will stand in no need of counsel but will be able to dispense it to others. It is probable that these two descriptions are to be taken together and understood as something like 'planner of wonders', meaning one who plans and executes astonishing things,[17] or 'a wonder of a counsellor', whose wisdom is supernatural.[18]

More than this, he will be the *Mighty God*. Deity is his. Already, in 7:14 he is said to be called 'God-with-us'. In Isaiah 10:20–21 'the mighty God' is equated with Yahweh, the God of Israel, besides

---

[13] *Contra* Wildberger, who misses this crucial point in arguing that a royal child in the time of Isaiah is in view, with titles similar to those accorded Egyptian monarchs on their enthronement. This can only be posited if the passage is isolated from the rest of the OT, and from the stern warnings against and denunciations of idolatry in this book; see Wildberger, *Isaiah 1–12*, pp. 398f.

[14] Oswalt, *Isaiah 1–39*, p. 246.

[15] Judg. 13:22.

[16] Isa. 11:2.

[17] Wildberger, *Isaiah 1–12*, p. 403.

[18] Motyer, *Isaiah*, p. 89.

whom there is no equal or rival (Isa. 44:1–8).[19] In this he is distanced from the purely human (cf. Isa. 31:3), while at the same time he is to be born, to be a child, and to grow in a normal human manner. The mighty God appears as an infant, a small child, a man!

Again, he is the *Everlasting Father*. This is also a clear ascription of deity. He is from everlasting, a phrase attributable only to Yahweh. He transcends the creaturely. As Father he provides for all who trust in him. The fatherly care of Yahweh for his people is particularly evident in Hosea 11:1–4 where he states that 'When Israel was a child, I loved him, and out of Egypt I called my son . . . it was I who taught Ephraim to walk; I took them up by their arms . . . I bent down to them and fed them.' This the son did and does.

He is also the *Prince of Peace*. He is the ruler who removes all hostile powers that threaten peace and attempt to bring discord. He secures peace. It is far more than *keeping peace*, as in some recent military exercises; a temporary and fragile exercise, the underlying hostilities unaddressed. Rather, he *makes peace*. He achieves it by subjugating the forces of enmity. Paul was to say that he achieved this by his cross (Eph. 2:14; Col. 1:20); peace between God and humans, peace between hitherto implacable enemies.

c. His invincible kingdom

Consequently, his kingdom is invincible (7). It will continually increase, with an ever-extending dominion in which peace will be decisively established in fulfilment of Yahweh's promise to David. The foundation of his kingdom will be *righteousness*. What is pleasing to God will triumph, for he ordains what is just and pronounces what is right. Underlying all this is his zeal for God, a zeal born out of love and of contending for the object of his love, his covenant people. In keeping with that, his kingdom will visit his wrath on those who attempt to usurp his people and undermine his righteous rule.

No, Yahweh was not going to leave matters in the hands of wicked King Ahaz, or Assyria, or Babylon, or anyone else for that matter. He was to give his people his true King, born of a woman, born in Judah, born of David's line, who would receive his kingdom, a rule that would increase 'till all his creatures own his sway'.[20]

---

[19] Oswalt rightly points out that *'ēl gibbôr* refers to God elsewhere in the OT (*Isaiah 1–39*, p. 247). Motyer regards the translation 'Godlike hero' offered by Wildberger as 'linguistically improbable' (*Isaiah*, p. 89); cf. Wildberger, *Isaiah 1–12*, pp. 403–404.

[20] 'The day thou gavest, Lord, is ended', John Ellerton (1826–93).

3. A shoot from the stump of Jesse (Isa. 11:1–13)

a. Judah's desolate condition (1–2)

While the main players in world affairs are described here as like the cedar forests in Lebanon (Isa. 10:33–34), Judah is a forest cut down and destroyed. Only the stump of a dead tree remains, with neither leaves nor branches. Its condition is pitiable. Instead of referring to the house of David, Isaiah mentions *the stump of Jesse* (1), one small family in the tribe. To all appearances he views the house of David as at an effective end, reduced to a rump. As future years rolled on, this grim vision was to become a reality. By the time the angel appeared to Mary, the line of David was living in greatly reduced circumstances.

b. An amazing change

However, as sometimes happens with a felled tree, new life emerges out of the ruined trunk. At some undisclosed time a small green *shoot* would appear, a mere twig. From the hidden underground roots, life was to emerge, however puny and insignificant. This small green shoot would grow and produce *fruit*. The seemingly dead and useless would spring to life and prove productive. This shoot is seen here to be a person; personal pronouns are used throughout, and while the masculine pronoun can also be used for impersonal things there are an abundance of personal characteristics attributed here to the shoot. On this shoot the Spirit of Yahweh was to rest. Yahweh would consecrate this descendant of the line of David with the sevenfold Spirit: *the Spirit of the LORD*, *the Spirit of wisdom*, of *understanding*, of *counsel*, of *might*, of *knowledge*, of *the fear of the LORD* (2).

c. The shoot's righteous judgment (3–5)

This shoot of *the stump of Jesse* is a ruler. His judgment is true, wise and righteous. He does not judge superficially. I remember two striking experiences. Once, while working on my PhD at Cambridge University Library in the mid-seventies, I walked past one of the college entrances at lunchtime when a man slumped in a wheelchair, heavily disabled, limp and pathetic, was being lifted over the steps leading up to it. The friend who accompanied me remarked that this crumpled man was one of the most brilliant mathematicians in the world – then unknown to the general public – Stephen Hawking. Again, in Oxford a decade later, while having lunch in a pub across from the Bodleian where I was doing research, a woman was holding forth about some poetry she had written. She was dressed in a dirty coat, egg stains all over it, and carrying plastic bags full of possessions. It turned out that this apparently unfortunate waif was arguably the leading poet in England, soon to be the subject of a feature article in *The Times* Saturday magazine. Superficial impressions can be quite wrong. The shoot, in this case, when sitting in judgment makes right decisions. His judgments are true (3). He acts in righteousness towards the poor and needy (4) and is implacably opposed to their oppressors (4b). The wicked will feel the full force of his judgment.

d. The shoot's impact (6–13)

He will establish peace between the most unlikely of forces (6–9). The Gentiles will trust him, the nations will rally to him (10–11), while Israel itself will benefit from his rule and its salutary effects (11–12). Old divisions will be healed (13).

4. Born in Bethlehem (Micah 5:2–5)

Micah foretells the future glories of Judah, but first of all there was to be destruction and exile (Mic. 4:9–10). Beyond this there would arise a ruler who was to lead the nation in peace and righteousness.[21]

a. A ruler in Israel (2–3)

This ruler would arise from *Bethlehem*. The focus continues to narrow. From within Israel, the details are concentrating on the place from where this great figure was to emerge. Bethlehem Ephrathah was an unimposing village. The word *Ephrathah* distinguished this Bethlehem from the one in Zebulun. 'Bethlehem' means 'house of bread', while 'Ephrathah' means 'fruit fields'. It was located in an area where plenty of food was available. However, it was very small. In John 7:42 *kōmē* (village) describes it. It was too small to be reckoned among the thousands of Judah and so lacked representation in the tribal councils.[22] In Anglo-Saxon lands, there is an expression 'the hundreds'; a Member of Parliament in the UK resigns by applying for the Chiltern Hundreds, a notional office of profit under the Crown disqualifying a person from representing his constituency. In the USA, my family lived in an area of northern Delaware known

[21] For highly technical – and critical – discussion of this passage, see William McKane, *The Book of Micah: Introduction and Commentary* (Edinburgh: T&T Clark, 1998).

[22] Ralph L. Smith, *Micah-Malachi*, WBC 32 (Waco: Word Books, 1984), p. 43.

as Brandywine Hundred, adjacent to the Brandywine River. So this Bethlehem was inconsequential in the political context, a small and insignificant backwater.

However, the origins of the ruler transcend the status of his birth-place. His *coming forth is from of old, from ancient days* (2c). His birth, upbringing and personal background in Bethlehem are merely a stage in his existence. It is unlikely, in fact anachronistic, to expect Micah to have comprehended what this meant. The immediate reference is to the Davidic kings and Yahweh's promise to David, so that this ruler – coming from Bethlehem as David did – was to be the son of David, the king promised in Isaiah.[23] Nevertheless, Micah's words suggest a superhuman origin. In the background were the appearances of the angel of the Lord to Abraham, Isaac and Jacob. The angel spoke in his own name and also as the Lord himself (Gen. 22:15–18). In fact, the expression *his goings out*, which more precisely renders *môsā'*, translated *coming forth* in the ESV, suggests repeated appearances in the course of history, whether goings out at creation, as the Word who effected it, or to the patriarchs as the angel of the Lord. John M. P. Smith wrote that 'the statement concerning the expected birth is evidently an allusion to Is. 7:14 and comes from a time when that prophecy was being given Messianic significance',[24] while Elizabeth Achtemeier refers to his origin from God in his providential purpose.[25]

Astonishingly, whereas Isaiah foretold the birth of a son who would rule as the 'Mighty God',[26] here the ruler is to be from insignificant little Bethlehem. That this was a common understanding among Jewish interpreters is clear from the answer given to the Magi who inquired as to where the king of the Jews was to be born (Matt. 2:4–6). If we were writing the script he would doubtless emerge with a blaze of glory in Technicolor splendour but with God the reverse is true, for he comes in obscurity, incognito.

However, until the ruler appeared Israel was to be in sorrow (3a), given over to the power of the nations. First there was to be exile in Assyria and Babylon. Then, after a remnant returned, the might of the Medo-Persian and Greek empires would ravage the land, to be followed by the hegemony of the Romans. The land of promise,

[23] Leslie C. Allen, *The Books of Joel, Obadiah, Jonah and Micah*, NICOT (Grand Rapids: Eerdmans, 1976), pp. 343–344; R. L. Smith, *Micah-Malachi*, p. 44.

[24] John Merlin Powis Smith, *A Critical and Exegetical Commentary on Micah, Zephaniah, Nahum, Habakkuk, Obadiah and Joel*, ICC (Edinburgh: T&T Clark, 1912), p. 104.

[25] Elizabeth Achtemeier, *Minor Prophets I*, NIBC (Peabody: Hendrikson, 1996), p. 339.

[26] Isa. 9:6.

occupying a strategic place in the ancient Near East, along the trade route from Egypt to the Mesopotamian basin, would be criss-crossed by opposing armies, the people reduced to semi-servitude. The people of Yahweh were to be a tiny pawn in a much greater game of international chess, the main players being elsewhere. The family of David would lose the throne and fall into poverty. Just as David was the youngest son of Jesse, overlooked as a contender for the throne, so his greater Son would be far from the limelight.

b. The ruler's blessings (3b-5a)

The rest of his brothers evidently refers to Judah and the Judeans, the ruler's own tribe of which Benjamin was a part. Judah would undergo punishment but a rescued remnant would return to Yahweh. The ruler will protect and feed his flock like a shepherd (4a). He will feed it in the strength of Yahweh. His standing to feed his flock indicates strength and perseverance over an extended period.[27] It reflects the point that David was called from the flock to be shepherd of God's people (2 Sam. 5:2) and points forward to Jesus as the good shepherd (John 10:11–12).[28] This ruler is not a tyrant, causing his subjects to fear and be terrified, but a protector who nourishes them in the strength of God.[29] He is gentle as he leads and directs them. He is 'the Mighty God'[30] endowed with 'the Spirit of might'.[31] The passage as a whole shows us something of what God is like. He comes to us in lowliness, on our level. In turn, this is to be a feature of our own life. God, in resisting the proud, gives grace to the humble.

His flock is *secure* (4b). He will be great and his greatness will be known to the ends of the earth. What a contrast from tiny Bethlehem! From humble beginnings to worldwide renown, the ruler will secure his flock from harm and bring them to maturity. This reflects the promise given to David whereby his greater Son would be great and reign on the throne of his father David forever.

This entails peace and security from their enemies (5a). It goes beyond the obvious point that the ruler will be the source of peace, the one who provides and maintains peace. More than that, *he himself* will be their peace. As Isaiah had said he is 'the prince of peace' since in his own person peace is secured permanently.[32]

[27] Achtemeier, *Minor Prophets I*, p. 340.
[28] Allen, *Micah*, pp. 345–346.
[29] Achtemeier, *Minor Prophets I*, p. 340.
[30] Isa. 9:6.
[31] Isa. 11:2.
[32] Isa. 9:6. Allen, *Micah*, p. 347; Achtemeier, *Minor Prophets I*, p. 340.

One of the human race, a descendant of Abraham in the line of Isaac and of Jacob, a member of Israel, a descendant of David, born in Bethlehem; the plot thickens, the clues accumulate.

> O holy child of Bethlehem
> Descend to us, we pray;
> Cast out our sin, and enter in;
> Be born in us today.[33]

---

[33] 'O little town of Bethlehem', Phillips Brooks (1835–93).

Isaiah 41 – 50
5. The Servant of the Lord (1)

These chapters contain a series of cameos, snapshots referring to the servant of Yahweh. The identity of this figure has been debated extensively. The contexts of the various Servant songs suggest a range of possibilities. Israel appears to be addressed in chapter 41, whereas the subject in chapter 42 could well be Cyrus, the Medo-Persian emperor who gave the edict for the Jewish exiles to return to Jerusalem.[1] Isaiah himself appears to be in view in chapter 49. Yet in each section the full scope of the various songs is not exhausted by the immediate situation.

1. Anointed ruler of the nations (42:1–9)

Here the Servant will carry out Yahweh's purposes for the nations. He is appointed by Yahweh, who has put his *Spirit upon him*, an expression used of the earlier prophets, and also of Saul (1 Sam. 10:10).[2] He will establish the rule of God quietly and unobtrusively. In contrast to the pomp and self-aggrandizing splendour of the general run of kings, the Servant will act effectively but without noise and clamour (2).[3] If Cyrus is in view it is noteworthy that he came

---

[1] Whybray states a preference, without supporting argument, for Deutero-Isaiah (R. N. Whybray, *Isaiah 40–66*, NCBC [Grand Rapids: Eerdmans, 1975], p. 71). Underlying this claim is his assumption about authorship. However, as we shall see, the passage fits Cyrus far better than an individual whose identity is both speculative and unknown. Watts agrees that Cyrus is in view here (John D. W. Watts, *Isaiah 34–66*, WBD 25 [Waco, Texas: Word Books, 1987], pp. 114–119). Westermann is wisely cautious and points to the limits of our knowledge, arguing that the identity of the Servant was and is something of a mystery (Claus Westermann, *Isaiah 40–66: A Commentary* [London: SCM, 1966], p. 93).

[2] Whybray, *Isaiah 40–66*, p. 72.

[3] Watts, *Isaiah 34–66*, p. 114; John N. Oswalt, *The Book of Isaiah: Chapters 40–66*, NICOT (Grand Rapids: Eerdmans, 1998), p. 111; Westermann, *Isaiah 40–66*, p. 96.

to power by diplomatic means, with the support of ethnic minorities, of which the Jewish exiles were one. Moreover, the Servant will nurture the weak (3), a wise policy, in view of the need to retain the support of the minority groups (4).[4] For the Jews it was to be beneficial. This is a dramatic example of the fact that history is governed by the God of Israel; we are in safe hands.

However, if we were to suppose that Cyrus was the figure envisaged here, there are elements that go far beyond his beneficent ethnic policies. Jesus Christ is said to be chosen by God, in whom his people are elect (Eph. 1:4–6). The Spirit of God rested on him at his baptism (Matt. 3:16–17) and the Father cited this very passage in identifying Jesus as his Son. God's determination concerning the nations is brought to effect in Jesus' kingly ministry (Rev. 1:5; 5:1–14). He came into the world without ostentation, born in a stable, incognito, living as one of the nation of Israel. He was meek and gentle, calling the weary and heavy-laden to find rest and salvation in him (Matt.11:25–30). On his resurrection, he established God's rule in heaven and earth (Matt. 28:18–20). He will not grow faint, while preserving a *dimly burning wick*. He will not be *discouraged*, and will not break a *broken reed*. He is God's covenant, the seed of Abraham, the son of David (Matt. 1:1); this could hardly be restricted to Cyrus (6). While Cyrus proclaimed liberty to the Jewish exiles, the language in verses 6–7 concerns his implementing the year of jubilee, giving release to the captives, sight to the blind, and *light for the nations*. In short, the Servant of the Lord – empowered by the Spirit of God – will established his righteous rule over the nations, supporting the weak, bringing the glory of God to expression (8). Moreover, his role relates to *the nations* (1, 6), a scope wider than the rule of Cyrus.[5] Oswalt rightly considers that the ultimate reference of the passage, and the identity of the Servant of the Lord here, is the Messiah.[6]

2. Yahweh's salvation in the midst of opposition (49:1–6)

Here, the servant appears on the surface to be Isaiah, called by Yahweh before he was born.[7] This is an intensely personal set of

---

[4] Watts, *Isaiah 34–66*, p. 119.

[5] Alec Motyer, *Isaiah: An Introduction and Commentary* (Leicester: IVP, 1999), pp. 320–322.

[6] Oswalt, *Isaiah 40–66*, pp. 109–119.

[7] Whybray again prefers Deutero-Isaiah (*Isaiah 40–66*, p. 135). He rightly remarks that 'in view of the fact that in the prophetical books generally the subject of speeches in the first person singular, when it is not Yahweh and not otherwise indicated, is normally the prophet himself, it is remarkable that this identification should have been contested in this case by so many commentators'. Watts also argues that the

affairs, comparable to the call of Jeremiah (Jer. 1:5)[8] or Paul (Gal. 1:15) and pointing to the sovereignty of God. He is depicted as the mouthpiece of God, his words akin to sharp swords, a prophet.[9] Both the swords and the polished arrows are kept concealed until the time comes for their deployment (2). Both overcome opposition. Moreover, Yahweh will be *glorified* in and through his servant and his words (3). While the servant is addressed here as *Israel*, he is distinguished from the nation in verse 5, and the tenor of the comments in verses 1–3 point more to an individual, one who embodies the nation through his calling.[10] Westermann points out that prophets are never addressed like this elsewhere in the OT – *you are my servant . . . in whom I will be glorified* – indicating that the servant is both prophet and king, a mysterious combination.[11]

Despite this the servant has an intense sense of failure: *'I have laboured in vain; I have spent my strength for nothing and vanity'* (4). The call of Yahweh would seem to guarantee visible success but the reality is quite the reverse. Isaiah's ministry was met by rejection. This was foreshadowed in the original call he received (Isa. 6:9–11), predicting that his words would harden Judah in unbelief. If this were a pastoral call, few would accept it! There is a powerful sense of dejection here. Is everything simply a waste of time? Has the work counted for nothing? Was the effort spent in vain? This is a common experience many of us may face. It is shared by many a pastor, and is by no means unusual for the faithful as they approach the end of their lives; it is frequent among sufferers of depression.

However, Isaiah's response reaches beyond his own time to the one he prefigures. The Servant of the Lord is a man and subject to genuine human concerns and emotions. His ministry met with widespread opposition and hostility. The establishment had him executed. At the time of his death he had a mere handful of disciples. He experiences the limitations of living as a finite human in a world that breeds disappointment and heartbreak, rarely realizing the fruit of his labour. Tiredness, frustration and dejection are not in themselves sinful; it depends on the context, the inner motivation. These are human attitudes and so fully possessed by the Servant. That this is not unbelief is evident from the second part of verse 4, where the

---

identity of the Servant here is the same as in Isa. 42 but in his case Cyrus is in view (*Isaiah 34–66*, pp. 185–187). While there are definite echoes of Cyrus' impact, vv. 5–6 go beyond anything Cyrus or his successor, Darius, could achieve.

[8] Westermann, *Isaiah 40–66*, p. 207.

[9] Ibid., p. 208.

[10] See Whybray, *Isaiah 40–66*, p. 136, and Westermann, *Isaiah 40–66*, pp. 208–209, for a discussion of the problematic 'Israel' in verse 3. Oswalt agrees that the identity of the servant is individual not collective (*Isaiah 40–66*, pp. 288–289).

[11] Westermann, *Isaiah 40–66*, pp. 208–209.

Servant affirms that *surely my right is with the Lord, and my recompense with my God.* At the same time that Jesus, on the cross, cried out in the words of Psalm 22:1 from his abandonment, he also confessed 'my God'.

Yahweh, in turn, affirms his God-given role. His task is to restore *Jacob* (5), which clearly differentiates the Servant from Israel. In the middle term, Isaiah's ministry would eventually point to the return of the exiles from Babylon to the land of promise. However, the true Servant will in the end banish ungodliness from Jacob so that 'all Israel will be saved'.[12] In addition, he will bring God's salvation *to the end of the earth* (6). This is more far-reaching than Isaiah could have conceived. The Servant will establish the rule of God throughout the world. No prophet, not even Israel itself, let alone pagan king Cyrus – however benevolent – could remotely do this. In fact, the language of verse 6 in both the Hebrew and the Septuagint expresses the point that the Servant is not merely the means or agent of God's salvation but that he himself *is* that salvation in his own person – *I will make you as a light for the nations, that my salvation may reach to the end of the earth* – demanding fulfilment far beyond the human characters of Isaiah's day.[13] Only the Son of God could be the salvation of God.

In order to appreciate the Servant's place in God's purposes it is necessary to step outside our limited and largely blinkered context and view the land from God's perspective; this requires divine revelation. Here is the divine revelation, the wider picture from the vantage point of the God who called his Servant in the first place.

> *It is too light a thing that you should be my servant to raise up the tribes of Jacob and to bring back the preserved of Israel; I will make you as a light for the nations, that you will be my salvation to the ends of the earth* (6).[14]

3. Faithful sufferer (50:4–9)

In this section the Servant is presented as a faithful listener and sufferer, facing his persecutors confident that Yahweh will vindicate him. In this setting, there is no hint that the immediate reference is to Cyrus. The language again is highly personal; it is about someone who suffers opposition and physical abuse but is confident of being sustained by Yahweh in the midst of it. This rules out a collective meaning and points in the first instance to the prophet, although

[12] Cf. Rom. 11:25–26.
[13] See Oswalt, *Isaiah 40–66*, pp. 293–294; Motyer, *Isaiah*, pp. 388–389.
[14] My translation, from the LXX.

again it cannot be restricted to Isaiah but is only properly fulfilled by the greater Servant who came later, in the fullness of time.[15]

First, *the servant listens so as to teach* (4). He knows how to use words to sustain the weary, those burdened by suffering and sorrow. In Isaiah's day the sorrow was occasioned by Judah's faithless defection from the covenant and its impending judgment. The sustaining words were not Isaiah's; they came from God.[16] His ability to speak words of encouragement was due to his listening to the voice of the Lord. Like getting up out of bed in the morning and going to school, Isaiah was a pupil in the school of Yahweh. He had to learn, to be taught, in order to teach and sustain his hearers at the appropriate time.[17] His was a prophetic work, effective because he was first of all a disciple.[18] But, as Oswalt points out, no prophet in Israel – let alone Israel itself – could ever lay claim to complete faithfulness in the manner described here.[19] Later, Jesus could say,

Come to me, all who labour and are heavy laden, and I will give you rest. Take my yoke upon you, and learn from me, for I am gentle and lowly in heart, and you will find rest for your souls. For my yoke is easy, and my burden is light.[20]

From a young age he learnt by debating with the leading rabbis of his day (Luke 2:41–50). His submission to the Father was the source of his sustenance of his followers. The author of Hebrews asserts that he is able to send us help in time of need (Heb. 4:16), connecting this to his obedience and godly fear (Heb. 5:7–8). Only he fulfilled these words.

Second, *the Servant is faithful as he suffers* (5–7). In the face of hostility he did not shrink from the challenge. He never turned backwards, never flinched. While this may have been true of Isaiah, it was undoubtedly the case with Jesus, who set his face like a flint to go to Jerusalem (Luke 9:51). He was obedient to his calling; he

---

[15] While reference to the original setting of Isaiah is necessary in order to understand the text and its significance, those commentaries, like the ones by Whybray and Watts, that stop there (leaving aside their questionable placing of these events in Babylon with its implicit assumption that predictive prophecy is ruled out) present an understanding of the text which is less than Christian. The apostles understood the Old Testament throughout to refer to Christ. To admit less than this is to place one's exegesis outside the Christian faith, and to assume that we know better than the apostles. If it takes us beyond the high places, it only conducts us to the synagogue. This is more than a question of exegesis; it is one of discipleship.

[16] Whybray, *Isaiah 40–66*, p. 151.

[17] Ibid.

[18] Oswalt, *Isaiah 40–66*, pp. 323–324.

[19] Ibid., pp. 324–325.

[20] Matt. 11:28–30.

submitted to Yahweh and followed him faithfully. He knew what the outcome would be but resolutely headed towards it. How unlike many of today's celebrity preachers, whose aim in life appears to be to gain as much applause as possible and heap glory to themselves! In the face of temptation to discouragement (Isa. 49:4) the Servant faced actual physical harm. For Isaiah, the calling of a prophet was dangerous. Tradition has it that he was sawn in two (cf. Heb. 11:37). In turn, Jesus was done to death by the establishment. He was struck, disgraced, faced ridicule and spitting but did not shirk the danger (6). In all this, he was confident that God would help him. 'For the joy that was set before him [he] endured the cross, despising the shame.'[21] These details were literally fulfilled during his arrest, trial and crucifixion (Matt. 26:67; 27:30; John 18:22).

Third, *the Servant is confident in the face of opposition* (8–9). He defends his position. He challenges his persecutors. In the ancient Near East, Westermann says, if one submitted to public humiliation one was accepting one's guilt.[22] In contrast, in the language of a law court, the Servant affirms that God will vindicate him; all accusations are false and groundless. He is sure of victory.[23] The joy set before him looms large through the gloom. Those who oppose the plans of God will not last. As a garment eaten slowly but inexorably by a moth, they will visibly wither. After persecution comes deliverance, after accusation vindication, after death resurrection. This is surely an encouragement to all who seek to follow Christ, that our service is not in vain but God will make it abundantly fruitful beyond our wildest expectations.

[21] Heb. 12:2.
[22] Westermann, *Isaiah 40–66*, p. 231.
[23] It is possible that this might refer to a trial the prophet had to face, according to Whybray (*Isaiah 40–66*, p. 152).

Isaiah 52:13 – 53:12
6. The Servant of the Lord (2)

This is the best known and most frequently cited of the servant songs. There are at least as many ideas about the identity of the Servant in this passage as there are commentators and scholars. Where two or three biblical commentators are gathered together there are three or four opinions. However, this is a particularly difficult text and its meaning has been disputed. Oswalt remarks that 'there must be something about the text itself that resists over neat conclusions'.[1] This does not mean that we cannot know what it is saying. The overall drift of the passage is clear.[2] It is clear that the details of this song could never have been realized by Isaiah, or indeed any other figure in Israel's subsequent history. The nation itself, in its persistent rebelliousness, could hardly be a candidate. When we reach the NT, we find it being applied by the apostles and evangelists to Jesus (Acts 8:26–38; John 12:36b–38; Rom. 10:16). The cautious Calvin says 'Isaiah goes on to speak of Christ, in whom all things are gathered together'.[3] If we are looking for a Christian interpretation of the passage we need hardly look beyond the apostles.[4]

---

[1] John N. Oswalt, *The Book of Isaiah: Chapters 40–66*, NICOT (Grand Rapids: Eerdmans, 1998), p. 377.

[2] Claus Westermann, *Isaiah 40–66: A Commentary* (London: SCM, 1966), p. 257.

[3] John Calvin, *Sermons on Isaiah's Prophecy of the Death and Passion of Christ*, trans. and ed. T. H. L. Parker (London: James Clarke, 1956), p. 26.

[4] Westermann correctly notes that 'here there is a point for point correspondence with the Church's confession as it is given in the Apostles' Creed – born, suffered, died and was buried' (*Isaiah 40–66*, p. 257). However, he stops short of the resurrection. On the other hand, Whybray's claim that 'the supposed references to the Servant's vicarious suffering and death and resurrection are illusory' is evidently based on assumptions that preclude the sovereignty of God, predictive prophecy, revelation, or the authority of Christ over world history. In short, he cannot provide a Christian exposition of the church's canon; R. N. Whybray, *Isaiah 40–66*, NCBC (Grand Rapids: Eerdmans, 1975), pp. 171–172.

1. He was disfigured yet surprisingly exalted (52:13–15)

The servant is said to *act wisely* or *prosper*. He will 'both know and do the right things in order to accomplish the purpose for which he was called'.[5] This occurs in three stages; he will rise up, he will raise himself higher, and he will stand on high. This suggests Jesus' eventual resurrection, ascension and heavenly session. Together the phrases point to a public and overwhelming vindication by God. Yet there is also a marring of his appearance, a grotesque disfigurement, in savage contrast to the ultimate exaltation. He was greatly disfigured. Many were horrified at him. So distorted was his face that it seemed to be beyond human resemblance. It was shocking and appalling. This occurred on a worldwide scale such that the nations and their kings were astonished. The sufferings and disfigurement, while physical, are not to be confined to that; they encompass mental and spiritual elements too. The effect is repulsive.

Once I knew a man, a theological student, who, shortly after he was married, was diagnosed with a malignant brain tumour. The effects of the disease, and the surgery he underwent, brought about a horrific change. His balance was precarious, his speech distorted. More than that, his face was transposed from that of a healthy man in his early thirties to an elderly invalid, twisted and deformed. He staggered around, the effects of the ghastly growths plain for all to see. Passers-by recoiled in horror. The Servant of the Lord shared that isolation, just as we believe my friend will share his glorious and exalted transformation.

In this, the Servant was to make the nations sit up in amazement. This sudden change from utter and appalling disfigurement to exaltation was to shock and startle them. *Kings shall shut their mouths* in amazement (15). They will see what they had previously not been told. They will understand what had never before occurred to them. The gospel will be brought to them, something far beyond their previous experience or expectation. Paul cites this verse, stating that it was fulfilled in his own ministry (Rom. 15:21).

2. Israel did not believe because his presence was unimpressive (53:1–2)

The Gentiles receive with wonder things not previously contemplated while God's own people take offence, placing no faith

---

[5] Oswalt, *Isaiah 40–66*, p. 378.

in things told them down the passages of time. The messengers, the watchmen, had brought glad tidings, all to no avail (Isa. 52:7–10). Yet human unbelief cannot nullify the truth of God (Isa. 55:11).[6]

The problem as far as Israel was concerned was that the Servant did not meet their expectations. He did not seem to have any special qualities. His background was singularly unimpressive (2a). The blessing of God is often symbolized in the OT in terms of a well-watered garden; but here is a parched plant, a *root*, nothing more. It seems that God's blessing has been withheld. There is nothing out of the ordinary about the Servant. He is like a tree chopped down, a small green shoot sticking out of a dead stump. The Davidic monarchy was to be cut off abruptly by the Babylonian exile. Jesus was to come from the stump of Jesse. Poor and miserable conditions were to be the basis of his life; born in a stable, raised in a rural backwater, of poor parents, the father dying while Jesus was comparatively young, he then having to provide for the family by carpentry. Meanwhile Israel itself had been a pawn in a large game of international chess, a small tribe subject to the whims of the power brokers of the day, the Babylonians, the Medo-Persians, the Egyptians, the Greeks and the Romans. Moreover, Yahweh did nothing to put this situation right, nor did he relieve the straitened circumstances in which the Servant found himself. Moreover, his career was brutally ended, cut off in its prime after a mere three years.

Even allowing for all this, the Servant had no presence (2b). John the Baptist could say that 'among you stands one you do not know'.[7] It required testimony to be borne to him by John and others, and even then his true identity was not self-evident, for only the Father could reveal it (Matt. 16:15–17; John 6:44–5, 64–65). His appearance was not impressive. He had no majesty, no charisma, no apparent leadership qualities. Nothing indicated anything out of the ordinary: '"Is not this Jesus, the son of Joseph, whose father and mother we know? How does he now say, 'I have come down from heaven'?" the Jews responded.'[8]

3. He was despised and ostracised (53:3)

No one of any importance gave heed to the Servant. Those of rank and status, the rich and the famous, the good and the great, the leaders of Israel and its grandees all drew back from him, as largely

[6] For alternative readings see Oswalt, *Isaiah 40–66*, p. 381.
[7] John 1:26.
[8] John 6:42.

is the case throughout history. They gave him no support. They deemed him unworthy of attention. Of those who followed him closely there was no one of distinction, no one that is until Paul appeared on the scene. The phrase *ḥădal 'îšîm* ('cessation of men') implies that people in general turned away from him, and did not consider what he had to say or what he did.[9]

Moreover, his life was painful. He was *a man of sorrows, and acquainted with grief* (3b). The sorrows were constant, their consequence excruciating. We already alluded to the death of Joseph and the demands placed upon Jesus to provide for the needs of his mother and the family. He learned to endure. His opponents remarked that he was not yet fifty years old, when in fact he was in his early thirties. Martyn Lloyd-Jones thought this indicated that he had prematurely aged due to the cares he faced and because he was living in a world stricken by sin and grief.[10] This does not mean that he was sickly, moving from one illness to the next. Rather, he was familiar with its effects on the human race and felt its grief keenly and sharply.

He was despised (3c). Not only did the rich and powerful spurn him but people turned away from him in disgust. *We esteemed him not*: we thought he was a non-entity, not worth considering, despicable, beyond the pale. We were blind to who he is. What a contrast Isaiah presents to the prosperity theology, to the culture of success and popularity!

4. He suffered and died (53:4–6)

The servant bore the burden of our sufferings (4a). *Surely* is emphatic; Handel summed it up well in his aria on this verse in his oratorio *Messiah*, where 'surely' is repeated, with emphasis. He *bore our griefs and carried our sorrows*, Isaiah says. Jesus went around healing people from their diseases. Sickness is part of the evil that flows out of human sin. When Adam sinned, death entered, with all its concomitants. While there is no necessary connection between this or that sickness and particular sins (although in some cases, such as drug addictions and sexual promiscuity there doubtless is), all illness ultimately is traceable to the disruption caused by Adam's sin, in which we all participated. The point here is that the Servant shared these burdens, carrying them as his own. He entered into fellowship with our sufferings and took them on himself. We had deserved to

---

[9] Oswalt, *Isaiah 40–66*, p. 383.
[10] D. Martyn Lloyd-Jones, *Studies in the Sermon on the Mount: Volume One* (London: Inter-Varsity Fellowship, 1959), p. 56.

bear and carry them; he took them away, delivering us from their sting and bite.[11]

However, we had thought of him differently (4b).We dismissed him as a person who had undergone intense misfortune. It seemed that God's vengeance had fallen on him. He was a religious guru who had failed, a false prophet who had brought divine punishment on himself by his misrepresentation of the truth – or so it seemed. And so he suffered a violent death (5). He was *wounded, crushed*. A violent calamity overtook him. The strongest language possible cannot exhaust what his apparent fate appeared to be from our point of view.

In reality he died because of our sins (5a). He was pierced, crushed, broken into pieces, dying violently due to our own rebellion; the Servant's death was the result of the people's sins. Sin deserved exile, at the time of Isaiah. Sin deserves death. Because of the suffering, the degradation to which the Servant submitted, the nation is spared. Our sins occasioned the death of the Servant. The Servant's death atones for our sins. His suffering and death are not in vain (5c). They bring our peace, our healing. They secure our well-being. In these statements the Servant is said to take our place as our substitute, to bear the penalty of our sin, and so deliver us from its liabilities. This is emphatic throughout this section:

> *Surely **he** has borne **our** griefs*
> *and carried **our** sorrows . . .*
> *But **he** was wounded for **our** transgressions;*
> ***he** was crushed for **our** iniquities;*
> *upon **him** was the chastisement that brought **us** peace;*
> *and with **his** stripes **we** are healed . . .*
> *the Lord has laid on **him** the iniquity of **us** all.*

The very burdens the Servant bears, which were the reason people disregarded him and considered him as a man of little consequence, are the means by which his people are delivered!

The Servant recovers us from our lost wanderings (6). We all have wandered away from God; we have followed 'the devices and desires of our own hearts'. We are like a flock of sheep that have, frightened out of their wits, run helter-skelter away from the fold, without a shepherd to guide us aright. We have wandered aimlessly.

[11] Oswalt effectively answers Whybray's rejection of any substitutionary meaning, in indicating that such an interpretation is alien to the context and fails to reckon with the sacrificial system and its teaching that it is only through substitutionary sacrifice that relations with God can be restored: Oswalt, *Isaiah 40–66*, p. 385; Whybray, *Isaiah 40–66*, p. 175.

We have erred and strayed from your ways like lost sheep; we have followed too much the devices and desires of our own hearts. We have offended against your holy laws. We have left undone those things we ought to have done, and we have done those things we ought not to have done, and there is no health in us.[12]

In this context, the Servant dies in our place (6b). *Yahweh laid on him the iniquity of us all*. He bore our sins. As a result, we are free, we no longer wander. As Peter was to say: 'He himself bore our sins in his body on the tree . . . By his wounds you have been healed. For you were straying like sheep, but have now returned to the Shepherd and Overseer of your souls'.[13] By his sufferings the servant has borne away our sins.

5. He was innocent as he suffered (53:7–9)

He suffered in silence (7). He accepted his sufferings without complaint. In this he is like a sheep; whereas we were compared to sheep in the negative sense of straying easily (6), here the Servant displays the positive qualities of meekness and innocence.[14] He was oppressed, treated harshly, abused. He was attacked, facing the physical brutality described in the Gospels and so typical of the ancient world, not to mention the modern. Yet he did not resist. The metaphor of the lamb sums it up; he was silently submissive, since this was the course of action on which he had embarked from the beginning. It was not the helpless submission of a professional victim but willing and purposeful acceptance of the plan of Yahweh. The extended sheep metaphor conjures up the idea of sacrifice.[15]

He was arrested and tried (8). This was no ordinary arrest. The Servant was coerced. All the proper judicial protections were removed. His trial was before a kangaroo court. No one sprang to his defence or gave consideration to the demands of justice. He was thereby *cut off out of the land of the living*.[16] This gross miscarriage of justice was not an inexplicable and meaningless tragedy but it was occasioned by the sins of the Servant's people: *stricken for the transgression of my people*. Moreover, he was cut off without offspring – a sign of the curse of God in Jewish culture, where to die without

---

[12] 'General Confession', *Book of Common Prayer*.

[13] 1 Pet. 2:24–25.

[14] Oswalt, *Isaiah 40–66*, p. 391.

[15] Ibid., pp. 391–392.

[16] The meaning of the preposition *min* has been debated at length. Some have argued for a local sense, the servant being delivered *from* oppression. The context favours a causal rendering. See Oswalt, *Isaiah 40–66*, pp. 92–93.

children was thought to be a denial of one's reason for being.[17] That the passage means that the Servant died literally is borne out by the normal use of *nigzar* (cut off).[18]

The Servant was assigned a burial plot with the dregs of society (9a). It is popular in many cultures to build huge shrines, mausoleums, to the dead, made of marble or other ornamental stone, so as to perpetuate their memory. The Servant, on the other hand, was put to death between two common criminals, with the intention that after his death he be buried among criminals – a detestable fate for a Jew. Despite this plan, it might seem that the text justifies the claim that he ended up buried among the rich and successful (9b), an ironic twist to the tale, for it was a member of the Sanhedrin itself who procured a comfortable and honourable resting place for the Servant after his ordeal. The Roman authorities handed over his body to Joseph of Arimathea, to be embalmed and placed in his own private tomb. The Hebrew parallelism would suggest, on the other hand, that *the wicked* and *the rich* are synonymous, in which case the idea is that the Servant's grave was with the oppressors, the wicked establishment.[19]

Previously the Servant was said, in his innocence, not to deserve the punishment that should have been meted out to his people. Here the thought goes even further. He had done no wrong, his words were totally lacking in deceit, and it was incongruous that his grave should be connected with the wicked or evildoers. He was innocent and so deserved no punishment at all. It is clear that the Servant could not be Israel, whose guilt is placarded across virtually every page of the OT. Nor could it even be Isaiah, who had confessed that he was a man of unclean lips (Isa. 6:5). As for the alleged 'Deutero-Isaiah', where on earth was such a person, other than in the imaginations of a coterie of OT scholars carried away with their own hypotheses? This servant cannot be found, even from the most diligent search of the OT or other ancient literature. His identity is only established in the record we have of the life and death of Jesus Christ.

6. He suffered in agreement with the will of God (53:10)

Yet, despite all appearances, the Servant's sufferings were part of God's plan (10a). The will of kings in the ancient world was law.

---

[17] Oswalt, *Isaiah 40–66*, p. 395.

[18] The *qal* usually has a literal sense, while the *niphal* (used here) occurs infrequently in the OT and only one instance can be said to be hyperbolic; Oswalt, *Isaiah 40–66*, p. 396.

[19] Although the burial of Jesus is mentioned in all four Gospels, this passage is not cited as being fulfilled.

Here human machinations are trumped by the purpose of God. This was not sadism or brutality, still less child abuse. Jesus was a willing sufferer, one with the Father in being and will (John 4:34; Heb. 10:7). He went to his death because, in love, he had determined to save his people from their sins and since there was no other way consistent with God's justice by which this could be achieved.

So the Servant became a guilt offering (10b). He sacrificed himself, priest and victim at one and the same time (Heb. 10:14). He offered himself. In the Levitical system in the OT the guilt offering was to be most holy (Lev. 7:1; 14:13). The fat portions were placed on the altar. There was no manipulation of blood by the priest. These offerings were for particular offences, including sins of ignorance. The priest was prominent, representing God. The offering was in compensation towards God, greater than the offence for which the offering was given. The lesson impressed on Israel was that God's justice requires satisfaction, the punishment outweighing the guilt incurred by the offence. The meaning of the Servant's suffering was that he should be an atoning sacrifice for sin.[20]

The Servant's sufferings were for him the path to glory (10c). God's purposes were worked out through his sufferings, not despite them. *He shall see his offspring; he shall prolong his days*: in contrast to the picture in verse 9 of his dying childless, the Servant will live to see his descendants, and live to a great age, the greatest blessing for a Jew at the time of Isaiah. This looks forward to Jesus being the light to the Gentiles, his salvation brought to the ends of the earth (Isa. 49:4–6).[21]

7. He was vindicated (53:11)

After his sufferings the Servant will see his offspring and know that his ordeal was not in vain. This looks forward implicitly to the Servant's resurrection. He will have a pleasing sight. In contrast to the cross comes 'the joy that was set before him'.[22] He will *make many to be accounted righteous*, having borne their iniquities. Yahweh pronounces formally that the Servant is *the righteous one*. This is in contrast to the pervasive sin that is the backcloth to what he did. He is truly vindicated before the bar of divine justice and publicly in his triumph over death.

Moreover, the Righteous One makes many to share in his righteousness through his bearing their iniquities. This is the seed of the

---

[20] Oswalt, *Isaiah 40–66*, p. 402.

[21] While Westermann agrees that this refers to 'an act done upon him after his death and on the far side of the grave' he resists going further to talk explicitly of resurrection from the dead (*Isaiah 40–66*, p. 267).

[22] Heb. 12:2.

biblical teaching of justification. It consists in the pardon, the complete removal and absolution of sin. Iniquities are buried in the depths of the sea (Mic. 7:19). It also entails being clothed in the righteousness of the vindicated Servant, having the same status before God as he does. This flows from the point that it is the Servant who is the Righteous One and that those who are accounted righteous are linked to him. Since he bore their iniquities, they share his righteousness. His sinful people are declared righteous. The Servant is the one foretold to be the deliverer from sin and death. Paul, reflecting on this, concluded that 'For our sake [the Father] made him to be sin who knew no sin, so that in him we might become the righteousness of God'.[23]

8. His reward (53:12)

The Servant is rewarded for his faithfulness unto death. The *spoil* here is a metaphor for a just reward for the expenditure of effort and dangerous toil. Once pitifully weak, the Servant is now triumphant. He seemed to be crushed beyond recognition (52:14) but he will now take his place among the great ones. From the lowest depths he is raised to the heights. Indeed, these grandees will do homage to him: *kings shall shut their mouths because of him* (52:15), they will 'prostrate themselves'[24] in submission to his regal rule. The reason is that *he poured out his soul to death*. As Paul was to put it 'he emptied himself',[25] not of what he was, such as aspects of his deity, but by becoming what he was not, taking the lowliest place as the Servant. Because he took the place of sinners, bearing their sins, and so continues to intercede for them, being in our nature at the Father's side, so he – as the Servant of the Lord – was raised to the heights.

Here the Servant is given his reward – *the many* – the entire number of those he delivers from the curse of sin. Meanwhile, *the strong*, the kings of the earth, are his spoil of victory, whom he has conquered and are at his disposal. This follows from his free and voluntary submission to death (*he poured out his soul . . .*), his identification with sinners (*was numbered with the transgressors*), his substitutionary atoning sacrifice (*he bore the sin of many*), and his mediatorial intercession (*he makes intercession for the transgressors*).[26]

---

[23] 2 Cor. 5:21. See Alec Motyer, *Isaiah: An Introduction and Commentary* (Leicester: IVP, 1999), pp. 441–442, who states that 'Isaiah 53:11 is one of the fullest statements of atonement theology ever penned'.

[24] Isa. 49:7.

[25] Phil. 2:7.

[26] Motyer, *Isaiah*, p. 443.

No wonder that, when asked by the Ethiopian as to the meaning of this passage which he was reading in his chariot, Philip 'told him the good news about Jesus'.[27] Hundreds of years of scepticism have failed to produce any convincing alternative focus for what Isaiah was saying. Centuries beforehand, the picture of the suffering and eventually triumphant Servant was already foretold. In the fullness of time, the details would be made known. Meanwhile the deliverer foreshadowed in Genesis, identified as a descendant of Abraham, in the line of David, and to be born in Bethlehem in remote obscurity, is disclosed as a supremely righteous sufferer who will be gloriously vindicated to lead his people. Thanks be to God!

[27] Acts 8:35.

Part Two
Christ incarnate

After the passing of the centuries, at last the promised deliverer arrives. Paul, in reflecting on this momentous event, writes that it happened at exactly the right time – 'when the fullness of time had come'.[1] God had prepared his people for this moment through many long years, and almost continual struggles. Ever since the late seventh century BC, they had been in exile. At first, Judah was driven from the land of promise to Babylon. Then, having returned, it was in a state of subjugation and dependency. Prophecy had ceased for over four hundred years. The voice of God was silent. It is at this low ebb that Christ came into the world to save sinners.

[1] Gal. 4:4.

Luke 1:26–38
7. Birth announcement

The record of the angel's appearance to Mary is so familiar that we may be inclined to overlook the many details. Moreover, the focus can easily drift to Mary rather than her son. Certainly, Mary was given a privilege greater than any other woman had or would ever have. No amount of concern at undue reverence for her should stop us recognizing that. However, this passage shows that right at the centre of her attention, and thus of Luke's, is the identity of the child she bore.

1. The identity of the Son (26–33)

Earlier Luke records the highly unusual events surrounding the conception of John the Baptist, who was to be the forerunner of the Christ. Zachariah and Elizabeth were beyond the age at which parents normally conceive children; they were also childless. Their son was to be a great prophet. He was to go before the Lord to prepare his way. He was the one foretold by Isaiah, a voice crying in the wilderness, drawing Israel's attention to the imminent realization of the remarkable prophecies of the OT. Yet the question remained – how was Yahweh to come to deliver his people? Here the answer is supplied by the angel Gabriel to a startled young woman. The connection with John is clear from the reference to Gabriel's visit being *in the sixth month* (26) of Elizabeth's pregnancy. The future task of John and the identity of the child described here are intertwined. This is pregnant with meaning. It will be clear from the fact that John is the climax, the end point, of OT prophecy. His ministry will bring to an end the OT, since the one on whom his ministry focuses is to be the complete embodiment of all the covenant promises of Yahweh.

a. Mary at the juncture of heaven and earth (26–27)

No wonder Mary was shocked and perturbed! Suddenly she had an unexpected visitor, a messenger from another dimension. *The angel Gabriel was sent from God to a city of Galilee named Nazareth.* His departure point was God; his destination was an obscure backwater in the far north of Israel. This was a conjunction of the spiritual realm and the material, heaven and earth. This great spirit appeared in bodily form. He left the presence of God; he arrived at a village in Israel. He spoke to Mary in Hebrew. These factors together aroused extreme agitation on Mary's part. Nothing like this ever had happened to her before. Added to this, she was young – *a virgin betrothed to a man whose name was Joseph* – legally married to Joseph, for that is what betrothal in Israel entailed, although the customary period of a year before the marriage was consummated had not yet passed.

Twice in verse 27 Luke records that Mary was a *parthenos*, a *virgin*.[1] As Nolland remarks, this is a clear barrier to the promised child just as Elizabeth's barrenness was to the birth of John the Baptist.[2] Both events are demonstrably the results of the sovereign power of God. On the other hand, Joseph – who features here only tangentially – is described as *of the house of David.* For that reason, the family are in David's line and the inheritance of the promises given to David in 2 Samuel 7 is of immediate relevance and about to be fulfilled.

b. Mary as the recipient of grace (28–29)

Gabriel's first words – words evidently *from God* – are words of greeting: *Hail, highly favoured one, the Lord be/is with you.* Mary is described as the passive receiver of God's grace. She has been favoured by Yahweh. Yahweh is with her. She is in a relation to God in which she has received God's favour and continues to do so. A

---

[1] The word could mean 'a young woman of marriageable age' (Johannes P. Louw and Eugene A. Nida [eds.], *Greek-English Lexicon of the New Testament Based on Semantic Domains* [New York: United Bible Societies, 1988], 1:109) but, as we shall see in a moment or two, the passage points unmistakeably to virginity. As Morris points out, 'the evidence of the Gospel as we have it is plain' (Leon Morris, *Luke: An Introduction and Commentary*, TNTC [Leicester: IVP, 1997], p. 79). Fitzmyer calls 'the normal understanding' of *parthenos* as virgin (Joseph A. Fitzmyer, SJ, *The Gospel According to Luke (I–IX)*, AB [New York: Doubleday, 1970], p. 343). See also Joel B. Green, *The Gospel of Luke*, NICNT (Grand Rapids: Eerdmans, 1997), pp. 85–86. The context (see v. 34) establishes this beyond question. For a detailed discussion of competing interpretations see I. Howard Marshall, *The Gospel of Luke: A Commentary on the Greek Text*, NIGTC (Exeter: Paternoster Press, 1978), pp. 68–70.

[2] John Nolland, *Luke 1–9:20*, WBC 35A (Dallas: Word Books, 1989), p. 49.

clear token of this is the announcement that follows. In these words there is not the slightest hint that Mary herself is a conduit of grace to others, still less a dispenser of the favour of God.[3] The participle is passive, not active. If Mary is representative of anything it is of the faithful who *receive* the bountiful goodness of God. Gabriel's statement is intended to reassure her in the face of the agitation and perplexity that gripped her as a result of the sudden intrusion of supernatural forces. It is tantamount to a declaration that her status with God is secure.

Nevertheless, even these words are not enough to banish all confusion from Mary's mind (29). She is terrified. She needs further words to convince her that there is no reason to fear (30). Only Gabriel's message will remove all distress and doubt. Even then, as seems characteristic of Mary, she ponders the meaning of the events and words that she sees and hears.

c. The announcement of the child (30–33)

There are good reasons for Mary not to fear but instead to rejoice (1:46–55). The angel repeats that she has found favour with God. The nature of this favour becomes evident in what follows. She will conceive *a son*. He is to be called Jesus, which means Yahweh saves.[4] In anticipation of the coming of the Christ, who would deliver his people and reign over the house of David forever, many a parent had given their son this name, in the hope that it might be he who would deliver the people, in a way analogous to Joshua, who led Israel into the land of promise. But this is different. Here is an explicit declaration from Gabriel, sent directly from God, that *this* is the child who will be the deliverer and saviour. The connection with the conception of John is again significant, for his work was to prepare the way for the saviour. That Mary knew of this, we may be confident; she and Elizabeth were cousins. Mary was well aware of her remarkable pregnancy and no doubt the angelic announcements that surrounded it, delivered by the same Gabriel who stood here now at this time and place.

The child Mary will bear will excel everything. He will be great. John was to be 'great before the Lord'[5] but Jesus' greatness will surpass every potential rival. *He . . . will be called the Son of the Most High* – in the Greek there are no definite articles, indicating Luke

---

[3] The Jesuit scholar Fitzmyer acknowledges that the later scholastic tradition went beyond the Lucan perfect participle (*Luke (I-IX)*, pp. 345–346). See Marshall, *Luke*, p. 65.

[4] On the meaning see Fitzmyer, *Luke (I-IX)*, p. 347.

[5] Luke 1:15.

has in mind the quality of the terms, demonstrating his absolute uniqueness. Furthermore, the phrase *the Most High* is often used in the OT to refer to God. In the background, perhaps, is the list of titles in Isaiah 9:6–7 where the child born to deliver the covenant people of God is termed the 'Mighty God'.

Additionally, *the Lord God will give to him the throne of his father David*. This child will be the one to receive and inherit the promises of the Davidic covenant (2 Sam. 7:12–16; Ps. 89:26–29). In contrast to the line of Davidic kings, who for the most part failed to follow the commands of Yahweh, Jesus *will reign over the house of Jacob for ever, and of his kingdom there will be no end*. In tandem with the Davidic throne comes the vision of the Son of Man in Daniel 7, who is given a universal kingdom that will never end. Here the point Luke made in verse 27 about Joseph becomes clear. Since Joseph will become Jesus' legal father, Jesus will indisputably be in the line of David, since in Israel legal paternity decided the matter. Jesus' opponents never questioned his Davidic claim. For Paul, it would be a crucial element of his view of Christ, 'born of the seed of David according to the flesh'.[6]

What a staggering announcement for Mary to take in! Even more so, since her marriage had not yet been consummated and the penalty for sexual infidelity by a betrothed woman was death.[7]

2. God's power (34–38)

a. The miraculous conception (34–35)

For Mary, this was to pile one shock upon another. As if the identity of her son were not enough to astonish and amaze her, the fact itself was beyond comprehension. The obvious point is that she was still a virgin. This was impossible. These things did not happen. Children were conceived by the regular traditional methods. Mary's question in verse 34 underlines this. *'How will this be, since I do not know a man?'* Green remarks that 'her question plays a vital theological role, for it accents the fact that she is still a virgin'.[8] People in first-century Israel were no more gullible or credulous than in our own day – possibly less so. One of the three main religious groups at the time, the Sadducees, were anti-supernaturalists, rationalists who opposed the idea of the resurrection and angels. For them, the very notion that the angel Gabriel had visited Nazareth was in the realm of fairy-tales; that is to say nothing about the details of his message.

[6] Rom. 1:3.
[7] Deut. 22:23–24.
[8] Green, *Luke*, p. 89.

So Mary was not taken in. She questioned the angel. However, it was not a question stemming from scepticism; her faith is evident in verse 38. It was the question of one who believes but needs to understand in some way what at first eludes or transcends the capacities of the mind. How can these things be? She believes but does not as yet understand.[9] This is not a description of any inner resolve to remain a virgin. There is no grammatical support for the claim of perpetual virginity or of any vow of that nature, a position which Roman Catholic exegetes are more and more abandoning.[10]

So Gabriel explains. His comment is poetic. It is presented in parallelism. Hebrew poetry rhymes ideas, not words, presenting them in successive lines, sometimes in similar ways and at other times in opposition.

> *The Holy Spirit will come upon you*
> *and the power of the Most High will overshadow you.*

That the angel frames his explanation in poetic terms indicates it remains deeply mysterious, beyond the bounds of ready definition. The truth cannot be captured merely in prose. The gist of his statement is that the imminent pregnancy will be due to the Holy Spirit. It will result from the action of God. The language reminds us of the account of creation in Genesis 1. There 'the Spirit of God was hovering over the face of the waters'.[11] The image is of the Spirit hovering over the waters of creation like a mother bird. Here, the angel relates that the Spirit, in overshadowing Mary, is to bring about a new creation. This is a new creative act on the part of God, the start of a new humanity of which the child is the head, a new creation that will stand and flourish for eternity.[12] This is the decisive point in the history of redemption, in world history as a whole. As with the original creation – and indeed all the direct mighty acts of God such as the resurrection – no one is there to observe the mechanics of it, to see what actually occurs at the instant the work is done. It remains a mystery, only known by revelation (cf. Job 38:1–11). As if to emphasize this, in our day we know that parthenogenesis (virginal

---

[9] Ibid.; Nolland, *Luke 1–9:20*, p. 55; Fitzmyer, *Luke (I-IX)*, p. 348.

[10] Fitzmyer, *Luke (I-IX)*, pp. 348–349.

[11] Gen. 1:2.

[12] Most commentators draw attention to a kindred phrase in Acts 1:8, to manifestations of the glory of God in the exodus and wilderness period or to the transfiguration, but miss this point entirely. Green is right, however, in asserting that 'these parallel affirmations do not suggest sexual activity, but do connote divine agency' (Green, *Luke*, p. 90). However, what element of divine agency is more compelling in this case than creation? Barth expresses it well when he describes the virgin birth as 'a creative act of divine omnipotence' (*CD* , IV/1, p. 207).

conception) can only produce a female, since, without the participation of a male, the Y chromosome is missing. This effectively
requires a supervening action of God to create what otherwise would
be absent.

The consequence of the Spirit's sovereign, creative action is that
the child to whom Mary gives birth will be called the *holy Son of God*.
There are a range of possible word orders in this sentence. In the final
analysis, the stress falls on the last words of the sentence – *huios theou*
(Son of God). In his humanity Jesus will be the *Son of God*. Israel
had been called God's son (Exod. 4:22; Hos. 11:1). The Davidic king
was the embodiment of sonship (Ps. 2:7) and Israel was anticipating
this to be developed by great David's greater son. Having already
described Jesus as *the son of the Most High* (32) and against the
backcloth of Isaiah 9:6–7, where the son born is 'the mighty God', it
is impossible to exclude from this statement an attribution of deity
to the child. This the church has recognized down through the ages
in calling Mary *theotokos* (God-bearer). Overall, Jesus' divine sonship
follows from the miraculous divine conception due to the work of
the Holy Spirit. It is this that fits him for the throne of David.[13]

However, other descriptions of the child Jesus are present here
too. He is a child and has a mother; so he is human. He is *holy*
(*hagios*); set apart for God, his call, and his purposes. Entailed in this
is separation from sin and its entailments. In Matthew's account of
the birth announcement – on that occasion the one given to Joseph
– Jesus is to 'save his people from their sins'.[14] In order to do this he
must be free from the entanglements that sin has brought into
the world.

b. Corroborating support (36–37)

Gabriel goes out of his way to reassure Mary that this is indeed her
future. First, there is Elizabeth's remarkable pregnancy. In Luke's
account earlier in the same chapter, there is no hint that this was
attributable to a direct action by the Holy Spirit. The reader is to
assume that conception occurred by the regular means, even though
the Spirit may have enabled it to occur. Besides, Zacharias and
Elizabeth had been married for years. There was no indication
that Elizabeth's pregnancy could have happened by extraordinary
means. Nevertheless, it was noteworthy due to the advanced age of
both husband and wife. Mary herself appears to be quite young.
Elizabeth was her cousin, but cousins can be quite distant in age due

[13] Green, *Luke*, p. 91.
[14] Matt. 1:21.

to the respective ages of their parents. This is how Luke presents it. Both Zacharias and Elizabeth were 'advanced in years'.[15] Zacharias affirms this to the angel, calling himself *presbytēs* 'an old man'.[16] He did not believe that Elizabeth would become pregnant.[17] Meanwhile Elizabeth herself was called 'barren' – a term of reproach for a woman –and when the child was eventually born a great celebration was held.[18] The evidence points to years of childlessness, following which her status as barren was widely recognized. Yet into this situation the power of God came with overwhelming force, and at last – beyond expectation – a child was conceived – and what a child, the direct forerunner of the Christ! So Gabriel's news was already foreshadowed. Mary's own cousin was the bearer of a staggeringly portentous son, and also in the most unexpected manner.

Second, the angel points to the invincible power of the word of God (37). No word from God is powerless; he always accomplishes what he says he will do. Again, Gabriel reflects on the creation account in Genesis. With the Spirit of God hovering over the waters, God said 'let there be light' and there was light.[19] He spoke; it was done. He created. He brought into existence what previously had no existence. He calls the things that are not as though they are. For Mary, this meant that what in human terms was impossible – to conceive a male child without the participation of a male – could be effected by the word of God in an instant. Luke points to the Holy Spirit and the word of God working together, inseparably, powerfully, effectively, effortlessly.

e. Mary's faithful response (38)

For Mary, this was to be an extremely difficult situation. We know from Matthew that after she became pregnant Joseph intended to divorce her for marital infidelity. Only after the intervention of 'the angel of the Lord' did he desist, and with Mary believed the angel's declaration and acted on it.[20] The penalty for sexual immorality by a betrothed woman was death by stoning, as pointed out above.[21] Since Joseph was a righteous man, before the angel visited him he had determined on a private divorce so as to protect Mary as far as possible. Either way, Mary's immediate future was fraught with

---

[15] Luke 1:7.
[16] Luke 1:18.
[17] Luke 1:20.
[18] Luke 1:7, 25, 57–58.
[19] Gen. 1:1–5.
[20] Matt. 1:20–21.
[21] Deut. 22:23–24.

danger. Besides the obvious changes that pregnancy would bring were the social problems that may have loomed larger. Beyond that, there would be the comments and the gossip about the unusual nature of Jesus' birth and her own participation in it – how many would believe the story of an angel? There is evidence that this was raised against Jesus by some of his opponents (John 8:41) and in the NT there is an awareness that his origins were unusual.[22]

Yet Mary's immediate reply is one of unalloyed faith: *let it be to me according to your word.* In this she echoes David's response to the word of the Lord through Nathan the prophet, concerning the promises about David's dynasty: 'and now, O LORD God, confirm forever the word that you have spoken concerning your servant and concerning his house, and do as you have spoken.'[23] In faith, Mary believes God's word, submits to it and follows it. Her own circumstances are secondary; indeed, they are out of the picture entirely. Faith is a matter of denying oneself, taking up one's cross and following Jesus. Mary, far from being a co-redemptrix, is a pattern for the church of saving faith. The whole scenario, as Barth stressed, portrays the relationship between the regenerating work of the Holy Spirit and the consequent response of faith.[24] Additionally, the virginal conception stands at the start of the Gospels with the resurrection at the climax, like book-ends framing the whole, pointing to the mighty acts of God constituting and establishing the entire drama of salvation.[25] Changing the metaphor, these are like frames around a picture, enclosing a portrait of surpassing beauty, of which we will catch a glimpse in the chapters that follow.

The tinsel and trappings that surround Christmas, with its overt commercialism and the welter of activity that goes with it, overpowers and effectively buries the message of the incarnation. Most of us do not have the time to reflect on its staggering nature and so we fail to integrate it into our grasp of what salvation entails. The consequences are that our faith and living are impoverished.

---

[22] Mark describes Jesus as 'the son of Mary' (Mark 6:3); a man would normally be seen in relation to his father. Paul uses *gennaō* for human begetting of sons and does so three times in Gal. 4 but when in the same context (Gal. 4:4) he refers to the birth of Jesus he uses *ginomai*. Tertullian insists on a reading of John 1:13 in the singular *qui non* (who was born not of bloods . . .) referring to the birth of Jesus, and castigates the Valentinian gnostics for intruding the plural *hoi ouk* (who were born . . .) in reference to believers. See Thomas F. Torrance, *Incarnation: The Person and Life of Christ* (Milton Keynes: Paternoster, 2008), pp. 88–94.

[23] 2 Sam. 7:25.

[24] Barth, *CD*, I/2, pp. 138–141.

[25] The finest exposition of the doctrine of the virgin birth is Torrance, *Incarnation*, pp. 94–104.

Luke 2:41–52
8. Growth and development

The scene here is from when Jesus was taken to Jerusalem for the Passover feast at the age of twelve. His parents went up at this time each year. It may have been the occasion when he had his *bar-mitzvah* (son-of-the-law) ceremony, although some scholars think that that occurred at the age of thirteen and so this was merely preparatory.[1] Jews were required to attend three feasts each year at the temple. Human nature being what it is, by the time of Jesus most people only went to one. Moreover, the dispersion of Jews following the exile made the original requirement somewhat impractical.[2] There were concessions for the poor. We know that Joseph and Mary were poor; when the time came for them to offer a sacrifice after Jesus' birth they were unable to pay for a lamb or goat and instead offered the alternative for those who could not afford it, a pair of turtledoves and two young pigeons.[3] After the *bar-mitzvah*, as a 'son of the law', came acceptance of full responsibility for the law, with all its obligations.

1. Jesus and obedience (41–45)

The episode at Jerusalem, where Jesus stayed behind, unknown to his parents, raises questions in some minds about whether he was living in submission to his father and mother as the Law prescribed

---

[1] See John Nolland, *Luke 1–9:20*, WBC 35A (Dallas: Word Books, 1989), pp. 128–229; Joseph A. Fitzmyer, SJ, *The Gospel According to Luke (I-IX)*, AB (New York: Doubleday, 1970), p. 440; Leon Morris, *Luke: An Introduction and Commentary*, TNTC (Leicester: IVP, 1997), p. 100; I. Howard Marshall, *The Gospel of Luke: A Commentary on the Greek Text*, NIGTC (Exeter: Paternoster Press, 1978), p. 126.

[2] Morris, *Luke*, p. 100; Marshall, *Luke*, p. 126.

[3] Luke 2:24; cf. Lev. 12:6–8.

(Exod. 20:12). The whole passage is summarized in verse 51 where Jesus is said to be *submissive to them*. Luke evidently wants his readers to know that the incident recorded here is to be seen in this light, not as an act of defiance. So as to understand what is happening we need to know about the conditions that prevailed at the feasts, especially at Passover (41).

Passover was attended by vast crowds. Some have estimated that there were as many as upward of three million in and around Jerusalem at the time. We have only to think of the huge numbers of pilgrims who travel to Mecca to see how this might be. Moreover, the roads to Jerusalem were often dangerous. Highway robbery was common and this journey would have passed through hostile Samaritan territory.[4] Such dangers were highlighted in one of Jesus' parables (Luke 10:29–37). Because of the threats from brigands, pilgrims often travelled in large convoys. These were normally divided into two sections; the men in one group, the women and children in another.[5] Jesus could have been in either group, in the thinking of his parents. He was of an age where he could easily have fitted into one or the other division of Mary and Joseph's convoy; they could both have supposed that he was in the other one from theirs, which explains how his parents might not miss him.[6] Only at nightfall, when the convoy stopped, would they look for him and discover to their consternation that he was not with them at all (43–44).

How about Jesus at this point? Why was he not with his parents? It is clear he had not decided to run away from home. Instead, he was preoccupied with other things, which assumed greater weight than the mere fact of returning to Nazareth. The nature of the things that had detained him becomes clear in the course of the paragraph. For now, the point to note is that his parents had assumed that he would be in the appropriate place and had not for one instant thought otherwise. In short, they trusted him implicitly at this age and had no concerns that he would have diverged from his customary behaviour. He would be where he ought to be. This is surely indicative of the fact that as a child his mother and father had grown to trust him to act in an appropriate way. He had inspired their fullest confidence. Indeed, in verse 40 Luke has said that during this time he 'grew and became strong, filled with wisdom'. This summary statement covers his entire childhood. It was evidently one of faithful obedience to his parents.

[4] Fitzmyer, *Luke (I-IX)*, p. 441.
[5] Morris, *Luke*, pp. 100–101.
[6] Marshall, *Luke*, p. 127.

2. Jesus and vocation (46–51)

What exactly was it that kept Jesus in Jerusalem? His parents found him in the temple after three days (bearing in mind the Jewish method of reckoning a part of a day as a whole, 46). This was not where they thought he would be: he was in his Father's house. May there be a hint here of Jesus' later comment recorded by John: 'Destroy this temple and in three days I will raise it up',[7] referring to his death and resurrection? The temple was the place where Yahweh and his people met; Jesus is the place where God and man meet. He is the fulfilment of the temple. His resurrection, on the third day, seals this point. However, at the time all this was in the future.

Jesus was deeply engaged in catechetical education with the leading rabbis of the day, asking and answering questions (46). This was the normal form of instruction in Israel. The rabbis were holding court, as was their custom, and Jesus was with them in intense debate. It is tempting to think of him instructing the rabbis but the point is that he is seen as a learner. The focus of this dialogical and catechetical method of teaching was the Torah, the law of God and the details of God's covenant relationship with Israel.[8] This method was – and is – a highly effective way of learning. It was Rudyard Kipling who wrote

> I keep six honest serving men,
>   (They taught me all I knew);
> Their names are What and Why and When
>   And How and Where and Who.[9]

It is also very appropriate for learning biblical truth and has been adopted by the church throughout its history. Paul's letter to the Romans is structured in large measure by a series of pointed questions.

Jesus showed amazing understanding (47). This was not the arrogant cocksure attitude of a know-it-all, one of those people who have a smattering of knowledge and think they are the masters of all they survey. Jesus was not some precocious upstart, trying to show he knew better than all the rabbis of Jerusalem. No, as verse 40 states, he was 'filled with wisdom' and 'the favour of God was on him'. The wisdom and knowledge he possessed came from God. In line with Gabriel's birth announcement, we may conclude, with the great

[7] John 2:19.
[8] Fitzmyer, *Luke (I-IX)*, p. 442.
[9] From 'The Elephant's Child', in Rudyard Kipling, *The Just So Stories*.

Puritan theologian John Owen, that the Holy Spirit upheld his humanity; having overshadowed Mary at his conception, the Spirit continued to shape Jesus' ongoing life.[10] This is a theme very clear in these early chapters of Luke; every episode of his life and early ministry is undertaken with the leading and enabling of the Holy Spirit.[11] Bobrinskoy writes of 'an exceptional convergence between the outpouring of the Spirit and the birth of Christ'.[12]

That the main factor driving Jesus at this time was the overwhelming impact of the Holy Spirit is demonstrated by his pervasive awareness of the Father. In reply to his mother's agitated concern (48), he replies that it was necessary for him to be in his Father's house (49). He realizes his true father is his Father in heaven: *Did you not know that it is necessary for me to be in the affairs of my Father?* This was to be the prevailing theme throughout his future ministry; his consciousness that he was sent by the Father to do the Father's will, to complete the work the Father had given him. This recognition – with the correlative knowledge that he was the Son – was unique in Israel. Certainly, Israel in its corporate sense had been termed God's son (Hos. 11:1) but for an individual to describe himself this way was not known, even if at this point it is by implication.[13] It shows that even at the age of twelve Jesus was aware that he was the Son in relation to the Father. Later, in his public ministry it is evident he knew this meant equality with God (John 5:1–18; Matt. 11:25–27) and identity with him (John 10:22–38). Whether he knew all this precisely at this stage is not disclosed and we cannot be sure. One thing the passage does demonstrate is that he advanced in knowledge by the very means he was using at the time; questioning the rabbis so as to come to a more exact understanding of the works and ways of God disclosed in Scripture. He was growing in knowledge (52) and to do this he used the means to advance in knowing God and his revelation. This leads us to suppose that it was a growth from implicit to explicit knowledge, from a latent and tacit to a clear and explicit understanding. As Michael Polanyi

---

[10] 'A Discourse Concerning the Holy Spirit', in *The Works of John Owen*, vol. 3, ed. William H. Goold (London: Banner of Truth, 1966), pp. 160f. See also Colin Gunton, 'Two Dogmas Revisited: Edward Irving's Christology', *SJT* 41 (1998), pp. 359–376.

[11] Elsewhere I have drawn attention to this theme in the early chapters of Luke; see Robert Letham, *The Holy Trinity: In Scripture, History, Theology, and Worship* (Phillipsburg: Presbyterian & Reformed, 2004), pp. 56–57.

[12] Boris Bobrinskoy, *The Mystery of the Trinity: Trinitarian Experience and Vision in the Biblical and Patristic Tradition*, trans. Anthony P. Gythiel (Crestwood: St Vladimir's Seminary Press, 1999), p. 87.

[13] Morris, *Luke*, pp. 101–102; D. R. Bauer, 'Son of God', in *DJG*, pp. 769–775.

argued, we know more than we can tell.[14] This was a way of bringing to expression what Jesus may have tacitly known but not yet articulated.[15]

Luke sums up the sequel well when he points to his parents' bewilderment. They simply did not understand; who could? Mary, as was her custom, *treasured up all these things in her heart* (51) and no doubt passed them on to the apostles – John perhaps, to whose care Jesus entrusted her on the cross – so that they eventually came into passages of Scripture such as this. She must have thought about them long and hard, trying to make head and tail of them. Meanwhile, asserting again that this was not an act of disobedience or defiance on Jesus' part, Luke states that he *went down with them* [away from Jerusalem] *and came to Nazareth and was submissive to them* (51). Jesus fulfilled the Law, obeyed the fifth commandment.

3. Jesus and growth (52)

This simple statement summarizes all that came before and points us forward to the ongoing course of Jesus' life from that time on until he was to burst forth into the public eye: *And Jesus increased in wisdom and in stature, and in favour with God and man.*

The picture is one of steady growth in a range of ways. Jesus was fully human and so advanced in height and strength, in physical and mental maturity, in social esteem and in relation to God. In no way was his life as human curtailed or abbreviated.

He progressed in wisdom and stature. He grew in size; he grew in knowledge; he grew in his ability to relate that knowledge to life situations. As a child this had been evident (1:40). Even then, he was filled with wisdom and his parents trusted him thoroughly. Yet as he got older he got even wiser, responding effectively to new challenges as they arose.

[14] Michael Polanyi, *The Tacit Dimension* (Chicago: University of Chicago Press, 1958).

[15] N. T. Wright considers that while Jesus may have had a sense of his Messianic vocation from before his baptism, this is 'by no means the same thing as Jesus having the sort of "supernatural" awareness of himself, of Israel's god, and of the relation between the two of them, such as is often envisaged by those who, concerned to maintain a "high" Christology, place it within an eighteenth century context of implicit Deism where one can maintain Jesus' "divinity" only by holding some form of docetism' (N. T. Wright, *Jesus and the Victory of God* [London: SPCK, 1996], p. 653). See also ibid., pp. 532, 536–537. It is difficult to know who Wright has in mind. He cites no sources and does not refer to the classic works of the patristics such as Athanasius and Cyril, or to recent scholars like Grillmeier, Kelly, Pelikan, Meyendorff, Weinandy and McGuckin.

He grew in favour with God. This implies that he advanced in his understanding of his relationship with the Father and so of his realization that he was the Son. As the author of Hebrews puts it 'although he was a Son, he learned obedience'.[16] This was not a progression from disobedience to obedience but from one degree of obedience to another.[17]

He grew in favour with man. This was not the odious, obnoxious front of a self-righteous prig who does everything right but in a way that is thoroughly distasteful. Jesus was known as a convivial companion; indeed, he was later maliciously accused of gluttony and excessive consumption of alcoholic beverages. His first miracle involved turning water into wine at a wedding reception. Jesus was appropriately gregarious. He was a leader. He was widely liked.

Did Jesus ever get into fights? The answer must be yes! Fighting is a process by which young males learn self-defence and so how to protect the weak from the threats of bullies. We must also affirm that he did so without sin. Just as the Bible allows wars to be fought for a just cause, and as Israel was also commanded on occasions to wage war, so a just fight in defence can be fought without taint of sin. Jesus was no wimp, no weak, effeminate, super-pious non-entity. He grew strong (1:40). He was recognized as a leader.

Jesus' growth and development followed normal human lines. He was a real creature of flesh and blood. Being and remaining the eternal Son of God, one with the Father, he became man and was subject to all the constraints that being human imposes in a fallen world. As E. L. Mascall put it so graphically: 'There are obvious difficulties in supposing that, in the plain and obvious sense of the words, the human mind of the Babe of Bethlehem was thinking, as he lay in the manger, of the Procession of the Holy Ghost, the theorems of hydrodynamics, the novels of Jane Austen, and the Battle of Hastings.'[18]

As human his knowledge and experience was human. His development was human in every way, with the one exception of sin. Into this equation we need to bring the reality that in terms of his personal identity – *who* he is – he *is* the Son of God (Luke 1:35). This marks him out as unique. Fitzmyer correctly warns against the idea of most theologians in the last century who seek to understand who Jesus is from a purely human perspective.[19] The Gospels tell us that what we see here is the action of God. He reveals these things to Mary

---

[16] Heb. 5:8.

[17] Robert Letham, *The Work of Christ* (Leicester: IVP, 1993), pp. 113–121.

[18] E. L. Mascall, *Christ, the Christian and the Church* (London: Longmans, Green and Co., 1946), p. 53.

[19] Fitzmyer, *Luke (I–IX)*, p. 447.

and so to us. Yet when we ask of *what* he consists we must say that he is also human, that the Son of the Father, the holy Son of God, became human, from embryo to birth, from a baby, and a toddler to eventual maturity.

This is astounding, that the eternal Son, one with the Father from eternity, should take our nature and from birth should experience our conditions, entrusting himself to the complete care of human parents, reliant on them for the everyday needs of life, and following the normal stages of human development thereafter. Such is the magnitude of the grace of God. Great is the encouragement for us that nothing we face is beyond the knowledge or experience of the Son of God; by this he is perfectly equipped to save, support and strengthen us.

Matthew 3:13–17
9. Baptism

1. Jesus is baptized by John the Baptist (13–15)

a. Jesus arrives from Galilee (13)

Jesus, arriving *from Galilee*, appears in this account in Matthew for the first time as an active agent. It is the point at which he enters his public ministry. The huge crowds who came to the Jordan to be baptized by John were from Jerusalem, Judaea and the region around the Jordan itself (Matt. 1:5). The fact that Jesus was the sole person from Galilee – as far as Matthew reports it – draws attention to him in distinction from the rest of those who sought baptism.

b. Why does Jesus receive John's baptism? (13b–15)

This is the obvious question John asks. He recognizes Jesus; since they were cousins, it is hardly surprising. However, his recognition extends beyond this. He realizes Jesus' significance, his true identity. John had been baptizing with a view to the people's confession of sins (3:6) and their repentance (3:1–2). He rebuked many of the Pharisees and Sadducees, calling on them to bring forth works befitting repentance, warning them of impending judgment (3:7–10). This was a baptism that had in view the sin and rebellion of Israel. In the light of this, Jesus was not a candidate for baptism. John understands who he is. He tries to prevent the baptism taking place. Jesus has no need of this baptism; John sees himself as standing in need of baptism at Jesus' hands. This is remarkable circumstantial evidence of the way Jesus was viewed by those who knew him, and particularly by those given by God the insight to appreciate what he had come to do. We know from elsewhere that John acknowledged that he himself was the forerunner of the Christ, a voice crying in the wilderness 'make straight the way of the Lord'.[1] While Jesus' true identity was hidden from the masses, evidently it had been revealed to John.[2] So he considered himself, as a sinner, a candidate for baptism by Jesus, while seeing the incongruity of baptizing him. Moreover, John specifically identifies Jesus as the Messiah, the Son of God, the long-expected saviour. As we have already seen,[3] originally God had promised that a member of the human race would deal a crushing blow to the serpent and so overcome the damage caused by sin (Gen. 3:15). Later, the focus had narrowed to a descendant of Abraham, in whom all the families of the earth were to be blessed (Gen. 12:1–3). This was focused further on a descendant of Isaac not Ishmael (Gen. 17:15–21), of Jacob not Esau (Gen. 25:19–26, 29–34; 26:1–5; 27:1–40). Further down the years, the deliverer was disclosed to be, from within that line, from the family of David (2 Sam. 7:4–17). He was to be born in the tiny backwater of Bethlehem (Mic. 5:2). Now John identifies him specifically and particularly – he who meets all these requirements. *This* is the man![4] As John's Gospel records, he announced clearly and publicly, 'Behold, the Lamb of God, who takes away the sin of the world.'[5] All the clues strewn around in the pages of the OT are identified as directed to this one man, Jesus of Nazareth.

Why, then, did Jesus insist on being baptized? His whole mission was to 'save his people from their sins'.[6] This meant identifying with them in their fallen condition. As Isaiah had said, he was to be 'numbered with the transgressors'.[7] By undergoing John's baptism, Jesus was identifying himself with his people, with Israel, as the first step towards saving them from their sins. He was taking a stand here with sinners, setting himself in opposition to the self-righteous, to the religious establishment of the day. His reply to John emphazises this: *Let it be so now, for thus it is fitting to fulfil all righteousness.*

What does Jesus mean by this phrase? Among a range of ideas, one strong possibility is that he is referring to his fulfilment of OT prophecy about the Messiah. Matthew, particularly in these early chapters, is keen to point out that the events surrounding Jesus, from his conception onwards, were all in fulfilment of OT Scripture. This is clear from the opening sentence of his genealogy, identifying Jesus

---

[1] John 1:23.
[2] John 1:19–27.
[3] Chs. 1–4.
[4] On John the Baptist's distinctive place as a witness to Jesus Christ, see Karl Barth, *CD*, I/2, pp. 120–121.
[5] John 1:29.
[6] Matt. 1:21.
[7] Isa. 53:12.

as 'the son of David, the son of Abraham'.[8] A second line of thought is that since he saw this as a necessary part of fulfilling his mission to identify himself with sinners so as to save them from their sins[9] it is a reference to the cross, where Jesus' obedience reached its zenith. In this sense, his baptism is of a piece with his crucifixion. This idea surfaces in a later statement of Jesus, in which he identifies the cross as his baptism.[10] In both Calvary and the Jordan, he takes the place appropriate for a sinner, even though he had committed no sins of his own. In this, he bore God's judgment on his people for their sins, the righteous on behalf of and in place of the unrighteous. The baptism is right at the start of his public ministry, while the cross is at the end of it. Both are like book-ends, within which the account of his life, teaching and works is laid out by Matthew for his readers. There at the cross Jesus fulfilled all righteousness on behalf of those who confessed their sins and looked for the forgiveness that John's baptism anticipated. Here in his baptism this is foreshadowed and represented.

2. Jesus and the Spirit of God (16)

Immediately after his baptism four things happen. He emerges from the water, heaven is split open, the Spirit of God descends as a dove and rests upon him, and the voice of the Father is heard from heaven. For now, we will focus on the first three of these essentially concurrent events.

Jesus is baptized and emerges from the water. He then climbs the bank of the river. It is most likely that he would have been immersed in the river, although that cannot be established beyond reasonable doubt. However, Matthew's interest does not lie with the details of the baptism but with what comes immediately afterwards and as a consequence of it. The picture is of a new creation. At creation the ocean was pervasive, covering the earth. The work of formation that followed made the dry land appear as a place fit for humans to live. So here, Jesus emerges out of the deep, the waters of the Jordan, on to dry land. From another angle, the imagery points to the exodus. There Israel passed through the waters of the Red Sea, in which the Egyptians were drowned. This was an act of grace and of judgment, just as the baptism of John was connected with the forgiveness of sins and the threatening judgment of Israel. It is striking that as Israel

---

[8] Matt. 1:1.

[9] R. T. France, *The Gospel According to Matthew: An Introduction and Commentary*, TNTC (Leicester: IVP, 1985), pp. 94–95; Craig S. Keener, *A Commentary on the Gospel of Matthew* (Grand Rapids: Eerdmans, 1999), p. 132.

[10] Luke 12:50; Mark 10:38.

then faced forty years' temptation in the wilderness, Jesus moved on from his baptism to be tempted in the wilderness for forty days by the devil (Matt. 4:1–10; Luke 4:1–13).[11]

In conjunction with this, *the heavens are split open*. This is an occasion for God to give a supreme revelation. It mirrors the great vision in Ezekiel 1, the statement of Jesus to Nathanael that from that time he would see heaven opened (John 1:51), and Stephen's sight of heaven open and the Son of Man standing at the right hand of God (Acts 7:56). It is unclear whether only Jesus was aware of this or whether the onlookers shared in it in some way.[12] Apparently, for a brief while the barriers between the creaturely and the divine realm were removed.

At this point *the Holy Spirit descends as a dove*. This was a public event, open to all. Mark describes it in purely private terms, as something purely for Jesus' own benefit (Mark 1:10), although he does not exclude the possibility that others observed it too. Whereas the splitting of the boundaries of heaven and earth is described in terms of what Jesus saw, this is reported as a settled fact.[13] Since in the ancient world animals and birds were not named with scientific precision we cannot be sure that the bird that appeared was identical to what we call doves today.[14] However, that is incidental to the main focus of the report. Back in Genesis 1, the Spirit of God was brooding over the waters of creation like a mother bird (Gen. 1:2). Here the Spirit descends as a dove in connection with the baptismal waters, themselves pointers to creation.[15] Moreover, there is a close conjunction, an inseparability, between baptism by water and baptism by the Holy Spirit. Indeed, while John discounts this connection in terms of his own ministry, he explicitly states that the coming one will surpass him in baptizing with the Spirit. It is clear from this passage that, in the light of Jesus and his work, the two – while distinct – are inseparable. The Spirit's descent seals the fact that Jesus' public ministry is to be a new creation. Moreover, while the Spirit of God in the OT was sometimes associated with the fire of judgment, here he is seen in the form of a harmless dove, possibly denoting the fact that Jesus had come to save, to deliver the poor and

---

[11] See also W. D. Davies and D. C. Allison, *A Critical and Exegetical Commentary on the Gospel According to Saint Matthew: Volume I*, ICC (Edinburgh: T&T Clark, 1988), p. 328.

[12] Leon Morris, *The Gospel According to Matthew* (Grand Rapids: Eerdmans, 1992), p. 66.

[13] Davies and Allison, *Matthew I*, p. 330.

[14] Morris, *Matthew*, pp. 66–67.

[15] See David Hill, *The Gospel of Matthew* (London: Marshall, Morgan & Scott, 1972), p. 96.

afflicted.[16] However, why the Spirit appeared as a dove is not entirely clear, as is seen by no fewer than sixteen suggestions listed by Davies and Allison.[17]

The Spirit rests on Jesus. The Spirit of God confirms Jesus' identity, status and worthiness. Jesus as the Son of God, the Christ – the anointed one, anointed here by the Holy Spirit in fulfilment of Isaiah 61:1 – is immersed not only by water but also by the Spirit of the living God.[18] Indeed, this shows what it is to be quintessentially human; it is to be endowed with the Spirit of God, resting upon one and enabling one to fulfil the ministry and calling of God.

3. Jesus and the Father's voice (17)

The voice from heaven is self-evidently the voice of the Father naming Jesus as his Son.[19] Jesus was already called God's Son (Matt. 2:15). The flight to Egypt to escape the murderous edict of Herod resulted in his eventual departure from Egypt back to Israel on Herod's death, recapitulating the exodus under the leadership of Moses. In Hosea 11:1 Israel was called God's son, who Yahweh had delivered from Egypt; Jesus, in union with his covenant people, is the true Son.

However, we have here something more advanced than that. Here God speaks directly, affirming him as *my beloved Son, with whom I am well pleased.* The Father himself directly proclaims that Jesus is the Son. The statement is a conflation of Psalm 2:7 ('you are my Son') and Isaiah 42:1 ('my chosen [one], in whom my soul delights'). The psalm focuses on a royal enthronement as king. In this Jesus is proclaimed to be the one who will reign over the house of Jacob forever, to whom the promises of the Davidic covenant belong. Jesus is the Son, the king, in relation to God as his Father. The other passage refers to the Servant of the Lord. The servant is seen in Isaiah 42 as endowed with the Spirit of God, beloved by God, in a right relationship with him, but destined to suffer and be vindicated at the last. In this compressed statement the whole future career of Jesus as the Christ is previewed. He is the Davidic Messiah, the Son of God and the Servant of Isaiah.[20]

[16] Morris, *Matthew*, p. 67.

[17] Davies and Allison, *Matthew I*, pp. 331–334.

[18] Ibid., pp. 334–335.

[19] For a discussion of the Jewish idea of the *bat qōl* (daughter voice), see Keener, *Matthew*, pp. 133–234. It was developed to account for indirect revelation after prophecy ceased in post-exilic times. Here the voice is that of the Father, which far transcends the *bat qōl*. See also Donald A. Hagner, *Matthew 1–13*, WBC 33A (Dallas: Word Books, 1993), p. 58.

[20] France, *Matthew*, p. 96.

This remarkable scene is a revelation of the Trinity. The Father speaks from heaven identifying Jesus as his Son, while the Holy Spirit descends from heaven and comes upon the Son and rests upon him.[21] In the second century, Irenaeus saw that here at the Jordan, is a key to begin to understand something of the Trinity.[22] Moreover, this self-revelation of the Trinity is connected with baptism. Christian baptism is 'into the [one] name of the Father, and the Son, and the Holy Spirit' and is spelled out at the climax of this Gospel; it is baptism into the one new covenant name of God, the Trinity.[23]

At Jesus' baptism, heaven itself is opened. From our perspective, the boundaries of our existence and God's are blurred. Mark uses the verb *schizō*, meaning to tear or to split. It is the same verb as he and Matthew use for the rending of the temple veil after Jesus' death, signifying that the way is now open into the presence of the Father by the blood of Christ (Matt. 27:51; Mark 15:38). At both events Jesus identifies himself fully and explicitly with sinners.

Jesus' baptism is his immersion in the Holy Spirit and fire (3:11). His death on the cross he describes as his baptism, a baptism in the fire of divine judgment on sin (Luke 12:49–50). Both grace and judgment meet at this point. Judgment fell on the Son at the cross, dying to atone for his people's sins (Matt. 1:21). Yet this judgment is the door to unanticipated and immeasurable grace. As Jesus identified himself with sinners in his baptism at the Jordan and in the greater baptism on the cross, so we share in this by grace, in union with him, saturated in the Holy Spirit whom he gives in his baptism. Heaven is ripped opened to us. As Calvin said, this is a mystery; we dare not step too far into it yet we dare not shrink back from it.

---

[21] In the light of this, we note the comment of N. T. Wright that 'Jesus did not . . . "know that he was God" in the same way that one knows one is male or female, hungry or thirsty, or that one ate an orange an hour ago' (*Jesus and the Victory of God* [London: SPCK, 1996], p. 653). We remarked on the deficiencies of some of Wright's claims in the last chapter. There he apparently disparages the orthodox Christology of the historic church but does not refer to primary sources. Wright can say this here by ignoring passages such as – *inter alia* – John 1:1–18; 5:19–47; 10:29; 20:28 and giving only a brief, superficial and at best tangential mention of Matt. 11:25–27, which H. R. Mackintosh described as 'the most important for Christology in the New Testament', speaking as it does of 'the unqualified correlation of the Father and the Son' (*The Doctrine of the Person of Jesus Christ* [Edinburgh: T&T Clark, 1912], p. 27).

[22] Irenaeus, *Against Heresies*, 3:17:1–3; 3:18:1–2 (*ANF*, vol. 1).

[23] Matt. 28:19–20. Robert Letham, *The Holy Trinity: In Scripture, History, Theology, and Worship* (Phillipsburg: Presbyterian & Reformed, 2004), pp. 59–60; John Nolland, *The Gospel of Matthew* (Grand Rapids: Eerdmans, 2005), p. 158.

Hebrews 2:10–18
10. Human experience

The author of the letter to the Hebrews has drawn attention to the fact that God has put the human race in charge of the coming world – the new heavens and the new earth instituted at the death and resurrection of Christ. We do not yet see this. But we see Jesus at the right hand of God, crowned with glory and honour. He who is equated with God in the first chapter (Heb. 1:1–13) is one with us in our humanity, on the throne of God. We will approach this passage topically and logically rather than sequentially.

1. Jesus shares with us a common humanity (10–12)

Jesus is the *archēgos, the source and leader of our salvation.* The *archēgos* is one who takes action first and then brings those on whose behalf he has acted to the intended goal. He is akin to a pathfinder, an advance party, who goes ahead into dangerous terrain in order to clear the way for the rest of the group. Mountaineering is a particularly apt comparison. The leader of the team will climb ahead so as to bring the remaining members of the party to the summit.[1] This metaphor points to two things; Jesus being the primary and foremost member – the captain – and also his being of the same nature as the rest of the team.

[1] The noun *archēgos* is difficult to translate succinctly. See F. F. Bruce, *Commentary on the Epistle to the Hebrews: The English Text with Introduction, Exposition and Notes* (London: Marshall, Morgan & Scott, 1964), p. 43; Philip Edgcumbe Hughes, *A Commentary on the Epistle to the Hebrews* (Grand Rapids: Eerdmans, 1977), p. 100; Paul Ellingworth, *The Epistle to the Hebrews: A Commentary on the Greek Text*, NIGTC (Grand Rapids: Eerdmans, 1993), pp. 160–161. Lane's commitment to a Hellenistic background leads him to compare the author's description of Jesus to Hercules. To my mind this fails to do justice either to text or to context; see William L. Lane, *Hebrews 1–8*, WBC 47A (Dallas: Word Books, 1991), pp. 56–57.

The expedition of which Jesus is the leader is salvation. The author has already written of the greatness of this salvation, and so of the need to pay close attention to it (2:1–4). It consists in deliverance from sin through the sacrifice of the Son (Heb. 1:3–4). Many of those who received the letter were tempted to revert to some form of Judaism and so to repudiate once and for all the only means of deliverance from sin and death, found in Jesus Christ.[2] The author warns them in the strongest terms of the dire consequences of such an action. Once repudiated there would be no possibility of the forgiveness of sins but only a fearful expectation of the wrath of the holy God (Heb. 6:4–8; 10:26–31; 12:25–29).

Jesus achieved salvation for us, as our pioneer and forerunner, through sufferings (10). This is a theme that will feature greatly in this paragraph but for now we simply note it. The point we want to stress now is that what he achieved results in *many sons . . . [being brought] to glory.* A vast number will be saved and the salvation consists in arriving at *glory.* Glory is consistently used in both OT and NT to denote what is distinctive of God. Salvation consists of a restored and heightened relationship to God, a closeness in marked contrast to the fearful prospect of falling into the hands of the living God (Heb. 10:31). We will consider this again later.

Jesus' achievement of salvation arose because he was one with us. He took our nature. He was the eternal Son made man. *He who sanctifies and those who are sanctified are all of one.* Jesus is the one who sanctifies; we are those who are being sanctified. The author sees sanctification not in the way we usually think of it. For us, sanctification is a lifelong process – a struggle, as often as not – in becoming more like Christ. For the author it relates more closely to the basic meaning of the word, in the way it was viewed in the OT, as consecration to God, being set apart from the common, the everyday. This was at the heart of the priestly ritual of Leviticus. Throughout, there were clear distinctions between the holy and the common.[3] So here, our salvation consists in being set apart for God, being brought into his presence by the sacrifice of Christ. The author sees sanctification as entailing the whole of salvation.[4]

In order to do this, the Son had to be one with those he was to save. Hence he and they *are all of one.* The following context points to this as meaning the sharing of a common humanity. Christ and

[2] On the wide variety of suggestions about the recipients of the letter, see the literature.

[3] Ellingworth, *Hebrews*, pp. 163–164.

[4] See Geerhardus Vos, *The Teaching of the Epistle to the Hebrews* (Nutley: Presbyterian & Reformed, 1975), pp. 122–123; Bruce, *Hebrews*, pp. 44–45; Hughes, *Hebrews*, p. 103.

his people are all of one nature by reason of his incarnation. *For this reason he is not ashamed to call them brothers.* This is an expression known as *litotes*, in which something is affirmed by denying its opposite. We often use the expression 'not bad' to mean that some state of affairs is good. Here Jesus is effectively said to be proud to call us brothers.

In support of this striking claim the author cites Psalm 22:22 (21:23 in the Hebrew Bible): *I will declare your Name to my brothers; in the midst of the congregation I will sing praise to you.*[5] Here the Christ is foretold as taking his place in the congregation of the faithful and joining with it in the worship of Yahweh. Moreover, he declares the character and acts of Yahweh to the people of God. He is both prophet and worshipper. In both cases he shares the nature of those among whom he stands. In citing this psalm, the author is implicitly referring its whole contents to the Christ, who is Jesus. The first section refers to the psalmist's intense sufferings, his abandonment by Yahweh (Ps. 22:1–21), while the remainder focuses on his anticipated triumph (Ps. 22:22–31). Ultimately, this is fulfilled at the cross and in the resurrection of Jesus from the dead. As David experienced both suffering and glory, so his son, the son of the covenant promises, tasted it in unfathomably greater measure. The exalted redeemer proclaims God's name and grace in his church to his brothers.

2. Jesus exercised with us a common faith (13)

Jesus' common humanity with us is demonstrated in his exercising faith, just as we are to do. The author makes two citations from Isaiah 8. Isaiah prophesied at a time of intense national decline due to dereliction of its covenant responsibilities. Judah was gradually enmeshed in idolatry and the inevitable injustice that followed. A large part of the prophet's ministry was to foretell the coming judgment of Yahweh, seen later in the exile in Babylon. The sanctions of the Mosaic covenant were hanging over the nation, like the sword of Damocles. The first citation, from Isaiah 8:17, describes Isaiah's faith in Yahweh as he seals the oracles of grace and judgment. He has met with no positive response from either the king or the people. Many will stumble and fall, be broken and snared (Isa. 8:15). Yahweh is 'hiding his face from the house of Jacob'. This must have

[5] In recent years, in an attempt to be inclusive, it has been common to talk of 'sons and daughters of God'. While the intention behind such language is laudable, it tends to obscure the reality that 'sonship' in the NT is not sexual in nature but denotes the point that we share the identical relation to the Father by adoption that Christ the Son has by nature. In this sense, 'sons' makes this identity patent.

been exceedingly hard for Isaiah to bear. Yet in this situation he says 'I will hope in him'.[6] So, the author of Hebrews says, Jesus placed his trust and confidence in the Father in the face of the opposition and rejection of the covenant people of his own day. In turn, the recipients of Hebrews were faced by persecution and some were tempted to give up their profession of faith in Jesus. The message is that Jesus shared our struggles and in doing so he placed his full confidence in Yahweh. His humanity is evident by his faith in the midst of opposition and persecution.

The second citation, from Isaiah 8:18 (the next sentence) takes this a stage further: 'Behold, I and the children whom the Lord has given me are signs and portents in Israel from the LORD of hosts, who dwells on Mount Zion.' The context is, of course, the same; national apostasy and impending judgment. Isaiah trusts in the mercy of Yahweh in promising deliverance to a world under his judgment. The names of the children are full of significance, as Hebrew names usually were. Shear-Jashub meant 'a remnant will return',[7] pointing to the eventual restoration of a remnant from exile in Babylon. Isaiah's other son, Maher-Shalal-Hash-Baz (poor chap), meant 'the spoil speeds, the prey hastens'.[8] In this case, the reference is to a closer event, when the combined forces of Syria and the northern kingdom ranged against Judah would be ravaged and destroyed by the Assyrians, and so Judah would enjoy a respite and a time for the covenant grace of Yahweh to be experienced.

By giving the two sons these names Isaiah showed his faith in the mercies of Yahweh, his commitment to his covenant even in the midst of the rampant unfaithfulness of his people. Applied here to Christ, the author is pointing to his obedient faith. The human surroundings were grim but he held firm to the promises of his Father and the work he had come to do. So too should you, the author encourages his people. There is of course a difference here. Jesus' faith was in God his Father. He did not exercise *saving faith* since he had no need of salvation himself. Our faith comes out of a situation of enmeshment in the mire of sin and rebellion, of endemic malfeasance, and is inextricably allied with repentance, a change of mind and conduct, from sin and death to righteousness and life. However, both Jesus' faith and ours share this in common; they are both trust in God and both are present in a world that is hostile to him.

---

[6] Isa. 8:17.
[7] Isa. 7:3.
[8] Isa. 8:1–4.

3. Jesus faced common temptations (18)

Temptation (*peirasmos*) entails being put to the test. In the Bible, when measured against the commandments of God, it refers to ethical and moral testing. Adam and Eve, in the garden, were given a command by God not to eat of the fruit of the tree of the knowledge of good and evil (Gen. 2:16–17). This prohibition went alongside their privilege of being able to eat from any of the other trees, of which there was a great profusion. They had the freedom of creation as bearing the image of God, and the task of tending the garden as his stewards. In short, this commandment was not onerous; it was simply a boundary marker, a test, in the midst of a sumptuous feast provided specially for them.

Temptation for our first parents came in the form of the serpent, which is later understood by Paul to be the devil, Satan (Rom. 16:20). It appeared as first a question about what God had said (Gen. 3:1), then an addition to his word on the part of Eve (Gen. 3:2–3), followed by an outright denial of its truth (Gen. 3:5–6). It was incitement to disobey God's commands, coming from an external source, with which Eve was complicit by her adding to the word of God. For us, temptation can come from external sources, as with Eve, but it also finds a positive response on the part of our own sinful propensities, inherited from our first parents.

Jesus, in being incarnate for us and our salvation, was exposed to temptation. Whereas Adam was tested in a beautiful garden, with every provision for which he could wish readily accessible on every side, Jesus was faced by the attacks of the serpent in a dreadful and barren desert. While Adam had food in abundance, Jesus fasted for forty days and forty nights. In both cases, the temptation was from an outside source. For both, part of the test was to seek to attain divine status by grasping for it. Adam and Eve succumbed; Jesus remained resolutely faithful, although for him he was and ever had been in the form of God.

Throughout his earthly ministry Jesus faced innumerable testings, from opponents, from demons, from wayward disciples. He was 'in every respect . . . tempted as we are'.[9] This does not mean he was tempted in every way that it is possible for a human being to be tempted. He never faced a temptation to be unfaithful to his wife, for he never married. Yet there was no area of life in which he could be immune from the attacks of the evil one. There is one difference between his temptations and ours; while with us there is that pull towards sin coming from within, with him he remained steadfast in

[9] Heb. 4:14–15.

his obedience to the Father. That does not make his temptation any less real or acute. Indeed, no one faced temptation like he did since no one resisted it as he did. Like walking into the force of a gale, the wind's power is more strongly felt than if one simply goes with the flow. Jesus' persistent, complete and comprehensive faithfulness to the Father meant that he experienced the force of temptation more graphically and urgently than any of us could ever do.

4. Jesus endured common sufferings (18)

Pre-eminently the reference is to the cross, where Jesus' sufferings reached their pinnacle. Already, Psalm 22 has been in the author's mind and we would not be far wrong in seeing the first part of that psalm as an appropriate backdrop here. There he suffered abandonment; 'My God, my God, why have you forsaken me?' he cried.

Yet Jesus' sufferings are not to be restricted to the crucifixion. Throughout his life he bore our griefs and carried our sorrows. We recall our earlier comment, worth repeating, that D. M. Lloyd-Jones thought that the Pharisees' statement that 'you are not yet fifty years old' implied that he had aged prematurely due to the intense burdens he bore as our Saviour in a world of sin.[10] Moreover, this verse implies that his sufferings were intensified by his faithful resistance.[11] As much in view at this point is the anguish he endured at Gethsemane, to which the author of Hebrews makes clear reference in chapter 5. As the *Heidelberg Catechism*, Question 37 states:

> What do you understand by the word *suffered*? Answer. That all the time he lived on earth, but especially at the end of his life, he bore, in body and soul, the wrath of God against the sin of the whole human race, in order that by his passion, as the only atoning sacrifice, he might redeem our body and soul from everlasting damnation; and obtain for us the grace of God, righteousness, and eternal life.[12]

5. Jesus underwent a common death (14)

The reality of Christ's humanity is never more pointedly evident than in his death and burial. This is the common lot we all face due to the sin of Adam. He took our nature and, having offered himself

[10] D. Martyn Lloyd-Jones, *Studies in the Sermon on the Mount: Volume One* (London: Inter-Varsity Fellowship, 1959), pp. 56–57.

[11] Hughes, *Hebrews*, pp. 123–124.

[12] Philip Schaff, *The Creeds of Christendom*, vol. 3 (Grand Rapids: Baker, 1966), p. 319, language modernized.

up on the cross by the Holy Spirit to the Father (Heb. 9:14), died and was buried. Earlier in the chapter the author has stated that he tasted death (2:9); the verb *geuomai* here does not mean that he merely had a brief sample of death but did not ultimately experience it, much like we might pick at food on a heavily laden buffet table but nothing more. It means he faced it and experienced it thoroughly. He hung on the cross. He gave up his spirit, committing himself to the Father. He was taken down from the cross, a lifeless corpse. He was wrapped in grave clothes. He was laid in a tomb. The tomb was closed by a huge boulder that took at least four able-bodied men to move. The boulder was sealed. He was dead.

To that extent, Jesus' death is of the same kind as ours. In physical and medical terms there is no difference. There are two things to note, however. In the first place, Jesus laid down his life. He was under no obligation to die since he was without sin and was, as the start of the new humanity, outside the corporate team headed by Adam. He did not inherit original sin. So he announced that no one took his life from him but he laid it down freely (John 10:15–18). Second, and in direct connection with the first factor, his death was an atoning sacrifice, effective, as the author says, for all time (Heb. 10:14). When we die it is a loss to our loved ones and a grim reality for ourselves but it does not have a huge bearing on the drift of world history. In contrast, Jesus' death is right at the centre of cosmic history. Together with his resurrection, it is the single dominant event, the Archimedean point, of the history of the cosmos, affecting all other persons and events, inaugurating 'the coming world' (2:5), the new heavens and the new earth in which righteousness dwells.

6. Jesus' death brings deliverance (14)

Indeed, by his death Jesus has destroyed the power of the devil and has brought about deliverance for those who were held in its grip. At first sight, his crucifixion might have seemed a defeat. Death on a cross was the most ignominious way to die. It was the death that accrued to a condemned criminal, a horrendous punishment, an inhumane torture forever associated with the brutality of Rome. It was shameful. This, surely, was no way for the saviour of the world to die.

This death might also have seemed to be a contradiction of what the author of Hebrews had said earlier. In chapter 1, he rehearsed a range of OT comments that identified the Christ with Yahweh, as the creator of all things, the ruler of the universe, the one to whom all angels bow. In chapter 2 he had explained that, according to his humanity, he is set in authority over everything on earth and in the cosmos, without rival, governing the new world he has established. In comparison with this, death by crucifixion, in agony, distress and shame, a focus of ridicule and abuse, could hardly be further removed. In essence, it seemed on all fronts to undermine any claim he might have had to homage, worship or discipleship.

Yet it is precisely because of this death, in this way, that death itself and all that flows from it, is decisively conquered. It is by the cross that the devil is rendered ineffective. It is at the cross that the serpent bruises the heel of the woman's offspring but that the offspring of the woman deals a mortal wound to the serpent's head (Gen. 3:15). Because it is at the cross that Jesus deals once and for all with sin, the root cause of human death, the results of sin are removed from ultimate significance.

The very purpose of his incarnation was *to render ineffective* (*katargēsē*) the devil. The devil had a certain power, subordinate at best; that power was vanquished. Now Christ has 'the keys of Death and Hades'.[13] He routed the devil because of who he was and the death he died. He is the Son of God, the creator, one in being with the Father from eternity. He is the Son of God who now had added human nature. The devil was no match for him! Of the kind of death he died we have already spoken. The devil was no match for that! The tyrant now defeated, death's prison doors have swung wide open and those held captive are now freed, rescued, liberated. We are now freed from the fear of death, for there is nothing about it that God the Son has not faced and experienced in a human manner. We will die – but he has been there before, as our pioneer. We will be buried – so has he, God in a human tomb. He has risen from the dead – so will we.

7. Jesus' sufferings ensure his effective sympathy (17–18)

Jesus was *made perfect through suffering* (10). This does not mean that he was imperfect or defective at any time but rather refers to his undertaking and fulfilling his office as mediator. His ministry as our Saviour and Mediator was brought to completion and total success. For that he had to live as one of us, to experience the gamut of human life, to be tempted, to suffer, to die. Having done that, he was equipped to be our saviour, to bring many sons to glory. He needed to identify himself with us, and this he did completely, being *made like his brothers in every respect* (17). This was essential, for God alone could not save us; since a man had sinned, deliverance must come through a man. As the Heidelberg Catechism put it in Question 16, 'Why must he be a true and sinless man? Answer.

[13] Rev. 1:17–18.

Because the justice of God requires that the same human nature which has sinned should make satisfaction for sin . . .'[14]

This completion in the work of representing us as our high priest was attained *through suffering* (10). Having suffered, he knows what our situation is, since he has experienced our lot. He knew temptation more than we do, as none of us resisted it like he did. So he is qualified both by experience and by conquest. He can send us help now that he is risen and ascended, 'the Son of God' 'who has passed through the heavens'[15] since he is able to do so. To sympathize and send effective help he had to suffer and to conquer death; he did both. As the high priest in the OT entered the holy of holies with the names of the tribes of Israel on his breastplate (Exod. 28:15–30), so Jesus at the right hand of the Father represents us before the throne of God. He can send us help and grace because he is qualified to do so. We can face no experience, however severe, that is greater than his capacity to understand, or to extend his powerful support.

8. Jesus' triumph brings us to glory (10)

The result of this is that the Father *brings many sons to glory* through the Son's high priesthood. The Father's sons are Christ's brothers. He is Son by nature, we are sons by grace.[16] He shared our lot – we will share his. He participated in suffering – we will share in the glory of God. As John Calvin put it, 'the goal of the gospel is to make us sooner or later like God'.[17]

What better words on which to end than those of John Henry Newman?

> O wisest love! that flesh and blood
> Which did in Adam fail,
> Should strive afresh against the foe,
> Should strive and should prevail.
>
> And that a higher gift than grace
> Should flesh and blood refine,
> God's presence and his very Self
> And essence all divine.[18]

---

[14] Schaff, *Creeds*, p. 312.

[15] Heb. 4:14.

[16] See Robert Letham, *Union with Christ: In Scripture, History and Theology* (Phillipsburg: Presbyterian & Reformed, 2011), pp. 85–128.

[17] John Calvin, *Commentarii in Epistolas Canonicas*, Ioannis Calvini Opera Exegetica (Genève: Librairie Droz, 2009), p. 328.

[18] 'Praise to the Holiest in the height', 1865.

John 1:1–5
11. The deity of Christ

John wrote his Gospel probably some time in the 80s AD in order 'that you may believe that Jesus is the Christ, the Son of God'.[1] He was writing to Jews of the Dispersion, probably living in Asia Minor. Years of preaching to Jewish audiences in Palestine would have given John ideas of the best way it could be done and in this great document he put these ideas on paper. Of course, these are more than ideas for they refer to great and ultimate realities.

1. Jesus' eternal deity (1–2)

Mark began his Gospel by tracing Jesus' ministry back to the time he was baptized by John the Baptist in the River Jordan and anointed by the Holy Spirit (Mark 1:1–11). Matthew and Luke begin further back with the events immediately preceding and surrounding the virginal conception of Jesus (Matt. 1:18–25; Luke 1:5 – 2:20). Both include genealogies: Matthew establishes that Jesus is the Son of David and the son of Abraham and so is the one foretold in those two covenants, whereas Luke traces Jesus' lineage back to Adam. In this Gospel, John goes back even further. His interest at this point is not so much in the human birth or descent of Jesus but in his origin in eternity. He reaches back before the creation of the universe: *In the beginning was the Word, and the Word was with God, and the Word was God* (1).

This statement is hugely reminiscent of the first verse of the Bible: 'In the beginning God created the heavens and the earth.'[2] The

---

[1] John 20:31.
[2] Gen. 1:1. C. K. Barrett remarks 'that John's opening verse is intended to recall the opening verse of Genesis is certain' (*The Gospel According to St John: An Introduction with Commentary and Notes on the Greek Text* [2nd ed., London: SPCK, 1978], p. 151). See also Barnabas Lindars, *The Gospel of John*, NCBC (Grand Rapids:

beginning of all things, the foundation of the cosmos, was the work of God. He brought it into existence. When it was created, having no previous existence, God was there. He was its creator. This is the context for John's statement here. If we were to stretch our imaginations back as far as they could go, the Word would be there. Westcott remarks that John uses the imperfect, a continuous tense, to denote his ongoing and uninterrupted existence.[3] Indeed, the verb *eimi* (to be) has no aorist or punctiliar tense. This may be why John selected it, for he uses *ginomai* (to become, to be made) when he refers to something created, repeatedly setting the two verbs in contrast.[4] There could be no time or place when he was not. Before God brought all things other than himself into being the Word was there. He is before all created things. Moreover, he himself is not created, for he has no beginning of days.[5]

What does John mean by *the Word* and why does he use this term? In Genesis 1 (we have already argued that this is the background for this expression) God spoke his word in creating light: 'And God said, "Let there be light", and there was light.'[6] God, the Spirit of God, and the word or speech of God; all three are present at the first record of creation. The psalmist reflects on this in Psalm 33:6: 'By the word of the LORD the heavens were made, and by the breath of his mouth all their host.' There is also throughout the OT the speech of Yahweh given through the prophets, 'the word of the Lord came to me, saying . . .'.[7] The word of Yahweh brings deliverance from great danger (Ps. 107:20). The word of the Lord is his self-expression, as words convey the inner thoughts of the speaker. But, as Rudolf Schnackenburg states, 'this "Word" is more than the "utterance" of God at the dawn of creation. It is the personal "Word" which became "flesh" at a given time in history, Jesus Christ'.[8] Here the Word is not merely speech but a person. So Jesus conveys the inner mind of God, since as the Word he is identified with God. As John argues throughout the Gospel, Jesus is the Christ, the Son of God, and

Eerdmans, 1972), p. 82; Leon Morris, *The Gospel According to John: The English Text with Introduction, Exposition and Notes* (London: Marshall, Morgan & Scott, 1971), pp. 72–73; Rudolf Schnackenburg, *The Gospel According to St John: Volume One: Introduction and Commentary on Chapters 1–4* (Tunbridge Wells: Burns & Oates, 1968), p. 232.

[3] Brooke Foss Westcott, *The Gospel According to St John: The Greek Text with Introduction and Notes*, vol. 1 (London: John Murray, 1908), p. 5.

[4] D. A. Carson, *The Gospel According to John* (Leicester: IVP, 1991), p. 114.

[5] Westcott, *St John*, pp. 4–5; Raymond E. Brown, *The Gospel According to John (I–XII)*, AB (Garden City, New York: Doubleday, 1966), p. 4; D. A. Carson, *John*, pp. 112–114.

[6] Gen. 1:3.

[7] Jer. 1:4; *et al.*

[8] Schnackenburg, *St John*, p. 232.

expresses to us the mind and heart of God. As Raymond E. Brown stated, 'there can be no speculation about how the Word came to be, for the Word simply was'.[9]

Moreover, he was *with God*. This refers to the identical circumstance mentioned in the first clause. The word *pros* can mean simply accompaniment, the Word being *with God*, but a more relational sense is preferred since, as Brown points out, the theme that John develops is life, which is dynamic rather than static.[10] The Word possesses an eternal relation to God, transcendent over time and space and all things created. The Word is therefore personal, not to be identified with human persons (as if we understand human personhood, which we don't) but in the sense that he is distinguishable from God as the Word in relation to God, yet simultaneously oriented to him. The Word belongs with God from eternity.[11] However, since only God is eternal, John progresses to the third clause of this majestic sentence.

The Word was not only in the beginning, in eternity, in the most intimate and ineffable relation to God, but *the Word was God*. The Word and God are identical yet there is a distinction. The Word and God are distinguished yet identified. There is evidently a sense in which they are to be regarded as distinct and another sense in which they are to be seen as one. It will help us at this point if we are to know that John, as other NT authors, commonly uses 'God' (*ho theos*) for the Father. Hence, the Father and the Word are eternally distinct but they are one being. Schnackenburg comments that 'the Logos is God as truly as he with whom he exists in the closest union of being and life. Hence *theos* is not a genus, but signifies the nature proper to God and the Logos in common'.[12] John is providing us with the building blocks for the Christian doctrine of God as Trinity.[13]

We should note at this point the well-known objection of the Jehovah's Witnesses that there is no definite article before the last occurrence of *theos*. This, so they say, means the Word is merely *a* god, one god among many and so not to be identified with God the creator in any way. This is a similar, although more far-reaching, claim than that of Arius and Eunomius in the fourth century. These two

---

[9] Brown, *John*, p. 4.
[10] Ibid., pp. 4–5.
[11] Carson, *John*, pp. 116–117.
[12] Schnackenburg, *St John*, p. 234.
[13] See Robert Letham, *The Holy Trinity: In Scripture, History, Theology, and Worship* (Phillipsburg: Presbyterian & Reformed, 2004), pp. 40–44; Arthur Wainwright, *The Trinity in the New Testament* (London: SPCK, 1963); Carson, *John*, p. 117.

argued that God became the Father when he generated the Son, on the analogy of human generation, which has a point at which it takes place. Therefore, for Arius and Eunomius, the Son began to be and is neither eternal nor of the identical being to the Father. However, there was a word for 'divine' (*theios*) that John could have used if he had wished to say this. The Jehovah's Witnesses, for their part, betray a lack of knowledge of the Greek of the NT period. Nominative predicate nouns preceding the verb normally lack the definite article.[14] This does not mean that they can be understood in English as having an indefinite article, for there is no indefinite article in NT Greek. It points to the quality of the referent of the noun; the positive nature of the Word is that he is *God* (*theos*). The literature on this matter is exhaustive.[15] This great statement has a balancing comment at the end of the Gospel, where Thomas acknowledges the risen Jesus as 'my Lord and my God' (*ho theos mou*).[16]

2. Jesus the creator (3–5)

a. The Word made the universe (3)

In Proverbs 8 Wisdom, personified, is Yahweh's agent in making the world (Prov. 8:22–36). John sharpens the focus here by asserting that the Word, who is one with God and yet distinct, is the creator of all things. Nothing came into existence apart from his creative power – *without him was not anything made that was made*. This statement is echoed elsewhere in the NT. Paul points out that 'by him all things were created, in heaven and on earth, visible and invisible, whether thrones or dominions or rulers or authorities – all things were created through him and for him'.[17] At Colossae the threat to the church was the veneration of angels, amongst which were the thrones and dominions to which Paul refers. In effect, Paul indicates that all created things owe their existence to Christ, including those most pertinent to the people at Colossae. This extends far beyond the human sphere, encompassing all animate and inanimate entities.[18]

The author of Hebrews, in stressing the Son's supremacy over angels, prophets, Moses and the OT priests, mentions that he is the one through whom God created the world (Heb. 1:2). This is a matter

---

[14] E. C. Colwell, 'A Definite Rule for the Use of the Article in the Greek New Testament', *JBL* 52 (1933), pp. 12–21.

[15] See Bruce M. Metzger, 'The Jehovah's Witnesses and Jesus Christ', *Theology Today* 10/1 (April 1953), pp. 65–85; Carson, *John*, p. 117.

[16] John 20:28.

[17] Col. 1:16.

[18] Schnackenburg, *St John*, p. 238.

understood through faith, for it follows from the realization that Christ is one with God from eternity: 'By faith we understand that the universe was created by the word of God, so that what is seen was not made out of things that are visible.'[19] The order and beauty of the world around us, the vastness of the cosmos and the intricacy of the sub-atomic, are all the workmanship of the eternal Word. How this took place is not explained by John, nor does he say exactly in what capacity the Word created all things.

All this could be accepted by Arius and Eunomius on the basis that God created the Son, who in turn brought all other created things into existence as the agent of God. The problem, which led to their condemnation as heretics, was that the Son himself was viewed as a created being. If this were so, he could not have saved us. The answer to the heresy lies, in common with many other places, here in this section where the Word is equated with God. It is his identity as one with God from eternity that is the crucial point. It is the main thing in John's argument in this Gospel. From this his activity in creating follows and it is this which identifies him as far more than an agent in creation.

b. In him is life (4)

By this John says two things. First, the source of life in the creation is to be found in Christ. He, as the creator, is the author and giver of life to all that he has brought into being. However, this rests on something more foundational still. The Word gives life because he himself *is* life. He is life itself. He is brimming over with life.[20] Later, the church would assert that this was the outflow of the fact that the Son is generated by the Father in eternity. Since the Father communicates life to the Son eternally, God is inherently dynamic and fecund. He is eternally bursting with life and productivity. Thus, in choosing to create, he has given life to his creatures and so is the eternal and ultimate source of life.[21] When his creatures opted to rebel against him, they were casting their vote for death, the absence of that productive, life-giving abundance that resides in the heart of God from all eternity. This life is reflected in the fact that man was created in the image and likeness of God, with the task of subduing the earth and multiplying (Gen. 1:26–28). The Western world in the

---

[19] Heb. 11:3.

[20] There are uncertainties here over how to punctuate the text, Greek manuscripts lacking punctuation. On the range of possibilities see Barrett, *John*, pp. 156–157, who prefers the reading here, since – *inter alia* – other alternatives are 'impossibly clumsy'.

[21] Herman Bavinck, *Reformed Dogmatics: Volume 2: God and Creation* (Grand Rapids: Baker Academic, 2004), pp. 308–310.

early twenty-first century has clearly determined to choose death, evidenced in millions of abortions, infanticide, calls for euthanasia, domestic and public violence, together with a determination to tear down or alter the ordinances of creation – such as marriage – established by God.

c. He is light – and shines in the darkness (5)

Again the background is the creation account in Genesis 1. There the earth was shrouded in darkness as originally created (Gen. 1:2). Darkness is the absence of light. Into that murky beginning the Word came, '"Let there be light!" And there was light'.[22] Light secured victory over darkness. So that light was the Word. Now the Word shines in the darkness of the world devastated by sin. People love darkness rather than light, because their deeds are evil (John 3:19) but into this darkness the light shines since Christ is the light himself. Paul uses similar imagery in 2 Corinthians 4. There he says that 'the god of this world has blinded the minds of unbelievers so that they cannot see the light' of the glory of God in the face of Jesus Christ, who is the image of God. Christ shines as 'we preach Jesus Christ as Lord' and a new creation dawns.[23] The Word who shone in creation shines also in the new creation to give light and life.

3. Later . . . Jesus the incarnate God

John underlines his teaching here later in his prologue and throughout his Gospel. In verse 14 of chapter 1 he makes the enormously portentous statement that 'the Word became flesh'. This took place in the incarnation. The Word, in becoming flesh, did not cease to be the Word since he is the subject of the following clauses. Nor, for that reason, did his becoming mean he was transformed into other than who he was and is. The Word was not mixed with flesh to form a third entity, like an ingredient in an ontological soup. He remained the Word. But he added flesh – human nature in its weakness and vulnerability.

In this context, Jesus claims equality with God (John 5:1–18). He is accused by his opponents of blasphemy. They take up stones to stone him. Jesus defends himself from the charges not by denying them or suggesting that he has been misunderstood but by reaffirming his statement that had occasioned such hostility (John 5:19–47). Again, he presses the matter further by stating that he is identical to

---

[22] Gen. 1:3.
[23] 2 Cor. 4:4–6; cf. 5:17.

the Father in the unity of the indivisible deity (John 10:22–30). The leaders of the Jews again prepare to stone him to death for blasphemy. Once more, Jesus defends his case by affirming that he is telling the truth and so is not blaspheming (John 10:31–39).[24] Has this ever been better expressed outside the Bible than by Josiah Conder?

Thou art the Everlasting Word,
  The Father's only Son;
God manifestly seen and heard,
  And heaven's beloved One.
Worthy, O Lamb of God, art thou,
That every knee to thee shall bow!

In thee most perfectly expressed,
  The Father's glories shine;
Of the full deity possessed,
  Eternally divine.
Worthy, O Lamb of God, etc.

True image of the Infinite,
  Whose essence is concealed;
Brightness of uncreated light;
  The heart of God revealed.
Worthy, O Lamb of God, etc.

But the high mysteries of thy Name,
  An angel's grasp transcend;
The Father only – glorious claim! –
  The Son can comprehend.
Worthy, O Lamb of God, etc.

Throughout the universe of bliss,
  The centre thou, and sun,
The eternal theme of praise is this,
  To heaven's beloved one.
Worthy, O Lamb of God, art thou,
That every knee to thee shall bow![25]

---

[24] For a fuller exposition of the NT discussion of the deity of Christ, including its unfolding in the Gospel of John, see Letham, *The Holy Trinity*, pp. 34–51.
[25] *The Congregational Hymn Book*, 1836.

John 1:14–18
12. The Word became flesh

1. The enfleshment of the Word (14)

This is the heart of the Christian faith: *the Word became flesh.*
Eternity and time intersect, Creator and creature are conjoined, God
and man united. The incarnation is a new creation. Athanasius
summed up this unique event in these immortal words:

> It is, then, proper for us to begin the treatment of this subject by
> speaking of the creation of the universe, and of God its artificer,
> that so it may be duly perceived that the renewal of creation has
> been the work of the self-same Word that made it at the beginning.
> For it will appear not inconsonant for the Father to have wrought
> its salvation in Him by whose means he made it.[1]

The verb *became* (*egeneto*) denotes the Word entering into something
new. The Word himself remained the same but the environment into
which he went was an experience that was different. In verses 1–4
John consistently uses the imperfect of *eimi* (to be) in referring to
the Word, indicating continuance. He reserves *ginomai* (to become)
for the creation in verse 3: all things *became* through him. He uses
this verb for John the Baptist in verse 6 who appeared on the scene
in the course of human history, in contrast to the Word who always
was and is. Yet here in verse 14 the Word is also said *to become*,
existing in the same manner as all other things created by him. In
fact, he appeared in human history just like John the Baptist did. It
is, as Schnackenburg stresses, a unique event, occurring only once.[2]

---

[1] Athanasius, *On the Incarnation*, 1 (*NPNF²*, vol. 4).
[2] Rudolf Schnackenburg, *The Gospel According to St John: Volume One:
Introduction and Commentary on Chapters 1–4* (Tunbridge Wells: Burns & Oates,
1968), p. 266.

118

However, this was not something that merely happened to him, as it did in the case of the Baptist. He chose it. It was his will that it be so. He was not humbled; he humbled himself. The subject of the verb is *ho logos* (the Word). The Word is the active agent. The subject of the clauses that follow is still the Word. The Word who always was and is, who is with God and who is God, who is the creator of all things, and who is life itself, having become flesh continues to be who he always is.

a. What does it mean?

At first sight it might appear that the Word changed into something else, in a metamorphosis akin to a caterpillar changing into a butterfly, the Word becoming flesh and so ceasing to be the Word that he always was. It would be the case that the Word, who was divine, changed into a human being and his being the Word came to an end. That this is not the case is clear from both the Word being the active agent, in control of what happened, and his continuing to be the subject of all that follows. Again, it might be supposed that the Word mingled with flesh and consequently formed a third substance, rather like ingredients in a recipe merge and become something other than what they were before they were added and mixed together. If this were so, the Word and flesh would have combined to form an entity composed of both yet different from either. Once more, we must point to the fact that John states that not only did the Word become flesh but he lived among us and we saw his glory; it is the Word who lived and was seen, not some composite entity.

If John does not intend to say that the Word ceased to be or changed into something else when he became flesh, but rather remained what he always was and is, what does he mean by saying that the Word became *flesh*? Clearly, while the physicality of humanity is obviously involved he intends something more than simply the flesh and blood of a human body. The flesh which the Word became is humanity in its weakness and dependence, creaturely existence in its vulnerability and smallness. Flesh draws attention to its fragility, prone as it is to decay and disintegration.[3] The Jews considered human beings to be a psychosomatic unity, body and soul together. This, as we have seen, Jesus was without dilution. He grew tired and hungry after a long journey (John 4:1–6). He was distressed at the death of a friend (John 11:33–35). He interacted with others just as they did (1 John 1:1). What happens is that the

---

[3] Barnabas Lindars, *The Gospel of John*, NCBC (Grand Rapids: Eerdmans, 1972), pp. 93–94; Schnackenburg, *St John*, pp. 267–268.

Word assumes, adopts and incorporates human nature, body and soul, into union with himself so that he now has a human nature of his own. He remains the Word – *ho logos* as we saw is the subject of the whole sentence both in the becoming and in the result of the becoming. What is there, and who is there, after the *egeneto* (the becoming) is the same as what was there and who was there before. The difference is that there is now an addition. The Word now has *flesh*, a full human nature.[4] In the words of Paul, he who was – and eternally is – in the form of God has now added the form of a servant. In doing so he has not ceased to be in the form of God. There is no subtraction, only addition. And it is the Word who is the subject of the whole event.

So if we are to ask *who* is the person about whom the Gospel record is written, *who* is Jesus of Nazareth, what is his personal identity, we must reply that he is the eternal Word of the Father, the Son of God who is one with the Father from eternity to eternity. On the other hand, if we are to ask of *what* he consists, what is the manner of his existence, we must reply that he is the Son of God who is incarnate in human nature.[5] Once again, the Word is still the personal subject of the sentence and all that follows the sentence. It is *the Word* who became *flesh*. It is flesh that *is added – permanently* – now and for eternity. The Word is the agent of the first and the new creation. He is not a hybrid of God and man; he is the eternal Son, now enfleshed.

b. He lived in a tent among us

In the OT Yahweh dwelled in the tabernacle, or tent, that was carried by the priests through the wilderness to the promised land of Canaan. The tabernacle sheltered the ark of the covenant, his 'throne', which was eventually inserted into the innermost part of the temple where Yahweh and Israel met, and became the centre point of the covenant relationship. Now the Word has his permanent tent-dwelling among his people. Jesus Christ is the place where God and his people meet face to face. He is the centre and the focus of the worship of his covenant people. In fact, as Jesus was to explain to the Samaritan woman, true worship is to be in the Holy Spirit and in the truth, the incarnate Christ, the Son, who is the way, the truth, and the life (John

---

[4] The idea of flesh (*sarx*) as corrupt and sinful, a theme prominent in Paul and evident in 1 John 2:16, is not in view here; see Schnackenburg, *St John*, pp. 267–268.

[5] The best description of the Christology of John that I have read is Thomas Weinandy's description of the Christology of Cyril of Alexandria, in 'Cyril and the Mystery of the Incarnation', in Thomas G. Weinandy, *The Theology of St. Cyril of Alexandria: A Critical Appreciation* (London: T&T Clark, 2003), pp. 23–54.

4:21–24; 14:6).[6] In all this God takes the initiative; it is his work from start to finish. The Word, since he is himself God, is in the driving seat throughout. As such, Jesus displays the *grace and truth* of God, pointing to his loyalty to his covenant and the promises it entails.[7]

2. The witnesses (14b–17)

a. The apostles (14b)

We have seen his glory. The law required two or three witnesses to establish a matter as true. Here there are more witnesses than can be numbered. First of all are the apostles, including John himself. He draws attention at the start to the mount of transfiguration. There Peter, James and John climbed with Jesus and saw his appearance changed into dazzling glory, whiter than could be imagined. They were scarcely able to bear the sight. It was a preview of Jesus' glorification as mediator (Matt. 17:1–8; Mark 9:2–8; Luke 9:28–36).[8] The presence of Yahweh in the tabernacle, the *shekinah*, the glory that he had revealed in a small way to Israel, was now fully embodied in Jesus Christ. Human beings could not look on the glory of Yahweh and live, but in Jesus this was reality. This was the glory of *the only-begotten Son of the Father.*[9]

However, Jesus' glory was radically different than might have been expected. He did not seek his own advancement, for he came as a servant. He took the lowest place, washing his disciples' feet, the action of a Gentile slave, the lowest of the low (John 13:1–20). His

---

[6] Note Basil the Great's striking turn of phrase when he writes of the Holy Spirit as the place of the saints, referring expressly to John 4:21–24; Basil of Caesarea, *On the Holy Spirit*, 26:62 (*NPNF²*, vol. 8).

[7] Lindars, *John*, p. 95.

[8] C. K. Barrett, *The Gospel According to St John: An Introduction with Commentary and Notes on the Greek Text* (2nd ed., London: SPCK, 1978), p. 166.

[9] The eternal generation of the Son was a teaching that formed the cement holding together the church's doctrine of the Trinity. See my forthcoming chapter 'Eternal Generation in the Church Fathers' in an as yet untitled symposium to be published by Crossway Books, and a book on the same theme by Kevin Giles, *The Eternal Generation of the Son: Maintaining Orthodoxy in Trinitarian Theology* (Downers Grove: IVP Academic, 2012), to which I contributed a foreword. The translation of *monogenēs* as 'only-begotten' has fallen out of favour among NT exegetes on the grounds that it means 'one and only'. However, while it is secondary to the truth of the doctrine, there is a case on both lexicographical and contextual grounds as well as theological ones for holding to the earlier translation; see Barrett, *John*, p. 166; Robert Letham, *The Holy Trinity: In Scripture, History, Theology, and Worship* (Phillipsburg: Presbyterian & Reformed, 2004), pp. 383–389; Lindars, *John*, p. 96; Schnackenburg, *St John*, p. 271.

glorification was at the cross where he hung as a condemned criminal (John 12:20–33). The Word, in becoming flesh, freely and sovereignly gave himself to self-abandonment by the Father so that we might become the children of God (John 20:31).

b. John the Baptist (15)

Jesus began his ministry after John the Baptist but John testified that Jesus would surpass him: 'he must increase but I must decrease.'[10] This was because he who came after John was before him, since before Abraham was, Jesus was (John 8:58).

c. All of us (16)

We have all received from his fullness, John asserts. Out of the fullness of his divine being we have received life and grace. All the power and grace of God is concentrated in Jesus Christ, the Son. He was full of grace and truth as witnessed by the apostles (14), so we receive from him as from a spring of living water (John 4:10; 7:37–39). John refers to the reality of his gifts and blessings to us, one after another, grace in place of grace. Whereas the Mosaic covenant of itself prescribed obedience, produced knowledge of the presence and reality of sin but was powerless to change us, Jesus Christ brought truth, grace and forgiveness (17).

3. The incarnation is the ultimate revelation of God (18)

We cannot know God as God – no-one has seen God as he is in himself, in his being. He is invisible (Exod. 33:20; 1 Tim. 1:17; 6:16). When he made himself known to us it was as man, on our level, in our nature. Christ was and is God but he made himself known as man. Only God can make God known. He did so as man.

And it is Jesus Christ who *has made [God] known*. The expression 'only begotten God' (*ho monogenēs theos*) has much greater textual support than the variants *only begotten Son*, supported as it is by both the Nestlé-Aland 28th edition and the United Bible Societies 4th edition. The reference is to the unique and only Son, begotten of the Father before all ages.[11] He is described as in an intimate, unbreakable and indivisible relation to the Father. There is a fellowship and

---

[10] John 3:30.
[11] Barrett, *John* , p. 169; Lindars, *John*, p. 98; Leon Morris, *The Gospel According to John: The English Text with Introduction, Exposition and Notes* (London: Marshall, Morgan & Scott, 1971), pp. 113–114; Schnackenburg, *St John*, pp. 269–271.

union of love within the Trinity from eternity.[12] From this, the Son has interpreted[13] the mystery of God to us, making known the indivisible love in the Trinity in self-sacrificial love to us.

[12] Barrett, *John*, pp. 169–170; D. A. Carson, *The Gospel According to John* (Leicester: IVP, 1991), p. 135.

[13] Barrett, *John*, p. 170; Lindars, *John*, p. 99.

Hebrews 1:1–14
13. The supremacy of the Son

One of life's greatest puzzles is the authorship of the letter to the Hebrews. As Origen said, 'the truth God alone knows'.[1] For our purposes this can remain a mystery, as it does not materially affect the meaning of this majestic chapter. Suffice it to say that the letter was probably written to a predominantly Hebrew church or churches, the members of which were facing acute temptation to revert to some form of Judaism.[2] The author warns in the severest terms of the consequences that would result from abandoning faith in Jesus Christ (Heb. 6:4–8; 10:26–39; 12:25–29). Since Christ is the only saviour, repudiation of him leaves a person with no hope of salvation.

In the face of such a dire prospect, the author sets forth the complete supremacy of Christ over all other figures in redemptive history. He is superior to the prophets (Heb. 1:1–2), the angels (Heb. 1:3 – 2:9), Moses (Heb. 3:1–6), Joshua (Heb. 4:1–10), and the OT high priesthood, together with the sacrifices offered in the tabernacle (Heb. 5:1 – 10:18). He is the mediator of a better covenant, founded on better promises and a better – because utterly and everlastingly efficacious – sacrifice. Therefore, he urges his readers, hold fast to your confession without wavering (Heb. 4:14–16), draw near to God in faith through the blood of Jesus (Heb. 10:19–25). This great theme is begun in unforgettable fashion here in the first chapter.

[1] Cited in Philip Edgcumbe Hughes, *A Commentary on the Epistle to the Hebrews* (Grand Rapids: Eerdmans, 1977), p. 21.

[2] On various proposals relating to authorship, recipients, dating and context see the literature, including F. F. Bruce, *Commentary on the Epistle to the Hebrews: The English Text with Introduction, Exposition and Notes* (London: Marshall, Morgan & Scott, 1964), pp. xxiii–lviii; Hughes, *Hebrews*, pp. 1–32; Donald Guthrie, *The Letter to the Hebrews: An Introduction and Commentary*, TNTC (Leicester: IVP, 1983), pp. 15–57; Paul Ellingworth, *The Epistle to the Hebrews: A Commentary on the Greek Text*, NIGTC (Grand Rapids: Eerdmans, 1993), pp. 3–86.

1. God's final word (1–2)

a. God's speech in the OT was piecemeal and incomplete

The author uses two adverbs, meaning *in many parts* and *in many ways or modes*. God spoke to Abraham, later to Jacob, then to Moses and Joshua, much later to Samuel, David, Isaiah and the rest of *the prophets*. A variety of persons were involved. God used various means: dreams, visions, direct speech out of a burning bush, and so on. Sometimes God spoke through the actions of the prophets – particularly in the cases of Isaiah, Ezekiel and Hosea. While the prophets are seen as the mouthpieces of God, his speech was aimed at the whole people – *the fathers*.

This broad variety of means together with the large number of instruments through whom God spoke indicates that his revelation at that time was incomplete, fragmentary. No one instance could be said to be of ultimate significance. Because of this, it was provisional, for it lacked a final unity. Moreover, the author uses the word *palai*, meaning *in the past*. This is used rarely in Scripture and conveys the idea that this form of revelation is over. It belongs in a bygone era.

Certainly, this revelation in the OT was authoritative. After all, *God spoke*. As Paul says, the OT Scriptures were 'God-breathed',[3] for, in Peter's words, he spoke in or by the prophets (2 Pet. 1:21). The tense here (an aorist participle) in verse 1 suggests completed action;[4] the whole OT revelation is summed up as one and as something that was completed and is now over.

b. God's speech in Christ is decisive and final

It is clear that the author considers that Christ is *the chief prophet*. Indeed, he is more than a prophet. The prophets spoke the words that God gave them. They could say, 'thus says the Lord', or 'the word of the Lord came to me'. But at other times they lived and spoke as ordinary people, no different than any of their contemporaries. On the other hand, Christ is the Son. Not only does he speak God's words but he *is* God's Word. He is the fulfilment of the words spoken by God to the fathers in or by the prophets. In this sense he is at one with the OT revelation of God since all that God said and did then was leading up to what he was to say and do in his Son. There is a unity to OT and NT, to God's speech in both epochs.

---

[3] 2 Tim. 3:6.
[4] Ellingworth, *Hebrews*, p. 92.

Moreover, Christ the Son is *the last prophet*. He is God's final word since he is God's Word, made flesh. The main clause reads *he has spoken to us in [his] Son*. The tense again denotes finality and completion. God spoke to the *prophets in former times* or *in the past* but now *in these last days* he has spoken in *his Son*.[5] God has spoken his ultimate word which cannot be superseded by another revelation. As F. F. Bruce says, 'the story of divine revelation is a story of progression up to Christ, but there is no progression beyond him'.[6] Christ is the one *Son*, whereas there were many *prophets*.[7] God has finished speaking because now that the Son has come there is nothing more that he has to say or can say.

Once, I was counselling a couple and, after several sessions, I came to the conclusion that I had given the matter everything that I could. All I could do was to reiterate the 'ghostly counsel and advice'[8] I had given repeatedly before. I turned to them and announced, 'there is nothing more that I can say'. In this other context, the author is insisting to his readers that the Son, Jesus Christ, is God's final word. God has given everything. There is simply nothing more that he can say. If these people were to repudiate Christ there will be no hope for them whatsoever.

This is so because of who the Son is. God has appointed him to be *the heir of all things*. Because he is the Son he is the heir of the universe. The whole cosmos belongs to him. He has taken permanent possession of it.[9] He has the right to rule and govern it. He will renew it and liberate it to hitherto undreamed dimensions. This is so because he created it in the first place. He is the one through whom the Father created the ages – 'the whole created universe of space and time'.[10] Our author is saying in his own words what John says in the first chapter of his Gospel. Since the Son is the creator of the universe it follows that he is God. As such he is the rightful heir, the one to whom the renewed universe belongs. Please note here that the author intends us to understand that this is true of the incarnate Son, the mediator, the Son by whom God has spoken, who has made known the Father in that perfect and complete manner – Jesus of Nazareth. In saying this, the author is implying that Christ, by whom God has spoken in human history, is – in terms of his personal identity – before all ages.[11]

[5] Hughes, *Hebrews*, p. 37.

[6] Bruce, *Hebrews*, p. 3.

[7] Hughes, *Hebrews*, p. 36.

[8] From the Warning for the Celebration of the Holy Communion, *The Book of Common Prayer* (1662).

[9] Ellingworth, *Hebrews*, pp. 94–95.

[10] Bruce, *Hebrews*, p. 4.

[11] See Hughes, *Hebrews*, p. 40.

2. The Son's nature (3a)

a. The Son is the radiance of the Father's glory

The author doesn't want to stop here. The Son is one with the Father, one with God. *Glory* refers to the outshining of light, the manner of being that is appropriate and peculiar to God.[12] He, the incarnate Son, is the radiant light of the glory of God. Paul said the same in 2 Corinthians 4:6, where he says that the light of the knowledge of the glory of God is seen in the face of Jesus Christ. As the sun gives off sunshine, so God radiates his glory in Christ the Son. In the OT the glory of Yahweh signalled his presence amongst his people; so here all the rays of God's glory are refracted in Christ. As on a sunny day a magnifying glass will concentrate the light and eventually burn up a section of grass, so God's self-revelation is focused in his Son.

b. The Son is the exact representation of the being of God

The image here is of a seal, or an impression engraved on an object such as a coin. However, in this case the Son is a living representation of God, not a static replica. This is a stronger image than the preceding one.[13] The Son brings before us what God is like since he is one with him. 'What God essentially is, is made manifest in Christ. To see Christ is to see what the Father is like.'[14] Of course, as humans we are incapable of seeing the glory of God. That is why he made himself known to us as one of us. Jesus Christ is the true and trustworthy representation of God the Father. As he said to Philip, 'He who has seen me has seen the Father'.[15] There is an exact correspondence between Jesus Christ and God. It follows, for the Hebrew recipients, that apostasy did not make sense.

3. The Son's activity (3b)

The Son governs the universe by his powerful word. Later in the letter, the author will say that 'by faith we understand that the ages were formed by the word of God'.[16] Here the attention is not on creation but providence, not on the bringing into existence of the cosmos but on its continued maintenance and rule. The Son's continuing utterance as he *upholds the universe by the word of his power*

[12] Ellingworth, *Hebrews*, pp. 98–99.
[13] Ibid., p. 99.
[14] Bruce, *Hebrews*, p. 6.
[15] John 14:9.
[16] Heb. 11:3.

keeps it in being. This is not seen as something difficult for him to achieve; he does it simply by his *word*. Indeed, without his word the universe would cease to be (cf. Ps. 104:29–30). Once again, the Son's word here in his providential direction of the cosmos is identical with the word of God in creation, since the Son is himself one with God from eternity.

Incidentally, this entails important connections between Christianity and science; how can the two be inherently opposed? Rather, true knowledge ultimately rests on a view of the world in which Christ's sovereignty is acknowledged. The alleged conflict between the Christian faith and science arises from the assumptions of sinful human autonomy, by which unbelievers attempt to exclude God the creator from their horizon, or from an anti-intellectual biblicism on the part of some Christians. It certainly does not result from the inherent compatibility between the Christian faith and the scientific activity that the Bible requires of us (Gen. 1:26–28; 2:18–10).

This image here in verse 3b, as many commentators have remarked, is not static.[17] It is not as if the Son is carrying the universe on his shoulders as a dead weight, merely supporting it. Instead, it conveys immense dynamism.[18] He carries the cosmos towards the destiny he intends for it. There is movement as well as support. Onwards and forwards to its consummation and renewal in a continuous process (note the present participle) irresistibly he lifts it!

4. The Son's exaltation (3c)

a. As priest he has done what we could not do

The scene shifts from the Son's rule as king of the universe to his work as high priest securing our salvation. He has achieved cleansing for us from our sins. Once again, the language entails completed action.[19] We were guilty and corrupt; the Son has cleansed us. He has made us clean. This we could never have done ourselves as there was no possibility for any efforts at self-purification. Christ's act by which we were cleansed from sin took place at the cross, in his death.

b. He is now installed in the place of highest honour

Christ has now *sat down*. This is in contrast to the priests of Israel who the author represents throughout the letter as still standing, going

---

[17] Guthrie, *Hebrews*, p. 67.
[18] *Contra* Ellingworth, *Hebrews*, pp. 100–101.
[19] Guthrie, *Hebrews*, p. 68.

about their work of offering the prescribed animal sacrifices. Evidently, this was written while the Jerusalem temple was still operational, before its destruction by the Romans in AD 70. Later, the writer will explain that the continuous offering of these sacrifices demonstrated their intrinsic inadequacy in dealing with human sin and corruption. Their very repetition showed that sin had not yet been decisively overcome, no ultimately purificatory action completed, by their means. Animals could not atone for the sins of humans.

Instead, Christ's work of cleansing is complete. Afterwards,[20] he *sat down*. He had no need to offer any further sacrifice as his was utterly sufficient. Moreover, he is seated on a throne, for he *sat down at the right hand of the majesty on high*, a paraphrase for God, specifically the Father in relation to whom he is the Son.[21] This is no literal location; rather, the reference to the throne denotes the Son's transcendence.[22] In the background is the declaration of Psalm 110:1: 'Sit at my right hand until I make your enemies your footstool.' He rules. He is king as well as high priest. His session at the right hand of the Father completes his resurrection and ascension.[23]

As the Son, he is perfectly equipped to be our mediator and deliverer. He is the chief and the final prophet, greater than a prophet since he is one with God the Father. He is the great high priest who has made atoning sacrifice for sin once for all and so cleansed his people from the guilt and defilement that this had brought. As our high priest and mediator he is also king, seated at *the right hand* of the Father, the creator and sustainer of the universe.

5. The Son's status (4–14)

It is possible that the recipients of this letter may have been influenced by the Dead Sea sect, which expected a dual priestly and kingly Messiah, with the Archangel Michael presiding. If so, the author asserts in no uncertain terms that they are looking in the wrong direction. Jesus is far *superior to the angels* (4). Again, the tense denotes completion. It refers back to his ascension to the Father. There and then he was exalted to the highest place, to rule the cosmos. *The name he . . . inherited*, which is superior to those of the angels, is the Son (cf. Rom. 1:3–4). This does not mean that he became Son at the resurrection and ascension, for it was the Son who was the final revelation of God during his earthly ministry and who is the express image of the Father both then and from eternity.

---

[20] Ibid.
[21] Bruce, *Hebrews*, p. 7; Guthrie, *Hebrews*, p. 69.
[22] Hughes, *Hebrews*, p. 48.
[23] Hughes, *Hebrews*, p. 47; Ellingworth, *Hebrews*, p. 102.

Rather, it points to his successful completion of the work of redemption, achieved by his faithful life, atoning death, and triumphant resurrection.

The rest of the chapter unfolds biblical reasons for this. In a series of citations from the OT, the author establishes that whereas the angels are described as the servants and ministers of God, as the Son he is self-evidently superior. Moreover, he is called *theos* (God) in Psalm 45:6–7 (Ps. 44:7–8, LXX), *kyrios* (Lord) in Psalm 102:25–27 (Ps. 101:26–28, LXX) and in Psalm 110:1 (Ps. 109:1, LXX).[24] In Psalms 45 and 110 God is distinguished from God. In short, the Son has the title and status of God, without jeopardizing the uniqueness and indivisibility of Yahweh.[25] The obvious corollary is that the readers should abandon any consideration of the worship of angels, any countenancing of the possibility of reversion to Judaism, and instead persist in the worship of Jesus Christ, to which the angels themselves are devoted (6, citing Deut. 32:43). The message to us is equally clear; each and every substitute for Christ is idolatry and so inherently futile. The pressures of militant atheism can lead believers to keep quiet about their faith for fear of ridicule or discrimination. We certainly need to be wise in a difficult environment. However, the reality is that the atheists and sceptics have nothing to offer. We need to draw strength from passages such as this, praying that God will grant this knowledge to the church's adversaries. What it means to be human is that we be worshippers of the Son and so remade in the image of God.

---

[24] The author of Hebrews quotes from the LXX , not the Hebrew text.
[25] Robert Letham, *The Holy Trinity: In Scripture, History, Theology, and Worship* (Phillipsburg: Presbyterian & Reformed, 2004), pp. 17–51.

Philippians 2:6–8
14. Suffering Servant

Paul is addressing an emerging problem of dissension in the church at Philippi. This is close to the surface in 2:1–2, where he urges his readers to be 'of the same mind, having the same love, being in full accord and of one mind', The repetition serves to underline the need for unity and to assume a certain and troubling lack of it.[1] In what follows the apostle diagnoses the cause of this malaise: 'do nothing from rivalry or conceit.'[2] Evidently some at Philippi were acting in self-interest and competing for prominence and power. The cure for this is 'in humility count others more significant than yourselves. Let each of you look not only to his own interests, but also to the interests of others'.[3] The cure for self-seeking and pride is to pursue the good of others. The over-riding proof is that this is the way Christ lived. Those at Philippi and, by extension, all who call themselves Christian, are called to live in the light of Christ. So, Paul says, 'have this mind among yourselves, which is yours in Christ Jesus'.[4] In this passage Paul addresses the community rather than individuals, although of course the community is composed of individuals.[5] It is in the church that the Christian life is grounded, in love for others after the likeness of Christ's love for us. Into this situation we recall the additional factor that Philippi was a Roman colony, under the protection of the *ius Italicum*, and so prided itself

---

[1] Ralph Martin, *Philippians*, NCBC (Grand Rapids: Eerdmans, 1980), pp. 85–86; Ralph P. Martin, *Carmen Christi: Philippians ii.5–11 in Recent Interpretation and in the Setting of Early Christian Worship* (Grand Rapids: Eerdmans, 1983), pp. xvi–xvii; Peter T. O'Brien, *The Epistle to the Philippians*, NICTC (Grand Rapids: Eerdmans, 1991), p. 166–167.
[2] Phil. 2:3a.
[3] Phil. 2:3–4.
[4] Phil. 2:5.
[5] Martin, *Philippians*, pp. 90–91.

on its civic status.[6] At a range of levels – pride in personal attainments and privilege, pride in belonging to a powerful and prestigious city – there were temptations to diverge from the path of true Christian humility. So traditionally this passage from verses 6 to 11 has been seen as an exhortation to follow the example of Christ. However, there are limits to such an aim. None of us can atone for sin as Christ did. The universe will – thankfully – not do homage to you and I.

There is another strand to Paul's argument that we need to consider. It appears that some at Philippi may have thought that it is possible to arrive at glory without having to suffer. In their eyes, since suffering was avoidable and not befitting an apostle, so Paul's sufferings undermined his assertion of apostolic status. These people thought they had arrived at the pinnacle of Christian faith by their trouble-free life and were inclined to belittle Paul, who had been forced to undergo deprivation, imprisonment and an impending trial. With this as background, Paul demonstrates how such ideas are altogether wrong. Christ's path to glory was by way of sufferings and the accursed death of the cross. The hymnic citation that follows from verse 6 has a definite metre, a rhythm broken at one point by a phrase Paul presumably adds himself; in talking of Christ's obedience unto death he adds *even death on a cross* (8).[7] Crucifixion was a Roman punishment reserved for the lowest of non-citizens. The Philippians would have despised such a death. For them, being citizens of Philippi exempted them from such a despicable fate.[8] Yet this was Christ's freely chosen path to glory. His destiny came by seeking the interests of others, in lowliness and obedience, in voluntarily undergoing the most accursed death of a condemned criminal with no rights whatever. There are a number of steps on this journey that Paul unfolds to the view of the church at Philippi. Salvation for Paul means union with Christ and it follows that the church is called to suffer with him as an intrinsic part of its path to glory.[9]

The discussion of this great hymn has been vast and the literature continues to pour forth like an unstoppable torrent. At the same time, as Peter O'Brien observed over twenty years ago, little scholarly consensus has emerged on any of the key questions.[10]

---

[6] Martin, *Philippians*, pp. 2–4. The *ius Italicum* was an honour given to a city by the Roman Emperor, with the effect that it was governed by Roman law, all born there being automatically Roman citizens.

[7] Martin, *Philippians*, pp. 99–100.

[8] Ibid.

[9] See Martin, *Philippians*, pp. 92–93.

[10] O'Brien, *Philippians*, p. 188.

1. Christ's humility in his pre-existence: he did not exploit his deity for his own advantage (6)

a. Christ is God eternally (6a)

Christ was and is *in the form of God* (*en morphē theou*). Much discussion has surrounded this phrase as, indeed, virtually every element of this sublime hymn. Some have argued that *form* (*morphē*) is a synonym for 'image' and 'glory', due to the OT background. There Adam was made *in* the image of God, made like God, but failed to live accordingly, whereas Christ, the second Adam, *is* the image of God.[11] Thus, Christ reflected God's glory as the image of the invisible God (Col. 1:15; 2 Cor. 4:4). However, while this is true, the parallel use of *morphē* in verse 7 – *the form of a slave* – can hardly mean that he had the glory of a slave, or even the image of a slave. A more suitable rendition of the word is something akin to 'status' or 'condition' since this would fit the statement in verse 7. In this sense, Paul is saying that Christ had the status of God.[12] O'Brien sums it up by saying that it pictures the pre-existent Christ clothed in the garments of divine majesty and splendour,[13] while Gordon Fee writes of 'that which truly characterizes a given reality'.[14]

The present participle (*hyparchōn*) may be timeless and so not necessarily indicate continuance on grammatical grounds,[15] but the overall statement requires continuance. Christ's being in *the form of God* is something that continues; it was, it is, and it continues to be so. It is hard to conceive of one who has the status of God ceasing to be what he always had been. In this, Paul is saying very much what John states in John 1:1, when he says 'in the beginning was the Word, and the Word was with God, and the Word was God'.

---

[11] Martin, *Philippians*, p. 95.

[12] This was argued by E. Schweizer, and is supported by Martin, *Philippians*, pp. 95–96.

[13] O'Brien, *Philippians*, p. 211.

[14] Gordon D. Fee, *Paul's Letter to the Philippians*, NICNT (Grand Rapids: Eerdmans, 1995), p. 204.

[15] '. . . the principle of a timeless *present* participle needs very careful application, since alternative explanations are often possible, and grammar speaks to exegesis here with no decisive voice' (James Hope Moulton, *A Grammar of New Testament Greek: Vol. I: Prolegomena* [3rd ed., Edinburgh: T&T Clark, 1908], p. 127). However, Fee thinks there is a temporal reference, as in 2 Corinthians 8:9 (*Philippians*, p. 203). In this he is in agreement with J. B. Lightfoot, *Saint Paul's Epistle to the Philippians: A Revised Text with Introduction, Notes, and Dissertations* (London: Macmillan, 1881), pp. 110–111.

b. Christ did not use his deity for self-advantage (6b)

No word has been debated at greater length than *harpagmos* here in the second line of the hymn. Christ, being in *the form of God, did not count equality with God as harpagmos*; what does Paul mean? Traditionally, two main interpretations held the field. The first, known as *res rapienda* (a thing to be seized) translated the word as *a prize to be grasped* or *an act of robbery*. This implied that Christ did not possess equality with God by nature, that he had the opportunity to seize it by force, but refrained from doing so. There is a clear parallel with Adam who, given the opportunity to eat the fruit and persuaded that if he did so he would become like God, seized it for himself. In stark contrast, Christ did not follow Adam's course of action but instead attained to equality with God by humble obedience.[16] This line of thought would be at variance with other NT passages that state that Christ was permanently and eternally of the same status as God. A more recent variant of this view has been advanced by James Dunn but, as with the older version, lacks corroboration from the text.[17] The second traditional interpretation was known as *res rapta* (a thing to be retained), which could translate *harpagmos* as *something plundered* or *a prize of war* implying that Christ, being in the form of God was also equal with God. In this case, he did not hold on to the status and position he always had in a compulsive manner, placing himself ahead of others, but rather he acted in the manner of a servant. This interpretation fits the overall teaching of the NT better but is still not entirely satisfactory.[18]

In recent years, the seminal work of Roy Hoover has been influential in providing a better understanding of *harpagmos* and so of the passage as a whole.[19] Hoover identified the predominant use of the word in classical and first-century Greek as referring to something lying within one's power that can be exploited to one's own advantage. Christ in the form of God was also equal to God, but he did not use his position, status and nature for his own ends, he did not look after his own interests but rather he attended to the interests of others. That was his path to exaltation as *kyrios* (Lord) in verses 9–11. This was in contrast to Adam and to the triumphalists at

---

[16] See Martin, *Carmen Christi*, pp. 139–143.

[17] James D. G. Dunn, *Christology in the Making: A New Testament Inquiry Into the Origins of the Doctrine of the Incarnation* (2nd ed., London: SCM, 1989), pp. 114–121.

[18] Martin, *Carmen Christi*, pp. 138–139.

[19] Roy W. Hoover, 'The Harpagmos Enigma: A Philological Solution', *HTR* 64 (1971), pp. 95–119.

Philippi. This way of love is what Paul urges his readers to follow.[20] I have noted elsewhere that this shows us what God is like and that here we are given access into his eternal heartbeat.[21]

2. Christ's humility in his incarnation: he took the lowest place (7)

a. He emptied himself (7a)

From the middle of the nineteenth century many claimed that in his incarnation Christ emptied himself of certain attributes of his deity – omnipotence, omniscience, omnipresence – that appear to be incompatible with being fully human. Some went further, asserting that he emptied himself of deity.[22] This latter idea is contradicted by the preceding comments in verse 6 about his being in *the form of God* and also by the strongly adversative *but* (*alla*) that separates it from the emptying and prevents *being in the form of God* and *to be equal with God* from being the subject of *he emptied*.[23] Moreover, both lines of thought run into the problem of what happened to the government of the universe when the Son supposedly took a leave of absence from his responsibilities over it. Both suggest that Christ emptied himself of 'something', and that there is a certain incompatibility between God and humanity that makes incarnation impossible and requires us to accept some form of metamorphosis instead.[24]

Moreover, Paul does not say that Christ divested himself of something that was always his. Instead, he continues to be who he always was and shall be. His emptying is of himself. The language is emphatic – *himself he emptied (heauton ekenōsen)*.[25] He emptied himself not by subtraction of deity but by addition of humanity. He emptied himself by *taking the form of a servant*. For the Philippians, with their advanced civic pride, the status of a servant or a slave was beneath their natural dignity. Yet this is what Christ, the eternal Son, did and what they in turn were to do. The background here is possibly the Suffering Servant theme we saw was prominent in Isaiah, the servant who lives in faithful submission to Yahweh, suffers

---

[20] See also N. T. Wright, 'Harpagmos and the Meaning of Philippians ii.5–11', *JTS* 37 (October 1986), pp. 321–352.

[21] Robert Letham, *The Holy Trinity: In Scripture, History, Theology, and Worship* (Phillipsburg: Presbyterian & Reformed, 2004), p. 403.

[22] For a discussion of the *kenosis* theory see D. M. Baillie, *God Was in Christ: An Essay on Incarnation and Atonement* (New York: Charles Scribner's Sons, 1948), pp. 94–98; Donald MacLeod, *The Person of Christ* (Leicester: IVP, 1998), pp. 205–220.

[23] O'Brien, *Philippians*, pp. 216–218.

[24] Baillie, *God Was in Christ*, pp. 94–98.

[25] Fee, *Philippians*, pp. 210–211.

grievously in solidarity with his people, and ultimately is glorified.[26] There may also be a reference to slavery in the Graeco-Roman world; the word *doulos* can mean either a servant or a slave. This would strike home with the Philippians pointedly. Since there was no synagogue at Philippi slavery may well be in Paul's mind,[27] but we must also allow for the fact that in every context to which he went he was concerned to root his teaching ultimately in the prior revelation of God in the OT.[28]

b. He took the form of a servant, being born in the likeness of men (7b)

In contrast to his being *in the form of God* (*en morphē theou*) Christ *added the form of a servant* (*morphēn doulou labōn*) by becoming human. He who was and is God lived as a man, fully and truly human. The record of the Gospels establishes it beyond doubt; we have seen that abundantly. Paul is not intending to stress that at this point. The *likeness of men* does not mean that Christ was merely like a human being. The reference is to how he appeared to those who saw and knew him, to the manner in which he took the form of a servant. In this he appeared as human in every way, in full identity with the rest of the human race.[29] The point Paul drives home is his humility. He focused on our concerns. He could have used his status for his own ends but he chose to identify himself with us. This self-humiliation led him to lay down his life in death, *even death on a cross* (8), the death of the accursed, the lowest of the low, the death of one who most definitely was not a Roman citizen but one bereft of all human privileges. That will be the theme of the next section of this book. So, Paul says, have this mind among yourselves, seek the interests of

[26] It seems to me almost too obvious that the OT Scriptures were foremost in the thought of the apostles. However, the consensus of NT scholars assumes that various non-canonical rabbinical writings of inter-testamental Judaism are to be our primary source for understanding the NT. Against this it must be argued that these sources are so diffuse and differ among themselves so widely that no coherent unity could be produced. Moreover – and ultimately telling – is that the NT writings frequently, pervasively, make explicit reference to the Scriptures but never to the rabbinical authors of Second Temple Judaism. At the same time, there are strong arguments against Paul primarily referring to the suffering Servant of Isaiah here, and instead leaning towards a comparison with the contemporary condition of a slave in the Graeco-Roman world; see O'Brien, *Philippians*, pp. 218–224, who has an extensive discussion of the range of interpretations suggested at this point, and also Fee, *Philippians*, pp. 212–213.

[27] This is favoured by many exegetes, including O'Brien, *Philippians*, p. 218.

[28] Tom Holland, *Contours of Pauline Theology: A Radical New Survey of the Influences on Paul's Biblical Writings* (Fearn: Mentor, 2004).

[29] O'Brien, *Philippians*, p. 224.

others before your own, for this is the mind of Christ and this is the way God is – and remember that there is no way that the church or its members can evade suffering as the divinely established path to glory.

c. He humbled himself and became obedient to the death of the cross (8)

The sequel to this process of self-humbling, which was in fact the goal for which Christ had come, was *the cross*. We have already remarked on how abhorrent this form of execution was to the Romans. We saw how from the Jewish perspective, death by hanging on a tree was an accursed death. Yet Jesus took this path since it was the one marked out for him, which he had freely chosen, and was necessary to accomplish the purpose for which he had come into the world. If this is a hymn Paul cites, we noted that he adds the phrase *even the death of the cross* to underline the gravity of his death. It marks the absolute nadir of his sacrificial humbling as the suffering Servant. To those events we will now turn.

Part Three
Christ crucified

Matthew 26:57 – 27:44
15. Jesus rejected and crucified

For our purposes we are going to focus on Jesus' trial rather than on some of the events surrounding it, such as Peter's threefold denial that he was a disciple, or the tragedy of Judas.

1. Jesus on trial (Matt. 26:57–68; 27:11–31)

a. Jesus before the Sanhedrin (26:57–68)

(i) The council's agenda (57, 59)
The Jewish ruling council was already in session when Jesus was arrested in the garden after Judas Iscariot had betrayed him. It is very likely that it was in the process of marshalling evidence to bring against him. With the public turmoil surrounding Jesus and the tumultuous reception he had received on entering Jerusalem only days previously, this was the prime item on the agenda. The danger of a public uprising for the Jews was that it would bring down on the nation the full might of Roman retaliation and possibly threaten their national existence. The Sanhedrin was traditionally supposed to consist of seventy-one members (elders, chief priests, and scribes[1]) although not much is known about it or how it functioned at this time and whether it had a fixed number of members.[2] According to the Jewish law a minimum of two or three witnesses were required for evidence in a legal case (Deut. 19:15) and in particular for a capital charge (Num. 35:30; Deut. 17:6; 19:15). This was no easy matter. The

---

[1] Leon Morris, *The Gospel According to Matthew* (Grand Rapids: Eerdmans, 1992), p. 680; Craig S. Keener, *A Commentary on the Gospel of Matthew* (Grand Rapids: Eerdmans, 1999), p. 615; David Hill, *The Gospel of Matthew* (London: Marshall, Morgan & Scott, 1972), p. 345.

[2] John Nolland, *The Gospel of Matthew: A Commentary on the Greek Text*, NIGTC (Grand Rapids: Eerdmans, 2005), p. 1123.

council was up all night struggling with the question. The imperfect *were seeking* (*ezētoun*) entails a process, a search for witnesses,[3] or more specifically *false testimony* (*pseudomartyrian*), clearly undermining the impartiality and legitimacy of the proceedings insofar as they wanted any charge that could possibly incriminate Jesus. The chances of bringing such a charge were receding by the hour. This may have been a preliminary hearing since capital trials could not be held at night.[4]

(ii) The search for witnesses (60–63a)
The evidence provided by the *false witnesses* in verse 61 was false in the sense that it was a misrepresentation of the truth, misconstruing an earlier statement Jesus had made as recorded in John 2:19. There he had said 'destroy this temple and in three days I will raise it up', referring to his body as a temple and to the resurrection that would follow. These *witnesses* interpreted the comment literally as an intention to destroy the Jerusalem temple and reconstruct it in an impossibly brief time. The temple, as the heart of Israel's worship and the place where Yahweh met his people, was sacrosanct and a threat to destroy it was inevitably damning. It was blasphemy.[5] It is clear that Jesus' saying had become distorted with the passage of time as it was passed on by word of mouth. Whatever may have occurred, such a declaration would have been a claim to be the Messiah (cf. Acts 6:14).[6] Jesus refused to answer these false claims, not dignifying them with any tacit acceptance of their legitimacy. Notwithstanding, the penalty for false witness in the OT Scriptures was death (Deut. 19:16–21). Here, presumably under cross-examination, the witnesses were shown to be false but yet the Council apparently did not charge them with the offence they deserved.[7] Matthew sees it as out to incriminate Jesus by whatever means it can employ.

(iii) Caiaphas' question (63b–66)
Into this void, the high priest Caiaphas questions Jesus under oath. This is a serious question. Jesus had to answer it.[8] *Tell us if you are the Christ, the Son of God.* Jesus answers but he does so by

---

[3] R. T. France, *The Gospel According to Matthew: An Introduction and Commentary*, TNTC (Leicester: IVP, 1985), p. 378.

[4] W. D. Davies and D. C. Allison, *A Critical and Exegetical Commentary on the Gospel According to Saint Matthew: Volume III*, ICC (Edinburgh: T&T Clark, 1997), p. 522; Nolland, *Matthew*, p. 1120; Keener, *Matthew*, pp. 644–645.

[5] France, *Matthew*, pp. 378–379.

[6] Ibid., p. 379.

[7] See Keener, *Matthew*, pp. 647–648.

[8] France, *Matthew*, p. 380.

distancing himself from Caiaphas' own understanding of what these terms mean. The high priest expected that the Christ would be a wonder-worker, displaying his full gamut of powers, a liberator. Jesus, on the other hand, was weak and vulnerable. Here he was, alone and without support, before the Jewish ruling council, in danger of his life. He draws attention to the content of Caiaphas' own question and then defines it in the true terms that reflect who he himself is and what he will be. In contrast to his current state of lowliness there will come a time when he will be *seated at the right hand of Power and coming on the clouds of heaven*.[9] Jesus avoided using the word 'God'; that would be blasphemy,[10] for it was a word the Jews did not use. Instead, he conflates Psalm 110:1 and Daniel 7:13–14 and ascribes them to himself. In Psalm 110 David refers to the Lord being seated by the Lord at his right hand, given authority over the nations and made a priest for ever, combined functions forbidden to the kings in the OT. The one thus enthroned has clear divine status. Daniel 7 presents the vision of a son of man coming on the clouds of heaven and being given a kingdom extending over the whole earth, indestructible and everlasting. Jesus had referred to himself as the Son of Man throughout his public ministry. Here he points to his future glory, his vindication and enthronement at the right hand of God.[11]

To Caiaphas, this was blasphemy. Jesus stood self-condemned. Correctly, for someone who did not believe Jesus, this was enough to secure his death. He *tore his robes*, an act prescribed by rabbinical law as an expression of horror at the voicing of blasphemy.[12] The council had the case sown up (65–66).[13]

However, another problem presented itself. There is some doubt as to whether the Sanhedrin had the power to carry out the execution by its own verdict alone.[14] There is evidence from the later martyrdom of Stephen that it did possess authority to exact capital punishment, although this has been disputed.[15] It seemed to the council that for

[9] Ibid.
[10] Ibid., p. 382.
[11] Ibid., p. 381.
[12] France, *Matthew*, p. 381; Keener, *Matthew*, pp. 651–652.
[13] Davies and Allison, *Matthew III*, p. 534; Nolland, *Matthew*, pp. 1132–1133.
[14] Keener, *Matthew*, pp. 664–665.
[15] Davies and Allison argue that it is possible that the stoning of Stephen was the result of mob action rather than a formal judicial process. Citing the later execution of James for blasphemy, they indicate that the high priest was deposed by the Romans for the deed. See Davies and Allison, *Matthew III*, p. 524. However, Paul appears to have said that he cast his vote for Stephen's execution (Acts 22:20; 26:10; cf. 8:1), implying a lawful judicial process preceding it. It is possible that such a right may have existed but only for exceptional cases.

Jesus to be executed there needed to be a sentence passed by the Roman authorities, some capital charge that could be sustained.[16] This needed careful thought. The council adjourned temporarily until morning, whereupon it decided on bringing a charge of sedition on the basis that Jesus had claimed to be king, in direct challenge to the authority of Caesar (27:1). That this adjournment was illegal, since the Sanhedrin could not recommence an adjourned meeting until a sunset had passed, did not bother them in the slightest.[17]

b. Jesus before Pilate (27:11–14)

The accusation then presented to Pilate was that Jesus made himself out to be a *king* and so was challenging the legitimacy of the Roman authorities and, behind that, Caesar. This was the question Pilate posed to Jesus when he was presented to him by the Sanhedrin (11). There is little doubt that such a claim would have undermined Rome in its own eyes, and so would justify a charge of sedition, upon conviction of which the guilty party would be executed. Jesus' answer to the charge is cryptic. He simply refers to Pilate's own question and gives no reply of his own.

His accusers, *the chief priests and elders*, are present at the hearing. They bring a whole range of accusations. Jesus remains silent. Pilate is astonished. Why does Jesus not answer these charges? This may well have implied for Pilate that Jesus was tacitly admitting his guilt and that he had indeed pronounced himself *King of the Jews* and so was guilty of sedition.[18] Did it indicate on Pilate's part a personal inclination to acquit Jesus, which the silence was threatening? Why, then, did Jesus not reply to his accusers?

Ultimately, it would seem that Jesus did not regard their accusations as worthy of a reply. The new context may have had something to do with it. Jesus was no longer before a meeting of the Sanhedrin, where he respected his opponents because of their office. Now he was in a court of the Gentiles and the Jewish leaders were not constituted as the ruling council as such but were merely witnesses for the prosecution.[19] However, there is something more far-reaching than that. In view of its heritage of God's covenant down through the centuries Israel had a huge responsibility. Israel had the promise of the Christ. Yahweh had prepared them for it over long years. They had rejected him with implacable hostility. He had failed to

---

[16] Davies and Allison, *Matthew III*, p. 554.

[17] Hill, *Matthew*, p. 347.

[18] This cannot be anachronistically related to the right, under English law, for the accused to remain silent.

[19] Nolland, *Matthew*, pp. 1158–1166; Keener, *Matthew*, p. 665.

fulfil their misguided expectations. By their consistent actions, they had made themselves unworthy of a reply. Jesus' conflict with the religious establishment, brewing and developing throughout Matthew, now comes to its finale. Davies and Allison think that this is a fulfilment of Isaiah's suffering servant, who remained silent and submissive before his accusers (Isa. 53:7).[20]

c. Jesus or Barabbas – a travesty of justice (27:15–26)

The custom of the Roman government was to grant an amnesty at Passover to a prisoner who the Jewish people requested. This was clearly a politically motivated policy to help assuage any potential insurgent nationalist sentiment. It was designed to keep the indigenous population happy and quiet and so facilitate Roman rule. However, there is no evidence for the existence of such a custom elsewhere than in the Synoptic Gospels.[21] This does not mean it did not happen or that the Gospel writers dreamed this up. These are as much historical records as the next piece of papyrus. What can be deduced from this is that it was not a widespread custom or one that featured large in Roman policy; it may have been a minor concession that was not deemed of much importance.[22]

Both Mark and Luke record that Barabbas had been thrown into prison for murder and insurrection, both capital crimes (Mark 15:7; Luke 23:19). If he had already been condemned to death then only Caesar could pardon him. The implication is that he had yet to be tried. The evidence of Jesus' trial is that he was crucified immediately afterwards, without delay.

The point of the injustice is obvious. Jesus had not been found guilty by Pilate of any crime. His own wife recognized that when she urged him to release Jesus (19). He should never have been placed in the same category as Barabbas. Even if Barabbas had yet to be tried and convicted, the charges against him were much graver; not only was he a leader of an insurrection but it was alleged he had committed murder. If he had been tried and convicted his proven guilt has to be weighed against Jesus' own innocence; not only was Jesus never charged with murder (!) but he had upheld the authority of Caesar whenever questioned about it (Matt. 22:15–22; Mark 12:13–17; Luke 20:19–26). According to legality, Jesus should have been released as of right; a bargain in relation to a murderer was out of the question. This was a violation of all principles of natural justice

---

[20] Davies and Allison, *Matthew III*, p. 582.

[21] France, *Matthew*, p. 389; Hill, *Matthew*, p. 350.

[22] See the discussion in Davies and Allison, *Matthew III*, p. 583; Nolland, *Matthew*, pp. 1166–1167; and Keener, *Matthew*, p. 668.

as well as Roman law. Pilate's wife corroborates this point. She – a pagan – was horrified at the prospect of an innocent man hounded to death and wanted her husband to keep out of it. Clearly Pilate did not regard her as 'she who must be obeyed'.

Pilate was swayed by the ferocious insistence of the Jewish leaders and by political expediency. Better an innocent man be executed than have a national uprising on his hands during his watch as governor. His second request to the mob effectively settled the matter (21–23). The time to resist the pressure was when his wife intervened. Once he had passed that threshold and gone to the crowds again his resistance was gone. He made a vain and pathetic attempt to absolve himself of responsibility for the deed (24), unwittingly admitting that Jesus was innocent, that he believed this, but was unwilling to stand against the concerted clamour of council and crowd. He showed himself a weak and indecisive leader, unfit to govern a Roman province, probably promoted above his abilities. It comes as little surprise that Christian tradition has him either executed for his official abuses or committing suicide.[23] To add to the cruel mix, he ordered that Jesus be *scourged* before crucifixion. Scourging, or unrestrained whipping with knotted leather straps often containing pieces of metal, was intended to weaken the prisoner and meant, in effect, being flayed to the bone.[24] It horrified even the cruel Emperor Domitian.[25]

d. Ridicule and blasphemy (27:27–31)

There followed mock worship by the execution squad. While they make preparations for the crucifixion, they blasphemously deride Jesus' kingly claim. They put *a scarlet robe on him*, scarlet being the colour associated with the Emperor. They place *a reed* – a symbol of regal power – *in his right hand*.[26] They cry out *hail, King of the Jews*, mimicking the usual greeting to the Emperor, 'hail, Caesar!'[27] Alongside it they make *a crown of thorns*, evidently to inflict pain, probably in the form of spikes as depicted on the crowns imprinted on the imperial coinage.[28]

The nature of this charade is mainly mockery. Certainly there is the physical pain. But it is a parody, as all ultimately Satanic activity

---

[23] R. Trevijano, 'Pilate', in Angelo Di Berardino (ed.), *Encyclopedia of the Early Church* (New York: Oxford University Press, 1992), p. 687.

[24] France, *Matthew*, p. 393; Hill, *Matthew*, p. 351; Davies and Allison, *Matthew III*, p. 593.

[25] Morris, *Matthew*, p. 708, n. 51.

[26] France, *Matthew*, p. 394; Hill, *Matthew*, p. 352.

[27] Keener, *Matthew*, p. 675.

[28] France, *Matthew*, p. 394; Nolland, *Matthew*, pp. 1182–1184.

is. In its perverse way, even the most demonic and depraved actions of a debased mind are unwittingly testifying to the kingly rule of Christ to which one day the savage brutality of the mockers will yield, too late, to abject fear and isolation.

When the mockery turns even sourer there is no doubt about the physical nature of the abuse. They strike Jesus on the head with the mock-royal reed. They spit on him. Ridicule merges with brutality and viciousness. Execution follows. Behind this is the action of the serpent, dealing a blow to the heel of the offspring of the woman (Gen. 3:15). It is the savage, pent-up fury of a defeated foe.

2. Jesus crucified (Matt. 27:32–44)

a. The departure from the city (32–36)

(i) Excommunication (32a)

As they went out the event unfolded. Jesus was to suffer 'outside the gate', a place of disgrace, outside the city, away from the place where Yahweh met his people.[29] This was the place where the carcasses of the sacrificial animals were thrown and burned. It was a place of rejection and abandonment. Klaas Schilder graphically portrays what this meant for Jesus. He was regarded as an *exlex* – one upon whom the full exaction of the law had been enforced but who was given over to suffer more than the law could demand.[30] He was now to go even further. He was to be accursed. God's justice as administered by humans had done the utmost it could do, even in its twisted perversity, in the grimness of execution. It had reached a point where all that could be done was to hand Jesus over to the unmitigated wrath of God. He is cast out of the gates of the city, out of the gates of human justice, to suffer and die in the place of the wretched and accursed.[31] 'A hanged man is cursed by God.'[32] As Schilder puts it:

> The thing we want to discuss now, as Jesus Christ goes out to the place of curse, is the awful weight of the justice of God which puts upon Christ a burden which to our mind is a superhuman one. This burden God places upon him in order that he may reach out from this maze of sin, from this knot of human falsehood, from these skeins of arbitrariness and injustice, in which he has

[29] Heb. 13:11–13.
[30] Klaas Schilder, *Christ on Trial*, trans. Henry Zylstra (Grand Rapids: Eerdmans, 1950), pp. 277–288, 415–549.
[31] Klaas Schilder, *Christ Crucified*, trans. Henry Zylstra (Grand Rapids: Eerdmans, 1944), p. 15.
[32] Deut. 21:23.

become entangled and been taken captive thus far – may reach out, we say, to the firm hand of God in order to submit to his justice, painful as it may be. He must submit to his justice now, to the one justice of God. That, and nothing else, he must do. For we can truly say that from the human side there is nothing but injustice here.[33]

This must be seen in a wider context. Jesus did not go to this place unwillingly. Certainly, it took a huge struggle in the garden in which his will was aligned with the eternal will of God. In this he did not move from unwillingness to willingness but rather from a human willing, limited in his incarnate state, to a full agreement with what he had always determined but now needed to bring clearly into focus.[34] Moreover, as the eternal Son of the Father he had planned this from everlasting. The question now was that he had to undergo this ordeal as man; that was something new. It is the eternal Son of the Father – one of the Trinity – who, according to the flesh, willingly goes to this place of execution on our behalf.

(ii) Exhaustion (32b, 34a)

Jesus had been awake all night. More than that, he had been assaulted and buffeted by the execution squad of Roman soldiers. He had been subject to interrogation by two tribunals. He was in a state of near-collapse. He was no longer able to carry his own cross, as condemned criminals were required to do.[35] The ordeal he had suffered was too much for him. The soldiers recognize that at this point. How is he to carry his cross to the place of execution? This was no disgrace. Jesus was, and is, human. As the Son, he had added human nature in the incarnation and grown from conception to adulthood, with all the necessary accompaniments to it. As man, as Calvin said, it is necessary that we consider him in the weakness of his incarnate lowliness.[36] He had taken 'the form of a servant'.[37]

---

[33] Schilder, Christ Crucified, p. 15.

[34] See the crucial letter of Pope Agatho to the Third Council of Constantinople (680-81): 'For when we confess two natures and two natural wills, and two natural operations in our one Lord Jesus Christ, we do not assert that they are contrary or opposed one to the other' for 'the divine will and operation he has in common with the coessential Father from all eternity: the human, he has received from us, taken with our nature in time'. In Henry R. Percival (ed.), The Seven Ecumenical Councils of the Undivided Church: Their Canons and Dogmatic Decrees, A Select Library of Nicene and Post-Nicene Fathers of the Christian Church: Second Series (Edinburgh: T&T Clark, 1997 reprint), pp. 330–331.

[35] France, Matthew, p. 395; Keener, Matthew, pp. 676–677.

[36] Institutes, 2:13:2, 2:15:12.

[37] Phil. 2:7.

Mercifully, a man was in the vicinity who the executioners *compelled . . . to carry [Jesus'] cross* for him. Mark implies that this man, *Simon* of *Cyrene*, was a Christian and the father of two prominent members of the church at Rome. He happened to be passing by at the time.[38] Was his passing by fortuitous or was he already some kind of disciple? We cannot know. Assuming he was later a believer it is possible that this may have been the occasion by which his interest in Jesus and his teaching was aroused. On the other hand, there must be a strong possibility that he was in the area because of the Passover and, being so, he could hardly escape coming into contact with the furore over Jesus and his capture by the authorities. Cyrene was in North Africa, so most probably Simon was a Jew of the diaspora, in this pointing forwards to the time – close at hand – when the kingdom of God would be extended beyond the boundaries of Israel.

Once the party arrived at *Golgotha*, the place of crucifixion, the executioners – realizing Jesus was drained – offered him a drink of drugged wine. This would alleviate the agony of what was to follow. The Talmud allowed for a condemned man, about to be executed, to receive a narcotic inserted into some wine in order to dull his senses.[39] Jesus was an obvious candidate for this in view of his previous ordeal. Yet he refuses the sedative. Why? There was a reason that went beyond the question of Jesus' own comfort. He needed to be fully conscious of the sufferings, pain and abandonment that lay ahead. He offered himself on the cross completely with his faculties unimpaired. For him to be drugged to a stupor would have negated his mission. He was the servant who had come to suffer, and to do so in the place of, and on behalf of, his people; to save his people from their sins (Matt. 1:21). He took a taste, realized what it was, and refused to drink it. As the psalmist had written, 'they gave me poison for food, and for my thirst they gave me sour wine to drink'.[40]

> We may not know, we cannot tell
> What pains he had to bear;
> But we believe it was for us
> He hung and suffered there.[41]

---

[38] Mark 15:21.
[39] France, *Matthew*, p. 395; Hill, *Matthew*, p. 353; Nolland, *Matthew*, pp. 1190–1191; Keener, *Matthew*, pp. 677–678.
[40] Ps. 69:21.
[41] 'There is a green hill far away', Cecil Frances Alexander (1818–95).

b. Execution (35–44)

Matthew is restrained in his descriptions of Jesus' suffering on the cross.[42] He was crucified (35a). For all who knew what that meant it would conjure up a dreadful cocktail of pain, shame and dishonour. There was no need for Matthew to elaborate. Indeed, for us much would detract from the purpose of his sufferings and death if we were to dwell on all the fine details involved at this point. His garments were removed and divided among the soldiers (35b). The soldiers themselves kept guard over him (36) so that it was impossible for his disciples to have come and taken him down – even if they had had for as much as one moment the courage to defy a military unit.[43] The normal practice of the Romans was to place an inscription over a cross informing the reader as to the reason for the execution. In Jesus' case the inscription referred to his claim to be *the King of the Jews* (37). If only the Jewish passers-by had thought carefully they should have seen the national rebuff this was. Any attempt at restoring Jewish independence would be met by a similar reprisal.[44] Israel was still a nation effectively in exile, even if living in its own land. There were two others crucified on either side of Jesus. According to some old Latin translations, Mark refers here to the fulfilment of Isaiah 53:12, he 'was numbered with the transgressors', pointing to Jesus' identification with us in our sin. While it may not be original to the text of Mark, it indicates a common very early understanding by the church.

Moreover, in addition to the intense pain – few if any tortures are regarded as worse than crucifixion in this respect – and the obvious shame, there was widespread public mockery. Again this in its widest context can be seen as a demonic parody, for at Christ's second coming every eye will see him and acknowledge universally that Jesus Christ is Lord (Phil. 2:9–11). Again, it was foretold in the OT (Ps. 22:7–8 has the words exactly, while Ps. 69:9 hints at it). We have here a group of three satanic witnesses attesting to their own rebellion and the demonic denial of the grace of God.[45] There are *those who passed by* – a disparate group of people who merely happened to be there. Presumably, they were ignorant of the psalm. The vast majority derided him, casting scorn on his prophecy of his resurrection by focusing on the literal interpretation of his temple saying (39–40). The temple had taken centre stage in Israel so as to amount to a virtual idolatry that blinded the minds of its adherents to the reality

[42] Hill, *Matthew*, p. 353.
[43] France, *Matthew*, p. 396.
[44] Ibid.
[45] See Keener, *Matthew*, p. 681.

to which it pointed. Second are the *priests*, *scribes* and *elders* who mock the fact that he is on the cross and has not displayed miraculous power so as to come down and rescue himself. They deride his claims to be king of Israel and the Son of God. They even cite the psalm they should have known foreshadowed this day (41–43). Third are the two *robbers* or insurrectionists crucified with him, one on either side (44), who mock him in the same way. So all branches of Jewish society join in the mockery – the leaders, the rank and file, and the dregs. 'He was despised and rejected by men'; 'numbered with the transgressors'.[46] Matthew says no more, although we find Luke, with his meticulous historical research, recording that one of these two came to his senses, acknowledged Jesus' innocence and his own guilt, confessed that Jesus was to enter his kingdom and called on him to remember him at that time (Luke 23:40–43). Evidently, he had heard of Jesus' teaching and had come to believe him. Jesus assures him of his salvation – a point that could only be known from Jesus himself after his resurrection! Even at this stage, there was the possibility of repentance and faith. Indeed, Jesus prayed that these people would be forgiven this sin due to their ignorance of the import of their actions (Luke 23:34). Justice and grace met together at the cross.

[46] Isa. 53:3, 12.

Matthew 27:45–56
16. The death of Jesus

1. Jesus on the cross (45–50)

a. The darkness (45)

For Matthew the time Jesus was on the cross was a period of super-natural *darkness*. It was the middle of the day, from noon to mid-afternoon; this was not the time for it to be dark. Moreover, darkness was over *all the land*. The reference could mean the whole earth but is more likely to denote the whole land of Palestine.[1] What was the meaning of this? Since Matthew has previously set the events of Jesus' life against the background of the exodus, he may be comparing the crucifixion with the plagues that Yahweh visited on Egypt. One of these was thick darkness, so dark it was impossible to see.

> Then the Lord said to Moses, 'Stretch out your hand towards heaven, that there may be darkness over the land of Egypt, a darkness to be felt.' So Moses stretched out his hand toward heaven, and there was pitch darkness in all the land of Egypt for three days. They did not see one another, nor did anyone rise from his place for three days, but all the people of Israel had light where they lived.[2]

[1] W. D. Davies and D. C. Allison, *A Critical and Exegetical Commentary on the Gospel According to Saint Matthew: Volume III*, ICC (Edinburgh: T&T Clark, 1997), p. 622; David Hill, *The Gospel of Matthew* (London: Marshall, Morgan & Scott, 1972), p. 354; R. T. France, *The Gospel According to Matthew: An Introduction and Commentary*, TNTC (Leicester: IVP, 1985), p. 398; Leon Morris, *The Gospel According to Matthew* (Grand Rapids: Eerdmans, 1992), p. 720; John Nolland, *The Gospel of Matthew: A Commentary on the Greek Text*, NIGTC (Grand Rapids: Eerdmans, 2005), p. 1205; Donald A. Hagner, *Matthew 14–28*, WBC 33B (Dallas: Word Books, 1995), pp. 843–844.

[2] Exod. 10:21–23.

This was the penultimate plague to strike Egypt, an act of divine judgment for its persecution of God's people, and the supreme OT demonstration of Yahweh's commitment to his covenant. There is a possible foreshadowing of the crucifixion in Amos 8:9, where the Lord says, 'On that day ... I will make the sun go down at noon and darken the earth in broad daylight' where the reference is to his coming judgment on Israel. So while the plague was directed against Egypt and Israel was vindicated, now at the cross there is a dramatic sign of judgment on *all the land* of Israel.[3] Additionally, this darkness demonstrated that God is the lord of creation. The death of Jesus has cosmic impact. As Paul (Col. 1:15–17), John (John 1:1–3), and the author of Hebrews (Heb. 1:1–3) say, he is the creator of the universe; it is hardly surprising that this crucial crime had deep impact on the universe itself.[4]

b. The cry of dereliction (46)

After three hours of intense darkness, Jesus cries, partly in Hebrew, partly in Aramaic,[5] *My God, my God, why have you forsaken me?*, a direct citation of Psalm 22:1, where the psalmist expressed his utter desolation, his sense of abandonment by God, agonized and bereft. We should see this cry in the light of the whole psalm, as the prayer of a righteous sufferer committing his case to God, trusting in his ultimate deliverance. This was how the psalm was generally interpreted by the Jews.[6] However, at this point the final triumph – the theme of the latter part of the psalm from verse 19 – is not yet in view. Only the anguish of the moment absorbs Jesus' mind as he endures the intense physical torture of crucifixion, the shame associated with it, the abandonment by his disciples and above all the overwhelming sense that God had let him go to this appalling trial.[7]

c. The vinegar (47–49)

Mistakenly thinking that Jesus was calling for *Elijah*, one of the bystanders supposed that he needed some wine vinegar and so fetched *a sponge* on which it could be administered. As we saw in

[3] France, *Matthew*, p. 398; Hill, *Matthew*, p. 354.

[4] '... it is an omen of divine displeasure or judgement, a sign of cosmic significance' (Davies and Allison, *Matthew III*, p. 622).

[5] For a discussion of this question, see Davies and Allison, *Matthew III*, p. 624; France, *Matthew*, p. 399; Nolland, *Matthew*, p. 1206.

[6] Hill, *Matthew*, p. 355.

[7] This, as Davies and Allison comment, was not a loss of faith but a cry of pain (*Matthew III*, p. 625). See France, *Matthew*, p. 398; Morris, *Matthew*, pp. 720–721.

chapter 15, this was often done to crucified criminals so as to assuage their pain and distress. It was apparently an act of kindness; the wine vinegar would have been diluted with water and would have a sedative effect, although it is possible that it could have prolonged the pain and so have been another act of hostility.[8] Again, one of the psalms of dereliction points forward to this minor incident. Psalm 69:21 states, 'they gave me poison for food, and for my thirst they gave me sour wine to drink'. Again, Matthew intends the reader to see that the abandonments spoken of by the psalmists were all realized in the sufferings of Jesus on the cross. At the same time, he may be commenting about the supposition that Jesus called for Elijah. The prophet did not die; he was taken up to heaven in a whirlwind (2 Kgs 2:1–12). A legend had developed that he would return to rescue the righteous sufferer at the point of his greatest need.[9] The onlookers' reaction is to wait and see if Elijah did in fact come back to deliver Jesus. Let us see if Jesus is really righteous, they are saying. There is a contrast here between the kind action of the one who brought the wine vinegar and the sceptical waiting of the crowd for the legendary figure to return.[10]

d. Jesus' death (50)

With a loud cry Jesus *yielded up his spirit*. There are two astounding actions here. Jesus is at his lowest ebb, all strength drained from him by the ordeal. Crucifixion was enough to destroy a person physically, leaving aside the mental and above all spiritual torment through which Jesus was passing. By this time he would have been an absolute wreck.

However, he makes *a loud cry*. This is in stark contrast to his physical condition. Clearly this indicates he was in full control of his great sufferings. Even at their most intense point, when death's mightiest powers had done their worst, he is able to cry out with vigour and power. Second, he does not die as a passive wimp. He is the active agent. He yields up his spirit to the Father. John records him saying that, as the good shepherd, he lays down his life for the sheep. No one takes it from him; he lays it down of himself. He is in charge throughout (John 10:18). Matthew corroborates this. At the point of darkest extremity Jesus has come to do the will of the Father, which he as the Son exhaustively shares. Moreover, elsewhere

---

[8] Davies and Allison, *Matthew III*, p. 627; Hill, *Matthew*, p. 355; France, *Matthew*, p. 399.

[9] Davies and Allison, *Matthew III*, p. 626; Hill, *Matthew*, p. 355; France, *Matthew*, p. 399; Morris, *Matthew*, p. 722; Hagner, *Matthew 14–28*, p. 845.

[10] France, *Matthew*, p. 399.

he is noted as calling on the Father to forgive his tormentors since they were acting in ignorance and unbelief. His death is an act of his own will, made for the good of those he had come to save from their sins (Matt. 1:21).[11] As Davies and Allison comment, 'there is terror in this text' for what it does is to 'portray the depths of irrational human depravity', 'the patient endurance of God' and 'the frightening mystery of God's seeming inactivity in the world'.[12]

2. Its immediate corollaries (51–53)

a. Jesus and the temple (51a)

At the point of Jesus' death, the *curtain of the temple was torn in two*, from the top downwards. The temple was the place where Yahweh and his people met for worship. The ark of the covenant was there. Into the holy of holies the high priest entered once a year to make atonement for the people, having first made sacrifice for his own sins. This was the centre of the covenantal relationship between God and his people. But as when the law was given at Mount Sinai (Exod. 19 – 20) there were 'keep out' signs everywhere. The Gentiles were forbidden to enter on penalty of death. Women were kept in an outer court. Only the high priest could ever enter the holy of holies and that only annually. The curtain, or veil, set the holy of holies apart, restricting access. There was also an outer veil to the temple, a thick curtain, eighty feet high, which may have been the curtain intended here, since it was apparently visible to the public.[13]

Now however, it was ripped apart. Again, two factors must be noted. The veil could not simply be cut; it was too thick and weighed too much. Second, it was torn downwards from *the top to the bottom*. This was no human action; it was done by God. Jesus had been mocked about his prophecies concerning the temple, its imminent destruction. Now he is vindicated at the moment of his death. Moreover, the connection between his death and the rending of the curtain is obvious; the former is the occasion of the latter. It indicates that the way to God is now open. The 'keep out' signs no longer apply. God is acting in judgment on the old system of worship, particularly in the light of the unbelief and rebellion of its contemporary practitioners. It looks forward to that grim and tragic day not many years in the future when the entire temple would be razed to the ground by Roman armies, when the sacrificial system – now

---

[11] France, *Matthew*, p. 399; Morris, *Matthew*, pp. 723–724; Nolland, *Matthew*, pp. 1210–1211.
[12] Davies and Allison, *Matthew III*, p. 639.
[13] Ibid., p. 631.

rendered obsolete – would finally be eradicated. By implication it attests that Jesus' death on the cross is the one perfect sacrifice for sins and that no other sacrifice is needed.[14]

b. Jesus and creation (51b)

At this moment there is a great earthquake and the rocks shake. The death of Jesus has immediate effects on the created order. His dying had been accompanied by an intense, anomalous and supernatural darkness, portending the judgment of God on Israel. Now the impact is extended to the rocks and the earth, to the whole fabric of the world he had made. Why was this? It was because he was its creator. Not as much as one thing was made apart from him, as John was to write (John 1:3). The great creator, who had assumed a house of clay, had been put to death in the flesh. No wonder the world was in turmoil. Is it any surprise that the rocks and the hills were on the point of bursting asunder? There is an inter-relationship between creation and redemption. The cosmos was created so that all things might be headed up by the Son in union with mankind, he having saved us from sin and death. Our salvation was planned and effected for the purpose that we might share with Christ the Son in the administration of the new creation. The two stand together. The material and spiritual realms together are unitedly to be ruled by the Christ. And this Christ had died according to the flesh, died as a condemned criminal. Salvation will only be complete with the resurrection of the body.

c. Jesus and resurrection (52–53)

Suddenly *the tombs* are *opened, many **bodies*** – Matthew stresses this – of OT saints come to life after Jesus' own resurrection, enter Jerusalem and are seen. This was evidently a selection of OT saints, not all of them or even a large proportion of them, but simply a sampling. They emerge after Jesus' resurrection. They are seen not universally but by many.

This is an odd happening, of which we read nothing elsewhere. However, it discloses a number of crucial inter-relationships. First, it demonstrates the unity of OT and NT. Jesus' death and resurrection has a liberating effect on the OT saints who had died. They are raised on the basis of the cross of Jesus Christ and his resurrection, just as we are. Jesus describes his death as the 'blood of the

---

[14] For an extensive discussion of eleven different interpretations of this dramatic event, see Nolland, *Matthew*, pp. 1211–1213.

covenant',[15] which ended the old covenant enacted at Sinai, so the OT saints are saved on the basis of this. Second, it signals the inextricable connection between Jesus' death and resurrection. Neither can properly be understood apart from the other. Resurrection, by definition, is resurrection *from the dead,* while the death had in view from the start the resurrection and glory that would follow: 'for the joy set before him' Jesus endured the cross (Heb. 12:1-2). Third, there is implicit a connection between Jesus' resurrection and the resurrection of the saints. It is *after* Jesus is raised that the OT saints come forth from their graves and appear *to many.* Paul makes this connection clear in 1 Corinthians 15, a passage we will address later in detail. Fourth, there is a connection between Jesus' death and our resurrection, since it is his atoning death that breaks open the curtain, inaugurates the new creation and so results in our renewal and eventual resurrection to glory. 'Jesus' death is a resurrecting death.'[16] Jesus, as a grain of wheat falling into the ground and dying, brings forth much fruit. Fifthly, this presages the final eschatological renewal of the cosmos. The 'last days' are associated with bodily resurrection in the OT (Dan. 12:2; Ezek. 37; Isa. 26:19) and this was reaffirmed by Jesus himself (John 5:29). The resurrection of these saints indicates that the last days had arrived.[17]

3. The aftermath (54-56)

a. The centurion and the soldiers (54)

The earthquake and the supernatural darkness – all these events spread terror into the minds of the witnesses. In some cases they elicited faith. This first group were soldiers all, and so were Gentiles. Matthew's aim in the gospel is to prove that Jesus is the inheritor of the promises of the Abrahamic and Davidic covenants. The Abrahamic covenant envisaged worldwide blessing through the offspring of Abraham. Here the Gentiles are filled with awe. Their response is to blurt out, *truly this was the Son of God!* There is no definite article before the word *son.* However, this is not a refined theological comment from the Roman soldiers. Besides, the focus

---

[15] Matt. 26:28.

[16] Davies and Allison, *Matthew III*, p. 633.

[17] What happened to these saints? Did they return to their graves, climb back into their coffins and close the lids?! Did they live for a while and then die a second time, as we suppose happened to Lazarus? Or did they share in Jesus' ascension, much as Elijah had done? We are not informed. However, with the mention of Elijah only a few sentences earlier, the balance of possibility may lie in that direction. Nolland tends to agree (*Matthew*, p. 1217).

of such anarthrous nouns is on the quality of what is ascribed.[18] From the untutored lips of pagan soldiers comes a confession of Jesus as the Son of God,[19] foreshadowing the discipling of the nations that forms the climax of Matthew's Gospel (Matt. 28:19–20). Moreover, Matthew sees it as an important witness to the truth. One assumes that, in connection with Jesus' crucifixion, they had heard at least a smattering of what he had taught. Now, in the face of the evidence of creation, they acknowledge Jesus' supreme status.

b. The women (55–56)

With the exception of John, the women were more faithful than the eleven. Women were not permitted to give evidence in a court of law in Israel. It is strikingly clear that the NT takes a different view, as did God. The women were selected as witnesses of these events. A minimum of two or three were needed to corroborate a matter in a law court in the OT. There is an abundance here, far more than necessary. There is no danger of a mistake about the reality of Jesus' death. It was corroborated by a plenitude of eyewitnesses and was well able to stand up to legal scrutiny. Jesus really died. These events actually happened. It brings about our salvation. It is the centre point of world history. It presages the renewal of the universe.

[18] E. C. Colwell, 'A Definite Rule for the Use of the Article in the Greek New Testament', *JBL* 52 (1933), pp. 12–21; Hagner, *Matthew 14–28*, pp. 852–853.

[19] Davies and Allison, *Matthew III*, p. 636; Hill, *Matthew*, p. 356; France, *Matthew*, pp. 401–402; Morris, *Matthew*, p. 726.

Matthew 27:57–66
17. The burial of Jesus

1. Joseph of Arimathea and Pilate (57–58)

According to Mark, Joseph of Arimathea was a respected member of the Sanhedrin, the Jewish ruling council (Mark 15:43). He is described here as wealthy. The two usually went together. Matthew says of him that he was *a disciple of Jesus*, presumably to this point a secret one. We might reasonably suppose that he had been opposed to the actions of the Sanhedrin but afraid to speak out. How many on church sessions or other leadership bodies are similarly reluctant to stand up for what they believe? Now, however, he has plucked up courage to identify himself openly with Jesus, even though evidently in a lost cause. He is paying his respects to a dead man. We must assume that the details of his discussions with Pilate were conveyed by Joseph himself and that he eventually firmly associated himself with the church. People come to faith in all sorts of ways and with Joseph it was clearly not an overnight transformation but a much more gradual process. At this point he is doing a good deed, committing the body of Jesus for a dignified burial after a grossly undignified death. His request of Pilate was a perfectly reasonable one to which no one could possibly object, even Jesus' detractors.

The Jews buried their dead straight away, unlike we in the modern West. The Romans often left bodies on their crosses until they decayed, although they would take them down if requested by relatives or friends. For the Jews, on the other hand, dead bodies were ceremonially unclean. The bodies of condemned criminals had to be removed from their place of execution by nightfall (Deut. 21:22–23). This was even more urgent when the next day, as was the case here, was the Sabbath. These bodies would be buried without honour in an open field. Their tombs could not be used again.[1] So in asking Pilate for Jesus' body, Joseph was giving it special honour. He was stating in practice that Jesus was not a criminal and therefore the procedure that had condemned him was unlawful. Jesus, in his estimation, was a righteous man. Moreover, Joseph was prepared to forgo using his tomb for the purpose for which he had bought it, so as to give pride of place to Jesus. In essence, he was denying himself, taking up his cross, and following Jesus. His actions here, at this moment, indicate he had accepted Jesus' terms of discipleship (Matt. 10:32–39; 16:24).

2. The security of Jesus' burial (59–61)

Note the care with which Matthew describes the preparation of the body. He is concerned to demonstrate that Jesus was accorded full burial honours and that the body was so encased in burial clothes and the tomb secured that there was not the slightest danger that anyone could contest the fact that not only had Jesus died but he had also been placed beyond controversy in a secured tomb.

The clean linen shroud in which Joseph wrapped the body was wrapped round and round the corpse. Together with the spices that the Jews used on the shroud it would form a casing as strong as cement. As for the tomb, it had been cut out of the rock. This was the normal place for a body to be laid. Inside there would be recesses in which individual corpses could be placed. Then Joseph rolled *a great stone to the entrance of the tomb*. Such was its size and weight that it was a major task to move it (Mark 16:2–4). Entrances to tombs were usually blocked in this way.[2]

Not only was the tomb secured but Matthew lists witnesses (61); *Joseph* himself – a reliable and respected man – *Mary Magdalene and the other Mary*. The women had watched Jesus die, now witnessed his burial and were the first to hear of his resurrection. Matthew wants his readers to know that there was no mistake about the place or time of the burial. There were the sufficient witnesses required by the Jewish law.

[1] R. T. France, *The Gospel According to Matthew: An Introduction and Commentary*, TNTC (Leicester: IVP, 1985), p. 403; David Hill, *The Gospel of Matthew* (London: Marshall, Morgan & Scott, 1972), p. 357; Donald A. Hagner, *Matthew 14–28*, WBC 33B (Dallas: Word Books, 1995), p. 858; Craig S. Keener, *A Commentary on the Gospel of Matthew* (Grand Rapids: Eerdmans, 1999), pp. 691–694; John Nolland, *The Gospel of Matthew: A Commentary on the Greek Text*, NIGTC (Grand Rapids: Eerdmans, 2005), pp. 1229–1231.

[2] France, *Matthew*, p. 403; W. D. Davies and D. C. Allison, *A Critical and Exegetical Commentary on the Gospel According to Saint Matthew: Volume III* (Edinburgh: T&T Clark, 1997), pp. 651–652; Hagner, *Matthew 14–28*, pp. 858–859; Nolland, *Matthew*, pp. 1231–1233.

In all this, where were the disciples, the eleven whom Jesus had chosen? Nowhere to be seen! Everything was too much for them. They proved unreliable and fickle; it would take a supernatural effusion of the Holy Spirit to put this right. At root, however, it was necessary that they should fail like that. Jesus had to suffer alone, to die alone, to be buried in obscurity. There could be no inkling of any other person sharing in these events, for this was the work of the Son of God and only he could put right the consequences of human sin.

> There was no other good enough
> To pay the price of sin;
> He only could unlock the gate
> Of heaven and let us in.[3]

3. Further precautions (62–66)

As if the record of the burial were not proof positive of the finality of the cross and its aftermath, a further line of security is introduced. The Jewish leaders, naturally enough given their commitments, want to ensure that there is no possibility of the theft of the body by disciples who might then take up Jesus' comments on his resurrection and so proclaim publicly that he was alive. They were concerned with what might happen to the people as a result. They had heard Jesus foretell that he would rise from the dead on the third day. They didn't believe it but they were fearful of pre-emptive action by the disciples. The last fraud would be the claim that he had risen and this would, in their eyes, be worse than his first claim to be the Messiah. They were anxious to have the tomb sealed completely. By now Pilate, having yielded to mob rule in order to forestall an uprising that would seal his own fate in the eyes of the Imperial authorities, has no energy left – or need – to obstruct their wishes.

So the Jewish establishment adds its own precautions. First, it seals the rock. Next, it utilizes the guard of Roman soldiers provided by Pilate on their request. These soldiers would guard the grave for their lives, for the penalty for dereliction of duty in such cases was often death.[4] No-one could have removed the body from the cross without Roman authority, since the soldiers were keeping guard there (27:54). This guard is continued at the graveside, throughout the Sabbath, so as to prevent any possibility of Jesus' followers

---

[3] 'There is a green hill far away', Cecil Frances Alexander (1818–95).
[4] France, *Matthew*, p. 410; Davies and Allison, *Matthew III*, p. 672; Hagner, *Matthew 14–28*, pp. 863, 876–877; Keener, *Matthew*, pp. 713–714.

claiming that his prophecies had been fulfilled. Matthew wants to refute Jewish criticism and remove every shadow of doubt from the events that were shortly to happen.

We should note that Matthew here records that the Jewish establishment *went and made the tomb secure by sealing the stone and setting a guard.* In doing this, they were exerting their final obstruction to the purposes of God throughout their history and now realized in Jesus. This was a gesture fraught with grim symbolism. Their answer to the grace of God was to kill Jesus and to seal his tomb so that he could never come out and trouble them again. It would be to the nations as a whole that God's covenant blessings would flow (Matt. 28:18–20).

4. The significance of Jesus' burial

The apostle Paul states that among those things 'of first importance' in the gospel is the statement about Christ 'that he was buried'.[5] On the one hand, it trumpeted to all the decisiveness of his death for our sins in accordance with the Scriptures, and was itself the clear proof of it. He died to atone for our sins, and by his burial they are cast into the depths of the sea (Mic. 7:18–19). Jesus' burial also establishes the truth of his resurrection from the dead according to the Scriptures (1 Cor 15:3–8). This burial was final. It was abundantly secure. All possible precautions had been taken to bury the body and to guard it from attackers or thieves.

There are also dramatic parallels between Joseph of Arimathea, here at the end of Matthew's Gospel, and the other Joseph at the start of the book. Both Josephs' actions are pious and godly. In both cases there are no records of anything they said; they are silent witnesses to momentous events. The first Joseph is faced with the problem of the virgin's womb; the last Joseph lays Jesus in a virgin tomb. In both cases Jesus is passive and helpless in terms of his humanity; he is conceived in one instance, buried in another, in neither of these events could he have any input or control. In both cases the Jewish leaders try to use Gentiles to harm Jesus; in both scenes their unbelief is unflinching.

The superlative final double chorus of Johann Sebastian Bach's *St Matthew Passion,*[6] one of the greatest achievements of Western cultural history, ends at Matthew 27:66 with the burial of Jesus.

---

[5] 1 Cor. 15:3–4.
[6] BWV 244.

Wir setzen uns mit Tränen nieder   We sit down in tears
Und rufen dir im Grabe zu: and call to thee in the tomb:
Ruhe sanfte, sanfte ruh!   Rest softly, softly rest!
Ruht, ihr ausgesognen Glieder!   Rest, ye exhausted limbs,
Ruhet sanfte, ruhet wohl.   Rest softly, rest well.
Euer Grab und Leichenstein   Your grave and tombstone
Soll dem ängstlichen Gewissen   shall for the unquiet conscience
Ein bequemes Ruhekissen   be a comfortable pillow
Und der Seelen Ruhstatt sein,   and the soul's resting place.
Höchst vergnügt   In utmost bliss
Schlummern da die Augen ein.   the eyes slumber there.
Wir setzen uns . . .   We sit down . . .

Here in these staggeringly portentous events the nations are in a ferment.

> The kings of the earth set themselves,
>   and the rulers take counsel together,
>   against the LORD and against his Anointed, saying,
> 'Let us burst their bonds apart
>   and take away their cords from us.'[7]

All seems lost. All is sorrow and tears. We sit ourselves down in tears and call towards the tomb. Meanwhile 'he who sits in the heavens laughs; the Lord holds them in derision'.[8]

[7] Ps. 2:1–2.
[8] Ps. 2:4.

Part Four
Christ risen

Matthew 28:1–15
18. The empty tomb

There is no description of the resurrection in the NT.[1] No one was present to see Jesus emerge from the grave clothes, to observe the angels remove the stone, to witness his departure from the tomb. All we see are the results: the empty sepulchre, the appearances to the disciples. Should this surprise us? Not if we consider all the mighty works of God. Was anyone present at creation to record exactly what happened? Can anyone explain the feeding of the five thousand? Was the process of the creative miracles seen and chronicled? How about the virginal conception, which in the Gospels is so closely related to the resurrection as a sign of the supreme and direct action of God?[2] No, in all such events, the production of which is the result of an immediate operation of the mighty power of God, the physics, the immediate procedure, the exact observance of what happened, is kept from us. We see the obvious and self-attesting result, like a crater after a bomb explosion – but we never see the bomb explode.

The emphasis of the accounts of the empty tomb is not on factual proof for the unbelieving world. Instead, the focus is on the impact on Jesus' bewildered followers and the restoration of broken relationships with him. Imagine their grief at Jesus' death and burial. All their hopes seemed to be dashed. For some, like Peter, there was the added shame that when the going had got tough they had buckled under the strain and had abandoned him to his fate. Personal failure was added to overwhelming sorrow. This was the situation of the disciples on those few days in Jerusalem. No wonder their accounts convey bewilderment and disorientation. As France comments, 'A

---

[1] R. T. France, *The Gospel According to Matthew: An Introduction and Commentary*, TNTC (Leicester: IVP, 1985), p. 405.
[2] Thomas F. Torrance, *Incarnation: The Person and Life of Christ* (Milton Keynes: Paternoster, 2008), pp. 96–97.

lack of precise agreement in independent accounts of such a bewildering series of events is hardly surprising.'[3] We could add that this is of the very nature of independent eyewitness reports. Each observer recalls his or her personal perspective[4] and in this case the event was of such cosmic significance that, by definition, it evaded simple explanation.

1. The women at the tomb (1–8)

a. The visitors to the tomb (1)

Visitation of the newly buried was standard practice in first-century Israel. It was the burial custom of the Jews, much like today a funeral is followed by a meal.[5] On the other hand, it may be that they went there simply to continue their vigil that had been interrupted by the Sabbath.[6] The striking point here is that the people involved in the tomb visitation and all that followed are women. Women were normally debarred from giving witness in the Jewish courts of the day.[7] Yet here, as with the shepherds at the birth of Jesus, those ostracized from the legal establishment are the ones God chose to be his witnesses. Again, as at the burial, it is *Mary Magdalene and the other Mary* (the mother of James) who are the ones who take the trouble to act, although Mark adds Salome to the list and Luke refers to Joanna (Mark 16:1; Luke 24:10).

The visit took place *after the Sabbath, towards dawn*. This is a rare use of the word and indicates Matthew's concern to relate all that occurs to the law. Clearly, the women refrained from visiting the tomb during the Sabbath but took the earliest opportunity they could to go through with their duty. However, Matthew's interest is not so much in their reasons for the visit but on what happens when they get there.

---

[3] France, *Matthew*, p. 405.

[4] I recall, having been at the Oval for the first day of the fifth test between England and Australia in 1972, travelling in by train for the second day on 11 August and reading two apparently conflicting reports of the first day's play by highly regarded observers. E. W. Swanton, in *The Daily Telegraph*, reported that 'Edrich batted with all his old customary assurance', while John Woodcock in *The Times* wrote 'Edrich was troubled by Lillee's pace'.

[5] W. D. Davies and D. C. Allison, *A Critical and Exegetical Commentary on the Gospel According to Saint Matthew: Volume III* (Edinburgh: T&T Clark, 1997), p. 664; Craig S. Keener, *A Commentary on the Gospel of Matthew* (Grand Rapids: Eerdmans, 1999), p. 700.

[6] Donald A. Hagner, *Matthew 14–28*, WBC 33B (Dallas: Word Books, 1995), pp. 868–869.

[7] France, *Matthew*, p. 406; Davies, *Matthew, III*, p. 662; Keener, *Matthew*, p. 698.

b. The dramatic intervention (2)

It might seem that when the women arrived at the grave, there was *a great earthquake* as there had been immediately on Jesus' death. However, the logic of Matthew's account requires the earthquake to have preceded their arrival. Either way, we see again the connection between the redemption brought by Jesus and the created order, between salvation and creation. The events surrounding his death, burial and resurrection have an impact on the entire universe. The OT had looked for an earthquake in the last days and here it is (Zech. 14:4–5). This quake happened in conjunction with the descent from heaven of *an angel of the Lord*. Earth and heaven were linked. Mark describes the angel as 'a young man'.[8] Angels often took human form and spoke in human language for the benefit of the people to whom they appeared.[9] In this case it was to calm the women and keep them from panicking, to explain what had happened and to instruct them as to what to do. On arriving at the tomb, the angel had *rolled back the stone and sat on it* (2). This was the scene that greeted the women on their arrival. It was entirely for their benefit that the angel had done this. There was no need for him to roll away the stone or to sit on it. It was not as if he was needed for Jesus to emerge; later the risen Christ would pass through locked doors and ascend into heaven in his risen humanity. Paul would attribute these events to the action of the Trinity – the Father raised Christ from the dead by the Holy Spirit (Rom. 8:10–11). An angel was not needed. No, it was the women who needed the angel's help.[10]

c. The angel's appearance (3–4)

The sight of the angel overwhelmed the Roman soldiers. The picture reminds us of the transfiguration of Jesus (Matt. 17:1–8)[11] and echoes the appearance of the angels in Daniel (Dan. 10:6–9). The angel is more than a messenger here. This is close to a theophany (an appearance of God in human form), although that is not required by the text. However, the results are similar. He strikes terror into the guard. In a supreme irony, the soldiers guarding Jesus' tomb *trembled and became like dead men*, whereas the dead

---

[8] Mark 16:5.

[9] Cf. Gen. 19:1–29; Dan. 9:20–23; 10:4–21; Matt. 1:20–21; Luke 1:11–20; 26–38.

[10] France, *Matthew*, pp. 406–407; Leon Morris, *The Gospel According to Matthew* (Grand Rapids: Eerdmans, 1992), p. 735.

[11] John Nolland, *The Gospel of Matthew: A Commentary on the Greek Text*, NIGTC (Grand Rapids: Eerdmans, 2005), p. 1247.

man they were guarding is now alive! Fear petrified *them*; the women are told *do not be afraid* (5). The pagan world must fear and become like the dead; Jesus' followers, in the midst of grief and bewilderment, need not fear at all for death has been swallowed up by life!

d. The angel's words (5–7)

The angel reassures and calms the women in the face of this intrusion from the spiritual realm. If Mary had been so frightened when Gabriel appeared with such staggeringly good news, what must have gone through the women's minds when at first they saw the angel in dazzling white, like lightning? The angel says five things to encourage them and then gives instructions as to how they are to proceed from there.

First, *they are not to be afraid*, unlike the quivering and catatonic imperial forces guarding the grave. The angel is fully aware of their intentions in coming to the tomb: *I know that you seek Jesus, who was crucified* (5). Their seeking of Jesus is to be without fear. There is something of comfort and encouragement the angel is going to say to them about the Jesus who they are seeking and whose tomb they have come to visit.

Second, Jesus *is not here* (6a). This was unusual. This was the place where they had seen him laid by Joseph only a couple of days before. Moreover, the tomb was protected by a contingent of soldiers. No-one could possibly have come to remove the body elsewhere unless it was at the behest of the Roman governor and undertaken by the army, and that was simply not possible or credible as the soldiers were still there. Evidently the angel was saying that the tomb was empty. Jesus' body had been removed.

Third, the angel goes on to explain what had happened, to solve the mystery of the absence of Jesus' body from the tomb. *He has risen* (6b). His body was not there. It had not been exhumed and stolen. He was alive, he had risen from the dead, he had gone elsewhere, but exactly where the angel did not disclose. However, that was a comparatively trivial matter beside the main assertion. This claim was unimaginably great. Yet the angel had supporting evidence for it, if any of the women were inclined to be sceptical. After all, *he is not here*; he has gone elsewhere. A lifeless corpse cannot do that. Moreover, there was the evidence of the semi-comatose soldiers, the great earthquake, the stone unsealed and rolled away, the angel whose appearance was like lightning, and his words of encouragement.

Fourth, the angel adds that this was *as he said* (6c). Jesus had foretold that he would rise from the dead on many occasions but the disciples had been obtuse and his comments had not properly registered with them (Matt. 16:21–23; 17:22–23; 20:17–19 and parallels). When the time came for him to face the cross they were so overcome by fear and sorrow that they had forgotten or re-evaluated what he had said. But Jesus' words stood over those of the rabbis in authority. He had proclaimed that he was the authoritative teacher of the Law. His words were those of the Father. He had taught that he would conquer death and now he had done so.

Fifth, the angel invites them to *come, see the place where he lay* (6d). This is an invitation to see that the old epoch is behind them, that just as his body is no longer to be sought in the tomb and that Jesus' life in lowliness as the suffering Servant is now completely fulfilled and terminated, so now he has entered into a new phase of human existence beyond the reach of the grave. They can see for themselves that this is so.

Then come the words of instruction: *Go quickly, and tell his disciples that he is risen from the dead* (7). The women are to be the first heralds of the risen Christ, the announcers of the arrival of the age to come, the last days, the new heavens and the new earth. This was urgent: *go quickly.*

Now there is a definite indication of where Jesus is or to where he is heading: *he is going before you to Galilee.* He is in a definite place and time. And the disciples are to go there and meet him, away in the far north, from where most had come, and away from the corruption in Jerusalem.

e. The women's reaction (8)

We can only conjecture at the depth of the women's emotions at this point. However, we are told two things, first about what they did and then about their state of mind. They were filled with conflicting feelings. They were still fearful. An encounter with an angel is usually a fearful thing. Where we read of it in Scripture it is often accompanied by terror or confusion. It is to come face to face with a being immensely more powerful than we. Part of the fear may have been generated by the fact that they were still trying to piece together in their minds what all this meant. On the other hand, they were also filled *with great joy* at the message they had received and the almost unimaginable news that Jesus had risen from the dead. As for what they did, *they departed quickly from the tomb . . . and ran to tell [Jesus'] disciples.* They followed through on the angel's instructions right away, without delay.

There was no need to remain at the tomb and fulfil Jewish burial customs!

2. Jesus' first resurrection appearance (9–10)

a. Matthew and John

There appears to be a conflict between Matthew's account and that of John. In John, Jesus appears first to Mary Magdalene in the garden after she had informed Peter and John that the body had been removed from the tomb. Additionally, there is no reference to her having seen an angel on her arrival at the tomb. Here, Matthew records the women, of which Mary Magdalene was one, meeting Jesus. However, John has Magdalene using the plural in her report to Peter about the empty tomb: 'we do not know where they have laid him.'[12] His omission of the incident with the angel may be because it was not relevant to his purpose, rather than due to ignorance of its happening. His intent is evidently to focus on Mary Magdalene and does not require that her encounter with Jesus in the garden was as a lone figure without others present. There is every reason to suppose that the passage here in Matthew is a shortened and edited version of the event described in detail but in greater focus in John 20.

b. The meeting

The striking thing about Jesus' appearance to the women in Matthew is that there is no confusion in their minds about his identity. Mary Magdalene, in John 20:14–16, mistakes him for the gardener, while the two disciples travelling to Emmaus, as recounted by Luke, converse with him for a lengthy period, invite him into their house and start a meal with him, supposing him to be a fellow traveller (Luke 24:13–31). A group of seven disciples fishing in the lake only identify him after a conspicuous miracle (John 21:1–7). Yet here the group of women – and if what we suggested above is valid it is the group as a whole to which Matthew draws attention – seem to have no problem in knowing who he is.[13] Jesus simply meets them as they are going on their way. This may be after they had informed Peter and John, according to John's chronology. Jesus approaches them and says *Greetings!*, the equivalent of 'Hello!'[14]

---

[12] John 20:2.
[13] Davies and Allison, *Matthew III*, p. 669.
[14] France, *Matthew*, p. 409; Hagner, *Matthew 14–28*, p. 874.

Their response is worship. They fall at his feet and worship.[15] This is what Mary Magdalene did in John's version of events.[16]

Note here the contrast between the women's encounter with the angel and their meeting with Jesus. The appearance of the angel engendered terror. With Jesus they approach him. They take hold of his feet. With Jesus they instantly recognize that there is fellowship, communion. He is not an angel, he is human like they are. This was a man of flesh and blood. John will stress that in no uncertain terms against those who suppose that Jesus is less than fully human: 'that which we have seen with our eyes, which we looked upon and have touched with our hands, concerning the word of life.'[17] Luke records how Jesus made a point of this in one of his resurrection appearances, inviting his disciples to touch him and see, since a spirit does not have flesh and blood. As if to underline this, he took and ate a piece of broiled fish (Luke 24:36–43). This is a physical resurrection. It is not a metamorphosis. He has risen bodily from the tomb. Yet in terms of his personal identity he is God, he is the object of worship. Angels, when faced with the worship of humans, refuse it (Rev. 19:9–10; 22:8–9).

Jesus repeats the instructions of the angel. He is going to Galilee and it is there that they must go so as to meet him. This would preclude neither his appearing later that day in Jerusalem, nor the following week in the same place or on the road to Emmaus (John 20:19–29; Luke 24:13–32). He would depart at his ascension outside Jerusalem at the Mount of Olives (Luke 24:50–53; Acts 1:6–11). But it was in Galilee that he would appear to the seven by the lakeside (John 21:1–23) and it was to be in Galilee that he would instruct them about the kingdom of God and the task of the church for the rest of the age (Matt. 28:16–20). Most strikingly, on this occasion in asking the women to inform the disciples of this he calls them his *brothers* – go and tell **my brothers** to go to Galilee, and there they will see me. These monumental events had so changed the relationship between God and man that his disciples were now brothers to the Son of Man, the one who was co-ordinate in knowledge and sovereignty with the Father (Matt. 11:25–27). Already, they were adopted as sons who could call God 'our Father, who is in heaven'.[18] So also are all who are united to him by faith.

---

[15] Nolland, *Matthew*, p. 1252; Morris, *Matthew*, p. 739.

[16] John 20:16–17. Davies and Allison draw attention to the fact that 'throughout world-wide folklore ghosts often have no feet ... then, the grasping of the feet indicates that Jesus is not a spirit – precisely the same thought found in Lk. 24.37-43' (*Matthew III*, p. 669).

[17] 1 John 1:1.

[18] Matt. 6:9.

Luke 24:13–49
19. The resurrection appearances

1. Conversation (13–24)

Luke describes how two disciples were walking the seven-mile journey to Emmaus, having left Jerusalem.[1] Discussing the recent events, they were dejected (17). They had heard the report of the women (22–23) and the others who went to the tomb (24) but this had left them bewildered. They had hoped Jesus was the one who was *to redeem Israel* but apparently their expectations had been dashed (21). At some point on the journey they were joined by Jesus but they did not recognize him. He appeared to be just like any other person, so much so that he was assumed to be simply another traveller (15–18). They were drawn into protracted discussion with him and invited him into their house for a meal without recognizing who he was.

2. Explanation (25–27)

a. Jesus explains the OT Scriptures

Jesus chides the disciples for their slowness to understand the Scriptures. This failure is due to their slowness of heart. He explains that the whole of the Scriptures, from the prophets (25, 27) and from Moses (27) spoke of the Christ and his sufferings as the prelude to the glory that was to follow. He explains that the purpose, the scope, of Scripture concerned the Christ, the anointed one. The focus of its teaching was that *[he] should suffer these things and enter into his glory* (26). It was necessary that the Christ should suffer before

---

[1] Cf. John Nolland, *Luke 18:35–24:53*, WBC 35C (Dallas: Word Books, 1993), pp. 1200–1201.

entering glory. This was something the Jews had not grasped. These two disciples as part of the nation shared in this failure of comprehension. They expected that the Christ was to bring immediate deliverance. Suffering and death – let alone death by crucifixion – was not part of the plan, so it seemed. Its intrusion undermined the whole promised salvation as they understood it. It scuppered their hopes that Jesus was the Christ. This was to pose a problem in later decades. Paul had to correct a similar misunderstanding in the church at Philippi.[2] There were those who thought that it was unworthy of an apostle to suffer, that the Christian life was one of unalloyed triumph, that glory bypassed the cross.

Jesus' comments shed light on how we should interpret the OT. Its focus is on Jesus Christ, whether directly or more obliquely. This applies to particular places but it also relates to the OT as a whole. The OT in general looks forward to the day when the Christ will come to bring deliverance. Moreover, it is to his death and resurrection that this prospective anticipation refers. Throughout, there are repetitive patterns of death, followed by resuscitation.[3] As Augustine put it, 'grace, concealed in the OT, is revealed in the New'.[4]

b. Jesus corrects their misunderstandings

As we remarked, the expectations of the two, shared with the bulk of Israel, were that the Christ would be a glorious leader who would restore the fortunes of the nation. In this he would liberate it from Gentile rule, and purify it from the corrupt practices that had become pervasive. In this conversation Jesus explained that Yahweh's purposes for his people were different. The identity of the Messiah was not what Jewish expectations held him to be. His task was to be correspondingly different. It would take forty days' instruction for the apostles to have their thinking and attitudes straightened out; it was too much to ask that these two unidentified disciples, presumably husband and wife, could be corrected in an hour or two. Misconceptions take a long time to eradicate. Consistent teaching on the nature of the kingdom of God was required (Acts 1:3). Clear new thinking on the necessity of sufferings was needed. The

---

[2] See ch. 14.

[3] Abraham passes through the promised land but has to spend time in Egypt due to a famine before he could return. Joseph is sold into slavery in Egypt but rises to rule. His family join him there due to famine, away from the land, but eventually are brought back. Judah goes into exile in Babylon but a remnant returns. Jonah is swallowed by a fish but then vomited up onto dry land. These are but a few – and the most prominent – of a range of similar patterns seen throughout the OT.

[4] Augustine, *De Spiritu et Littera*, 27 (*NPNF*[1], vol. 5).

prophecies of Isaiah had to be seen in the light of the promised seed of Abraham and David.

3. Revelation (28–35)

a. An ordinary meal transformed (28–30)

The disciples asked Jesus, still not recognized, to stay with them, have a meal and spend the night, in keeping with regular practices of hospitality. This was nothing out of the ordinary; it was the custom. And so a dinner was prepared and they all sit down to eat. However, this is a meal with a difference. Luke describes it in similar terms he has used for the Last Supper: 'And he took bread, and when he had given thanks, he broke it and gave it to them.'[5] Here the identical pattern is present: . . . *he took the bread and blessed and broke it and gave it to them* (30).

Luke follows the same sequence in his description of Jesus distributing the bread in the feeding of the five thousand, a creative miracle, took – blessed – broke – gave: 'And taking the five loaves and the two fish, he looked up to heaven and said a blessing over them. Then he broke the loaves and gave them to the disciples to set before the crowd.'[6] Luke wants us to see the connection between these events. The terminology he uses is sacramental.[7] Paul uses the same language in his description of the supper in 1 Corinthians 11:23–26, describing it as what had been handed down to him by the Lord and what he was now passing down to the church as a sacred tradition. Here at Emmaus Luke sees this ordinary meal as transformed and raised to the status of a sacrament by the risen Christ's actions. The Lord presides, the Lord takes charge. It is a supper but it is the Lord's Supper since the Lord himself is present, blessing and distributing the bread. Moreover, in connecting it with the feeding miracle, Luke sees this meal as a creative miracle, revelatory of the new creation, the kingdom of God about which the disciples needed instruction and which would serve to reorient their thoughts and living from this time on.

[5] Luke 22:19.
[6] Luke 9:16.
[7] Contrary to Alfred Plummer, *A Critical and Exegetical Commentary on the Gospel According to S. Luke*, ICC (Edinburgh: T&T Clark, 1896), pp. 556–557. Nolland sees a parallel here (*Luke 18:35–24:53*, p. 1206). We note that there is no evidence that the two disciples ate the bread, neither is there wine mentioned, so it would be going beyond the text to affirm that this was an actual Eucharist. However, the correspondences between this possibly aborted meal and the actions at the Supper are more than coincidental.

b. Recognition dawns (31)

As Jesus broke the bread, the disciples' eyes *were opened*. Before this their eyes were closed, their hearts slow to understand, and so they were completely unaware of who the stranger was. But now they know! In this both were passive (*diēnoichthēsan*). Their eyes were opened from an outside source. The action of the Holy Spirit, in conjunction with the manifestation of Christ enables them to perceive the stranger for who he is, the risen Christ, the Lord of all.

Ludwig Wittgenstein pointed to the fact that people can see the same arrangement of shapes and lines differently, depending on the frame of reference with which they view them. In particular he referred to a drawing of the face of a rabbit which could instead be seen as a duck, the rabbit ears perceived instead as the duck's bill.[8] In Luke's account, the Spirit gave the disciples the capacity to see Jesus for who he is.

And he vanished from their sight (31). That this was to be no return to the previous arrangements that obtained before the crucifixion is clear from Jesus' immediate disappearance. He had risen from the dead; that was clear from the conversation, his exposition of Scripture, his sitting down with them for a meal. But this was something different. It was equally clear that he was no longer living in the same realm as before. People don't vanish from sight like that.

c. The supper and the word, Christ and the Spirit

Luke means us to consider that the risen Christ is made known to us *in the breaking of the bread* (35), in the Lord's Supper. In the breaking and distribution of the bread and wine Christ is seen by the illumination of the Holy Spirit. It is his supper, his table. It is a thanksgiving (*eucharistia*), for he was crucified to atone for our sins but is now alive from the dead and present with us by the Holy Spirit.

There is also a connection with the declaration of the word of God. Immediately, the two disciples reflect on the conversation on the road from Jerusalem. There the risen Christ had expounded the various sections of Scripture, the OT. He had *opened to us the Scriptures* (32); explaining what had been in comparison a closed book, interpreting to them the things relating to himself throughout its pages. The Scriptures had been opened by Christ; their hearts burned – or glowed[9] – within them; their eyes were opened by the Holy Spirit. These were sovereign actions of the Trinity.

[8] Ludwig Wittgenstein, *Philosophical Investigations*, trans. G. E. M. Anscombe (Oxford: Basil Blackwell, 1989), p. 194.

[9] Plummer, *Luke*, p. 558.

No wonder the two of them hurried back to Jerusalem as fast as they could! They were bursting to let the rest of the disciples know the great things that had happened. It was getting late – but they could not delay. One imagines they covered those seven miles much faster than on the way out! On their arrival, they told the apostles and the others about what had happened to them, no doubt in breathless excitement. The eleven and the cohort of followers had their own news: *The Lord has risen indeed, and has appeared to Simon!* (34). Simon had denied being Jesus' disciple three times; now he was one of the first to see him resurrected.

4. Confirmation (36–49)

a. Peace proclaimed (36)

While the two groups were excitedly comparing notes, Jesus suddenly appeared, passing through locked doors. He pronounced *peace be to you* (36); peace with God based upon his death, peace among themselves as a result. Was this part of what he taught the apostles during the forty days (Acts 1:3)? It was expounded at length later by Paul (Rom. 3 – 5; Eph. 2:11–21). On the other hand, it was a standard Jewish greeting, equivalent to 'Hello'. Yet in the context of these momentous happenings, and the density of Luke's language, it seems to me to go beyond the banal and points to the wider and far-reaching relationship the disciples sustain to Jesus himself.

b. Bodily resurrection established (37–43)

At first the disciples were all terrified. They thought they had seen *a spirit* (37). Jesus' sudden disappearance earlier may well have reinforced this supposition. However, Jesus points out that there is no need to be terrified; it reminds us of what he had said to the women at the tomb. To support this he shows them *his hands and his feet*. Singling out the hands and feet was significant since they would have the marks of the nails from the crucifixion. As Jesus says, *see my hands and my feet, that it is I myself. Touch me and see, for a spirit does not have flesh and bones* (39). They could see that Jesus had flesh and bones and so was not a spirit and that it was not in some non-material form that he was present among them. He could be touched. The women had known that. John was to emphasize it later (1 John 1:1–3). Their reaction was joy and astonishment mingled with incredulity (41a).

At this point, as if to make sure that his followers knew clearly that he was alive from the dead, and that this entailed physicality,

Jesus asked for something to eat. *They gave him a piece of broiled fish, and he took it and ate it in front of them* (42–43). A spirit does not eat fish. Here is a man that had died the most cruel death imaginable, now restored to life, who can pass through locked doors, and who can disappear suddenly from sight. A transformation has occurred. Yet at the same time it is evidently the same Jesus. Moreover, he has flesh and bones, real hands and feet – the same hands and feet that had been pierced – and can join the others in a meal. There is no need for us to assume that the resurrection body of Jesus is in the same need of food as we are; the purpose of the eating is to assure the disciples of the reality and physicality of his resurrection.[10]

c. The OT Scriptures interpreted again (44–49)

Jesus reminds the disciples that he had foretold all this during his ministry. *Moses* (the law, the Pentateuch*), and the Prophets and the Psalms* (all three sections of the OT) spoke of him and had to be *fulfilled*. The OT focus is on the death and resurrection of Christ. That meant that it referred throughout to him.

This has enormous implications for biblical exegesis and for preaching. Just as we cannot understand the NT aright apart from the OT, neither can we grasp the proper meaning and orientation of the OT apart from its fulfilment in Jesus Christ. It follows that our preaching from the OT is incomplete unless it opens out to embrace the saving purpose of God that has come to fruition in his Son. How many OT sermons could equally well be preached in a synagogue? One thing that has pained me while preparing this book is the captivity of many biblical scholars to a model of academic study that precludes a Christocentric view of Scripture. While the Bible is capable of being studied academically, it has been given by God to the church not to the university. To approach the Scriptures – and particularly the OT – without reference to Christ is to misunderstand them and ultimately to abuse them. It is a blind alley that leads nowhere and the result is the blind – be they ever so clever and learned – leading the blind. In this, some of the church fathers (Athanasius, Chrysostom, Cyril and Augustine to name a few) can help us, for they understood the Bible to be a unity that is fulfilled in Christ, drawing their preaching and teaching from the whole of Scripture.

Here is the solution to this horrible situation (for it is horrible when the word of God in all its glorious scope is obscured) in the words that follow. *He opened their mind* (*ton noun*) *to understand*

---

[10] Plummer, *Luke*, p. 560.

the Scriptures (45). A twofold opening is needed to grasp what Scripture – in this case, the OT – says and means. The Scriptures themselves must be opened (27, 32), so that their manifestation of Christ can be made clear. Then, secondly, the minds of its readers and hearers need to be opened. Naturally, these minds are closed. Sin blinds us, enabling us to shut out the truth. We need to be given sight to see the riches that are there that unfold the glories of the Saviour. We desperately need our minds to be opened to receive that truth, to be capacitated to understand, believe and obey. Both the text and the interpreter need the illumination of the Holy Spirit. Moreover, the eyes of the two at Emmaus were opened so as to recognize the risen Jesus (32). In dealing with Christ, and his word, supernatural and divine action is needed to enable us to understand and recognize.

In detail, the OT spoke of the sufferings and death of Christ, his resurrection on the third day, the gospel of repentance and the forgiveness of sins and its spread to all nations, starting from Jerusalem. The apostles are the witnesses. The apostolic testimony was to become part of the gospel (Acts 2:32; 3:15; 5:32; 10:39–41; 13:30–31; cf. 1 Cor. 15:1–9). For our part, we pray that the Lord will open our hearts to receive his word, to recognize him in the sacraments, and to follow in the joyous announcement of his risen power.

1 Corinthians 15
20. Paul on Christ's resurrection

1. The heart of the gospel (1–11)

a. First things (1–4)

Paul urges the Corinthians to return to the things of first importance. They were in danger of moving from this base as a result of the sectarian divisions that had emerged (1 Cor. 1:10–17) and their doubts over the resurrection (1 Cor. 15:12–19).[1] This is the gospel Paul preached originally when he first visited Corinth. It is the message of salvation, in which all Christians are in the process of being saved. It is never something that they, or anyone else, can leave behind. Whatever else is learned can only be grounded on these matters of first and utmost importance. As every part of the rim of a wheel is connected to the hub by spokes, so all branches of revealed truth are in some way related to the heart of the Christian gospel. We can never outgrow it.

Paul insists that this is not something of his own devising, nor has it been concocted by a group of theologians with too much time on their hands. Instead, he received it and in turn passed it down to the Corinthian church he planted. While there are certain traditions to which the NT is opposed (the tradition of the elders, Matt. 15:1–9; pagan traditions, Col. 2:8), it is unequivocally positive about the Christian tradition. This is the teaching given by Christ to the apostles, who in turn handed it down to the church with express instructions that it be passed on to faithful men who would continue the transmission of the truth to others (2 Tim. 1:12, 14; 2:2).

---

[1] On the latter see the extensive discussion of the history of interpretation on the Corinthians' problems with the resurrection in Anthony C. Thiselton, *The First Epistle to the Corinthians: A Commentary on the Greek Text*, NIGTC (Grand Rapids: Eerdmans, 2000), pp. 1172–1178.

Paul refers to the details of the Lord's Supper in similar light, as something he received from the Lord and passed on to the church (1 Cor. 11:23–26). There is a necessary continuity, a handing over and receiving from one generation to the next (Deut. 6:4–9; Ps. 145:4–12).

Paul may be citing an early creed or summary of the gospel.[2] The statement in verses 3–4 has a certain liturgical feel to it. Paul acknowledges that this is the heart of the gospel that he received himself and passed on to the Corinthians (3).[3] Whatever its origin – and it may well have been used for catechetical purposes – it grounds Christian belief in clear-cut historical events and provides equally clear theological explanations for them.

The heart of the gospel is that *Christ died for our sins in accordance with the Scriptures, that he was buried, that he was raised on the third day, in accordance with the Scriptures.* Paul considers the death of Christ to be an atoning sacrifice for sin. Moreover, he sees it in substitutionary terms. This, he states, was both foretold and required by the OT. It was an integral, central, utterly crucial and necessary part of God's covenantal plan for the redemption of the world as he planned and revealed it ever since the fall of man in Genesis. All the Scriptures point to Christ, and they do so in connection with his death. This is also a stupendous mystery, for it was Christ – the anointed one, the Son of the Father – who submitted to human death. God's eternal plan took a form the reverse of all human expectations!

Also in the bulls-eye of the gospel darts board is Christ's burial. We saw how this neglected part of his work is so important. Paul declares it to be indispensable for a proper understanding of the central message of the Christian faith. It signalled the reality of his death for our sins, and is the absolutely necessary prelude to the resurrection, for it establishes that he was really and truly dead, that his sufferings and death were actual. It parades the fact that the sins of Christ's people have been buried in the depths of the sea (Mic. 7:18–19).

The resurrection posed a problem for many at Corinth. For Greeks in general, the body was somehow of lesser importance than

[2] Thiselton, *First Corinthians*, pp. 1186–1187; Gordon D. Fee, *The First Epistle to the Corinthians*, NICNT (Grand Rapids: Eerdmans, 1987), pp. 718–719.

[3] In Gal. 1:11–12 Paul states that he did not receive the gospel from the apostles or other human sources but by direct revelation from Jesus Christ. Fitzmyer argues cogently that Paul is not contradicting himself here in 1 Corinthians, since in Galatians he refers to the content of the gospel as a whole, whereas here he insists on the precise formulation that has been passed down (Joseph A. Fitzmyer, SJ, *First Corinthians: A New Translation with Introduction and Commentary*, AB [New Haven: Yale University Press, 2008], pp. 545–546).

the soul or spirit. It was hard for them to conceive of resurrection. If a large group of Jewish thought – represented by the Sadducees – could not accept the possibility of the resurrection of the body, we must reasonably suppose other nations had a similar difficulty. Especially would this apply to Greeks. Therefore Paul stresses the reality of the bodily resurrection of Christ and insists that it is not of peripheral interest but right at the heart of the Christian faith.

First, Paul makes clear that the resurrection was an historical event. It happened *on the third day*. Scholars have disputed the exact year of Jesus' death but Paul was living much closer to the event than we. As he makes clear, it was well within the lifetime of most of those alive at the time he wrote. Following this, it was an event in which Jesus himself was passive. He *was raised* (*egēgertai*). The active agent was the Trinity. In Romans, Paul attributes the resurrection to the Father, who brought it about by the Holy Spirit (Rom. 8:10–11). We know that in all the works of God, all three persons are inseparably involved, although each work is particularly attributable to one of the persons. So the Son was also at work, but according to the flesh, in terms of his incarnate state, he was the one to whom the action was applied. Paul also underlines that this great climactic event was also *in accordance with the Scriptures* of the OT. Foretold in such passages as Psalm 16:8–11, the whole tenor of the OT and the promises of the covenant demanded it. At each stage of covenant history there are a plethora of patterns of death and revival, exile and restoration, that presage Christ's conquest of death. The fact that he, as the creator, is life itself demonstrates that death could have no hold over him.

b. Superabundant witnesses (5–9)

As if the Scriptures themselves were not enough, God had provided a vast overflow of witnesses to this reality. The Law required two or three witnesses to establish any point in a trial (Deut. 17:6; 19:15); in this case there were literally hundreds. First of all, there was *Cephas* (5a). Peter was one of the first to the tomb. Jesus singled him out for special attention in view of his previous lapse and his eventual leadership (Mark 16:7). Paul says that Jesus *appeared*; it was an event in this world, open to public scrutiny. As an appearance it indicated that the time of waiting for Yahweh to deliver his people and to make known his glory had now come to an end.

Second, he appeared *to the twelve* (5b). Since Judas Iscariot had by now committed suicide, this reference to the twelve must include Matthias (Acts 1:21–26), even though his election and ordination did not take place until after the ascension. It is possible that this is not intended as a statistical reference but merely denotes the office of apostle under its hitherto customary designation. If so, the list of witnesses may have been part of the putative catechetical statement which Paul now cites; this would find support in the fact that the witness of the apostles is seen in Acts as part of the gospel events (Acts 2:32; 3:15; 5:32; 10:39–41, 13:30–31). The reference to the twelve may also indicate the continuity of the NT apostles with the tribes of OT Israel. The apostles had been followers of Jesus from the time of his baptism.

Third, Christ appeared to *more than five hundred* on one occasion, of whom the majority were still alive when Paul wrote (6a). The identity of this appearance is not clear and probably is not among those listed in the Gospels. Paul feels under no obligation to identify it and assumes that it will be sufficiently well known to need no explanation, particularly in view of the fact that there were hundreds present who could testify – and surely must have done! – to what happened.

Fourth, Christ appeared *to James* (7a). This is presumably his brother, who later became the presiding elder of the Jerusalem church, the author of the letter of James, and was still alive when Paul wrote. The evidence in the Gospels points to James' scepticism, along with other members of Jesus' family. It may have been that this was the occasion of James' coming to believe in Jesus.

Fifth, Christ appeared *to all the apostles* (7b). Possibly Paul is making a veiled reference to the fact that Thomas was not present on the third day, at the time in Jerusalem when the disciples were gathered together behind locked doors (Luke 24:36–40; John 20:19–29). If so, Thomas – together with James – would stand as a witness who initially was in some sense reluctant to accept the full reality or significance of Jesus' claims, or of the reports of his resurrection. The witnesses were not credulous simpletons – if indeed any of them ever were – but included some who were hard-headed and wanted clear and verifiable evidence.

Finally, Paul lists himself as a witness of Christ's resurrection (8–10). If James and Thomas were somewhat sceptical, Paul was violently hostile. He *persecuted the church of God* and regarded the Christian faith as blasphemous; its assertion of the deity of Christ, its attitude to the temple and the law, each and together was, for him, an assault on the very substance of Yahweh's covenant with his people Israel. So he rounded up church leaders and had them imprisoned and brutalized. He cast his vote in favour of the execution of Stephen.

So he describes himself as *an aborted foetus* or *a prematurely born dead foetus*. His apostleship is an abnormality. He was unworthy of the office and came to it in an exceptional way. Not only was he not one of those who had been a disciple of Jesus since his baptism (Acts 1:21–26) but he had actively opposed the apostles for a number of years. His calling was a gift of God's grace. Yet he was chosen by Christ, who appeared to him on the Damascus road, and so constituted him a witness of his resurrection.

2. Christ's resurrection and ours (12–58)

a. Christ's resurrection and ours are one reality (12–19)

At this point Paul argues that not only is Christ's resurrection central to the entire gospel but our own resurrection at the end of the world is of a piece with his. The two are one reality. The church is united to Christ and so shares in his resurrection, experiencing its own in the future. This is clear by Paul's arguing back and forth from one to the other, so as to establish that they stand together. Deny Christ's resurrection and one has denied the general resurrection of the dead. Deny the latter and one has rendered impossible Christ's resurrection. The two are linked inseparably.

So, if we preach Christ's resurrection, how can we deny *the resurrection of the dead* at the end (12)? Moreover, if there is no general resurrection Christ is not risen (13). Paul repeats this argument in verses 16–17. He concludes that if Christ has not risen *our preaching is in vain* (14), which he repeats and intensifies in verses 17–19, where he concludes that we would be false witnesses to God and supremely deluded. There would be no point in being Christian if Christ had not been raised from the dead; he would have been a mere man who had died.

Dynamically, this connection results from union with Christ. Christ took our humanity into union with himself in the incarnation. In our humanity he lived and died on the cross. In our humanity he rose from the dead. Further to this, Christ's people are united to him by the Holy Spirit through faith, so that Paul can say elsewhere that we died with him and are raised from the dead with him (Rom. 6:1–9). Christ is like a captain of a team; his actions are those of the team. He was raised to life sometime around AD 30; we will be raised in the indefinite future. The resurrection is one reality, behaving identically in both aspects. The rest of the chapter proves that this is the case.

b. Christ's resurrection and the future (20–28)

(i) Christ is the first fruits of the full harvest (20)
The first fruits of the harvest come first in time in relation to the rest of the harvest; the first apples precede the rest. However, the first

fruits – while distinguished from the whole harvest in this way – are identical to the rest of the fruit. The first fruits of the apple harvest are apples! In the OT the first fruits were offered in thanksgiving to Yahweh as a pledge of the remainder of the harvest. So Christ's resurrection as the *firstfruits* has a temporal priority to our resurrection. It also has a representative role, for his resurrection represents the whole. Moreover, it is a promise and pledge of more to come, the guarantee of the full harvest at his return, the earnest of the whole, and is of the same kind as the rest.[4]

(ii) Christ and Adam, death and resurrection (21–22)

The whole human race was in solidarity with Adam and so participated in his sin. He was the captain of the team in which all persons in the human race are members. When he sinned, all sinned. The penalty of death which Adam received fell upon the whole race in union with him. As a result the world came under the curse of the Adamic covenant. On the other hand, Christ as the second or last Adam, as captain of a new team, rose from the dead in our humanity, conquering death and bringing life and immortality. Christ bore the curse of death at the cross. In solidarity with him, we rise to newness of life and at his return participate in the resurrection of the body in him.

(iii) The order (23)

This *order* means 'that which has been arranged'.[5] It is a properly arranged order. First is the resurrection of Christ, which has occurred already. Then those who belong to him will be resurrected at his parousia (his coming), from our limited perspective in the indefinite future.

(iv) Christ's reign (24–27)

Paul does not map out the end precisely as some might wish he had. But it will come, and we will rise from the dead, when two things happen. First, Christ hands over the rule to God the Father. This does not mean that he and the Father are two separate beings. Nor does it imply that the Son is somehow less than the Father, a subordinate god or under the Father's rule himself. It simply points to the conclusion of his mediatorial task in redemption. It also relates to his incarnate condition in which he was sent by the Father, did

---

[4] Thiselton, *First Corinthians*, pp. 1223–1224; Fitzmyer, *First Corinthians*, p. 569; Fee, *First Corinthians*, pp. 748–749.

[5] Thiselton, *First Corinthians*, p. 1229; Archibald Robertson, *A Critical and Exegetical Commentary on The First Epistle of St Paul to the Corinthians*, ICC (Edinburgh: T&T Clark, 1999), p. 354.

the Father's will and completed the work the Father had given him to do. Second, Christ annihilates all hostile powers, structural and demonic, and subjects all his enemies to his rule, in fulfilment of Psalm 110:1. This is necessary (*dei gar auton basileuein*). It is God's eternal purpose. It is not something postponed to the far future or to a limited time. It is already taking place. It will reach its consummation at Christ's return, when every knee will bow and 'every tongue confess that Jesus Christ is Lord, to the glory of God the Father'.[6]

The last enemy to be destroyed is death (26). This will of course take place at Christ's return when the dead are raised in union with him. In this case the resurrection of the wicked is not in the picture. Note that Paul puts the verb *katargeitai* in the present indicative; death is already in the process of being destroyed, the final *coup de grâce* to be administered when Christ comes back in glory. The process of the annihilation of death has already started; it began with Christ's resurrection and will be completed at his parousia. In short, this is a prophetic present. It also links Christ's resurrection and ours.

c. The nature of the resurrection body (35–49)

Paul later addresses the question of what the resurrection body, in which we will participate and of which Christ is the first fruits, is like. It was considered in some branches of Jewish apocalyptic literature that in the resurrection the body would be an assemblage of particles of the rotting corpse, configured as before so as not to differ from the present body.[7] That seems to be the reason for Paul's outburst, 'You fool!'[8]

(i) The resurrection body is not precisely identical to our present body (35–38)

The model Paul chooses is agricultural, drawn from sowing and reaping. Since he has already used the analogy of harvests, this represents a continuity with his previous discussion. The sequence is of a seed that is sown, dies, and comes to life in a different form, having been transformed (36–37). It follows that the resurrection entails a transformation to a different level of existence. Yet underlying this dramatic change is an ongoing continuity. The transformation takes place through a process of death, with new life following. *What you sow is not the body that is to be*, for *what you sow does not come to life unless it dies* (36–37). The picture is of a seed or kernel that

---

[6] Phil. 2:10.
[7] Robertson, *First Corinthians*, p. 368.
[8] Fitzmyer, *First Corinthians*, pp. 587–588.

ends up as grain. In this case, what is sown is the present body; death follows, and life emerges in a different form. In the case of the resurrection body it comes from God as a gift – *God gives (didōsin) to it a body as he wills* (38). Paul will reiterate this in his second letter to the Corinthians when he describes the resurrection body as 'from heaven'.[9] The sovereign will of God determines the nature of the resurrection body. There will be order, differentiation and variety. We cannot predict it, it is in the hands of God. However, since our resurrection and Christ's are the same reality it seems reasonable to conclude that ours will be patterned on his. Christ was recognized as a human being, engaged in conversation, ate food, cooked breakfast, and was mistaken for other people. When full recognition dawned it was clear that it was he and no other. Hence, while there is not an identity between our present and future bodies, there is to be continuity.

(ii) There is a wide diversity of bodies (39–41)
The difference between the two bodies is underlined in this section. A radical transformation is in view. The raised body will be different from the body that dies. It will not be the same as the one that rots in the grave. The diverse range of material entities in the creation is proof of this. Humans, animals, birds and fish all differ. The sun, moon and stars are quite different than physical objects or beings on earth. Furthermore, they all differ among themselves.

(iii) There will be discontinuity between the Adamic body and the resurrection body (42–44)
These two bodies (what we receive from Adam and the resurrection body) are classed as the body that *is sown* and the body that *is raised*. The differences and continuities are within the power of God to do as he pleases. Paul lists four pairs of contrasts: perishable/imperishable, humiliation/splendour, weakness/power, natural/spiritual. These four pairs highlight the dramatic transformation that occurred in Christ's resurrection, which we will share at his return.

In these contrasts the present body is described as *perishable*. This was always the case. Even before the fall, Adam's body was capable of decay should he have sinned, being potentially perishable. This potentiality became actual for Adam and his team upon his transgression and the breaking of the covenant of life. Consequently, the present body is subject to decay. Its powers decline, it gets weak and exhausted, and eventually dies. The present body is also lowly, pitiful, full of misery and shame. It is weak, fragile, with limited

---

[9] 2 Cor. 5:1.

capabilities, subject to frustration and failure. It is a natural (*psychikon*) body, facing the common lot of the human condition in this fallen world, designed at its best for the mundane realm to which we are accustomed.

In contrast, the resurrection body is *imperishable*. It flourishes, achieving the ultimate purpose God has designed for humans made in his image. It is glorious; *glory (doxa)* signifies what belongs to God. As such, the body will be suffused with the glory of God, as we are fully partakers of the divine nature. Glorification is the end and goal of the Christian life and of the redemption won by Christ, consisting of our sharing the glory he has with the Father (2 Pet. 1:4). It will be a body marked by *power* in contrast to our present *weakness*; decay, disease, frustration will be no more. Above all it will be *a spiritual body (sōma pneumatikon)* in contrast to a *natural* one *(sōma psychikon)*. It is designed for the immeasurably greater work we will have in the new heavens and the new earth. By this Paul does not mean it will be a spirit and that there will be no bodily resurrection; that would be contrary to his argument in the entire chapter. What he means is that the resurrection body will be under the undiluted sway of the Holy Spirit.[10] Wherever Paul refers to *pneuma* he means the Holy Spirit, unless there is clear evidence to the contrary. Christ's resurrection body was marked by the Holy Spirit, so much so that Paul in his second letter to Corinth almost equates Christ and the Spirit (2 Cor. 3:17). It will be a body that is not less than physical for it will be more than physical, constituted by God the Holy Spirit. It will be enhanced over and above and beyond its present limitations. There is a body for the created realm, and there is a body for the new creation, the realm of the Holy Spirit, which includes the physical.

(iv) Adam and the risen Christ (45–49)

Paul now sharpens the contrast. His two poles are now the two heads of the two teams that make up the human race. Adam was made *a living being*, with a life that could potentially be lost in death. His body was correspondingly provisional. He was given life. On the other hand, the risen Christ, *the last Adam*, is *a life-giving spirit*. His risen identity is inseparable from the Holy Spirit. He is the author and giver of life. Adam received life. The risen Christ gives life and is the source of life, for he is life. In short, the resurrection is not a return to this mode of existence. It is an advance beyond our present imagination. It is a new creation (2 Cor. 5:17). We have glimpses of

---

[10] Herman Ridderbos, *Paul: An Outline of His Theology* (Grand Rapids: Eerdmans, 1975), pp. 540–548; Richard B. Gaffin Jr, *The Centrality of the Resurrection: A Study in Paul's Soteriology* (Grand Rapids: Baker, 1978), pp. 78–92.

this in the resurrection appearances of Christ and in his revelation to Paul and John from glory.

There is a proper order to this progression. First is the natural order, from the earth's soil, in weakness and vulnerability, subject to mortality. Then we will bear the imprint of the last Adam, the second man, the man from heaven, raised by the Holy Spirit to power and dominion. We have borne the image of the earthly Adam. Then – but not yet – we will be like Christ in glory.

d. Transformation and resurrection (50–58)

In order to enter into heaven and the renewed cosmos holiness is indispensable, a transformation of body and soul to be conformed to the glory of God. So resurrection and transformation are the same event. Mystery exists in both the biblical sense of something hidden but now revealed and also in the sense that this is something beyond our present grasp. Both are instantaneous: *in a moment, in the twinkling of an eye* (52). The *last trumpet* itself bespeaks a sudden and dramatic event, for the sound of the trumpet in the OT was a manifestation of God, a call for all to hear (Exod. 19:16; 1 Chr. 16:6; Ps. 47:5; Joel 2:1; Zech. 9:14). At that point the *sōma* will *be raised* without degenerative decay; rather, the reverse, for it will flourish unimpeded by the ravages of sin and its effects. Yet in the midst of such change there is recognizable continuity. It is *this perishable body* that puts on *the imperishable*, *this mortal body* that puts on *immortality*. If it were not so, it would not be we who were saved. Paul is speaking of a recognizable identity in a different form. This is not akin to the transformation that changes a caterpillar into a butterfly, for not only is that a purely natural immanent process but the butterfly is unrecognizable from what precedes it. This will be a recognizable transformation and fulfilment. The result is that we will be incapable of dying, even as Christ is now raised from the dead, never again to die. As Augustine put it in his *Sermons for the Feast of Ascension*, 'is he who was able to make you when you did not exist not able to make over what you once were?'[11] So, with the church down through the ages, in the words of the Nicene Creed, we 'look for the resurrection of the dead and the life of the world to come'.

Christ is risen!
He is risen indeed!

---

[11] Cited by Thiselton, *First Corinthians*, p. 1297, n. 195.

Part Five
Christ ascended

One recent writer has remarked that 'the ascension is, I think, a subject richer and more instructive than is commonly recognized'.[1] Yet we hear very few sermons on it. Throughout the Western church the focus has been on the cross, on Jesus' death to atone for our sins. This is all very good, as the cross is right at the heart of salvation. The resurrection has also quite rightly taken a prominent position, largely due to hostile attacks on the supernatural. The reality that Jesus rose from the dead has been stressed over the years but often the consequences that are spelled out in the NT have been missed. As Paul says, the death of Christ for our sins and his resurrection from the dead are 'of first importance',[2] so we can have no quibble with this. However, the ascension has somehow been eclipsed. Perhaps some of us have a concern about the physical dimensions of Jesus ascending. Levitation is hard to comprehend. A description of the event occurs in only two places in the NT, both written by Luke; that may lead us to assume that it lacks a significant place in the teaching of the Bible. Yet, as we shall I hope see, if we neglect the ascension we will leave a gaping hole in our grasp of the gospel. The NT refers to it far more often than those two places we mentioned, and it is also foreshadowed way back in the OT as well.

---

[1] Douglas Farrow, *Ascension and Ecclesia: On the Significance of the Doctrine of the Ascension for Ecclesiology and Cosmology* (Edinburgh: T&T Clark, 1999), p. x.
[2] 1 Cor. 15:3.

Luke 24:50–53; Acts 1:6–11
21. The ascension[1]

1. The OT background

Among the many ways in which the ascension is prefigured in the OT, pride of place must go to the psalms of enthronement (Pss 24; 47; 68; 110), which feature the installation of the royal king. Behind these psalms lie events recorded in 2 Samuel 6 and 1 Chronicles 13 – 16. There King David brings the ark of the covenant up to Jerusalem with shouts of joy. The ark was the central place in Israel's worship, the place where Yahweh met his people in the person of the high priest. It was placed at the very centre of the tabernacle, in which the sacrifices were offered by the high priest in the holy of holies, that sacred area into which only the high priest could enter – and only once a year, on the Day of Atonement (Lev. 16:1–34). Years before, after a long period of faithlessness and idolatry on the part of Israel, and as a penalty for their rebellion, the ark had been captured by the Philistines (1 Sam. 4). In its exile, its captors were struck down by tumours and hastily arranged its return to Israelite territory (1 Sam. 5:1 – 7:2). Not for decades, until David was firmly established on the throne, was the ark brought to Jerusalem. David himself led the triumphant procession.

The enthronement psalms reflect these events. In Israel, one always went *up* to Jerusalem and leaving it was always a movement *down* from the city. This was so regardless of the geographical direction of travel. Jerusalem was in an elevated place in more ways than one. So Psalms 24, 47, 68 and 110 portray an ascent to royal sovereignty, the enthronement of Yahweh as king of his people.

---

[1] This chapter is the substance of a lecture given in the Faculty Lecture series at Calvin College, Grand Rapids, Michigan, in September 2004.

In tandem with these are the psalms of ascent, where the people go up to the temple or to Jerusalem in festal procession (e.g., Ps. 24:3–6; 122:1–5). The regular phraseology of 'going up' to Jerusalem is of significance here also. We can imagine the procession climbing the road to the temple, to the place where the ark was located, to the worship of Yahweh.

We recall too the earlier occasion where Yahweh invites Moses to ascend Mount Sinai to meet him in the clouds on behalf of the people (Exod. 19:3, 20, 24; 24:1–2, 9–11, 12–18; 32:30; 34:1–4). Repeatedly Moses climbs the mountain and descends from it. He goes up to Yahweh and descends to the people. He enters the cloud and the darkness, the cloud and fire, privileged to meet with Yahweh high above the assembled crowds below. In particular, at the establishment of the Mosaic covenant, Moses and Aaron, Nadab and Abihu and seventy of the elders of Israel ascend Sinai (Exod. 24:9–11), where they see the God of Israel, and eat and drink. Peace with God and communion with him are to be found in the heights of the mountain of God.

Even earlier than that, at creation itself, Adam was put in the Garden of Eden to cultivate it to the glory of God. He lived in communion with his creator. God provided a superabundance for his varied needs. Moreover, 'a river flowed out of Eden to water the garden, and there it divided and became four rivers'.[2] The place where Adam had fellowship with God was in an elevated position, rivers flowing out, and presumably down, from it to lower-lying ground elsewhere. From the beginning the place where God met his people was on high ground.[3]

If we move further on through the course of the years, the prophet Elijah ends his ministry in the most unusual way. Aware in advance that he was to be taken away from Elisha, his successor, 'chariots of fire and horses of fire separated the two of them. And Elijah went up by a whirlwind into heaven'.[4] Elijah ascended and he did so 'into heaven', to the place where Yahweh dwells. He was no longer to be found in the terrain of Israel (2 Kgs 2:15–18). He was transferred from regular interaction with his contemporaries to the realm of God, this being signalled by a powerful upward movement evidently stemming from the direct action of Yahweh. For us, this is a deeply mysterious event. It is beyond our experience; like a bolt from the blue, we cannot grasp what it actually portends. We could try to compare it to something known to us from our daily life but we cannot do so.

[2] Gen. 2:10.
[3] John V. Fesko, *Last Things First* (Fearn: Mentor, 2007).
[4] 2 Kgs 2:11.

All these events and circumstances, taken together, point us to the idea that God's place is elevated far above ours. It suggests that in order to worship him and have communion with him, we are to ascend beyond our own sphere, taken up as it were by the powerful hand of God to meet him in the clouds.

2. The ascension described

a. In Luke (24:50–53)

We have already noted that in the NT only Luke describes the ascension. In Luke 24:50–53 it brings to an end the first volume of his historical record:

> Then he led them out as far as Bethany, and lifting up his hands he blessed them. While he blessed them, he parted from them and was carried up into heaven. And they worshipped him and returned to Jerusalem with great joy, and were continually in the temple blessing God.

Here Luke gives us the following details: (1) Jesus lifts up his hands and blesses his disciples; (2) while he blesses them he is parted from them; (3) he is carried up into heaven. Benediction, parting, being taken up into heaven, these are the salient features.

The act of benediction is a priestly act. It is the last thing the apostles see Jesus doing. It is to be characteristic of his ongoing ministry. It signals the nature of the circumstances that will follow his departure. His disciples, headed by the apostles, will receive the blessing of the risen and ascended Jesus.

The parting is decisive and distinguishes this event from the previous resurrection appearances. Then Jesus simply disappeared, and for a time only; this is permanent. Then he returned, usually after a short period of a few days. Now he will no longer be in the personal interaction that he had with them over the course of the previous years. It signals a departure that will continue.

One further point here is that *Jesus is passive*; the Father takes him up to heaven, to his right hand. Jesus is the one upon whom the action takes place. It is from elsewhere that the movement originates. Jesus is God incarnate; in his incarnate condition he is dependent on the Holy Spirit and works in pursuance of the Father's will. Here the pattern is underlined. In this the ascension mirrors the virginal conception Luke describes in chapter 1. There he likens the incarnation to a new creation; in both contexts the Spirit takes the initiative.

195

b. In Acts (1:9–11)

In Acts 1:9–11, Luke describes the same event from another perspective. Coming at the end of the first volume and the beginning of the second of his two-volume work, Luke is stressing the pivotal significance of this event in connection with everything that precedes and all that follows. The entire preparation of the OT, the life, ministry and death of Jesus, recorded in the Gospel, and all that will follow in the history of the church, beginning with the role of the apostles in Acts, is summed up here, at this point, in this action. This, as Douglas Farrow says, is 'the hinge' upon which the two volumes turn.[5]

Jesus has just informed the apostles of the imminent coming of the Holy Spirit, and their international task as his witnesses. After this

> . . . when he had said these things, as they were looking on, he was lifted up, and a cloud took him out of their sight. And while they were gazing into heaven as he went, behold, two men stood by them in white robes, and said, 'Men of Galilee, who do you stand looking into heaven? This Jesus, who was taken up from you into heaven, will come in the same way as you saw him go into heaven.'

In this account, Jesus is lifted up, and a cloud receives him while he passes out of their sight. During this sequence, they are looking on. He is taken up into heaven. Again, we have the thought that the Father is taking him to be with himself, the seal of divine approval on Jesus and all that he has done.

There is *a physical removal*, a lifting up. We cannot avoid this element, although we will need to explain it in the terms Luke sets it. In order to see what exactly Luke has in mind, we should first ask about the other aspects of this remarkable scene.

It is important to grasp that the reference to *the cloud* receiving him is more than merely a weather report (as if, incidentally, it was partly cloudy, with a high around 25°C, with winds from the southwest at 15 miles per hour). While Luke pays careful attention in Acts to the surrounding conditions, and nowhere more so than in his account of the shipwreck in which he and Paul were involved, he has other ideas in mind on this occasion. For one thing, the language reminds us of the description of the son of man in Daniel, who comes 'with the clouds of heaven' and to whom is given 'dominion and

---

[5] Douglas Farrow, *Ascension and Ecclesia: On the Significance of the Doctrine of the Ascension for Ecclesiology and Cosmology* (Edinburgh: T&T Clark, 1999), p. 16.

glory and a kingdom, that all peoples, nations, and languages should serve him; his dominion is an everlasting dominion which shall not pass away, and his kingdom one that shall not be destroyed'.[6] Jesus here, in his ascension as the Son of Man, is receiving his kingdom which shall embrace 'the end of the earth'.[7] The rest of Acts unfolds the ways this process begins. Luke has already, in his Gospel, explained the things 'Jesus began to do and teach';[8] now he will recount the things he continues to do and teach through his apostles, extending the kingdom of God to the Gentiles and ending at the heart of the leading world power, Rome (Acts 28).

Moreover, throughout Scripture *clouds are associated with the glory of God*, especially by Luke himself. In his record of the transfiguration (Luke 9:28–36), a cloud overshadows the three disciples, who are consequently struck with fear. Out of the cloud comes the voice, 'This is my Son, my chosen one; listen to him!' The Father speaks, refers to his Son, and does so out of the cloud. The cloud that envelopes Jesus is the glory of the Father, and it is in this context that the apostles are to listen to Jesus, for it is in this way and no other that he is to be understood. Similarly, John writes of Jesus as coming at his parousia 'with the clouds';[9] this is in line with Luke's own report of the angels' announcement to the apostles that Jesus will one day return in the same way as they had seen him disappear – with the clouds (10–11). His return will be in his full glory as the eternal Son of the Father. His disappearance, concealed by a cloud, represents his passing into the presence of God; he as the God-Man, our mediator, goes from being with the disciples to being with the Father.

That *the disciples see this* – for Luke stresses that they are *looking on*, repeating the point – takes us back to the ascension of Elijah (2 Kgs 2:1–14). There Elijah promises Elisha a double portion of his spirit – the portion of the first-born – *if* he sees Elijah taken up to heaven. This he does: 'And Elijah went up by a whirlwind into heaven. And Elisha saw it.'[10] Thereafter, the record is of twice as many miracles by Elisha. He received the double portion, the portion that belonged to the first-born of the father. Here, the apostles – promised the Holy Spirit – see Jesus taken up by the Father to the glory of God in the cloud. They are gazing intently. They see him go. They are *looking on . . . gazing into heaven*. Then, a few days later, the Spirit of Jesus, the Holy Spirit, is unleashed in mighty power, with consequences reported throughout the book of Acts.

[6] Dan. 7:13–14.
[7] Acts 1:8.
[8] Acts 1:1.
[9] Rev. 1:7.
[10] 2 Kgs 2:11–12.

Farrow's comment, mentioned earlier, on the centrality of the ascension to Luke-Acts is very perceptive.[11] From this it follows that Peter's sermon on the Day of Pentecost (Acts 2:14–36) is a sermon on the ascension of the risen Jesus to the throne – to Israel's throne and the throne of the presence from which the Spirit goes forth.

3. What happened?

So much for the bare details. Now we need to probe further and ask what Luke intends us to grasp from this epoch-making event. What actually happened? What does it all mean? From our own perspective it is certainly odd. Things like this don't take place every day.

a. The physics of the ascension

While the ascension remains deeply mysterious and elusive to us, we can nevertheless point to boundaries to keep us from viewing it in unhelpful ways. On the one hand, *it is not to be reduced, in crassly literal manner, to the level of a primitive form of space-travel.* We saw that the reference to the clouds was not intended as a weather report but as a reference to the glory of God. As Yahweh in the wilderness went before Israel in a pillar of cloud by day (Exod. 13:21 *et al.*), as Moses in ascending to his meeting with Yahweh entered the clouds (Exod. 24:18), as Yahweh rides on a swift cloud (Isa. 19:1), as the son of man comes with the clouds of heaven (Dan. 7:13), and as the Father spoke from the cloud at the transfiguration (Luke 9:34–35), so Luke points us to Jesus' removal from the immediate realm of human interaction to the presence and place of God.

On the other hand, *we must avoid the opposite danger of reading the event in an entirely spiritual manner.* As he parted from them, Jesus' hands were raised in priestly blessing. The physicality of the event is clear. The ascension affirms, par excellence, Jesus' continuing humanity. Our human flesh is taken to the right hand of God, invested with the glory of God, received by the Father. That this event took place in our own time and space was *necessary* since what is at stake is the continuation of our humanity.

In short, *the ascension bridges our present world and that of the age to come.* It is a movement, in T. F. Torrance's words, 'from man's place to God's place'.[12] Jesus moved from regular interaction with

[11] Farrow, *Ascension and Ecclesia*, p. 16.
[12] Thomas F. Torrance, *Space, Time and Resurrection* (Grand Rapids: Eerdmans, 1976), pp. 106–158.

his contemporaries to the place where God dwells, in the clouds of glory. It follows that this event took place in this world at a definite time and place but that it also has extra dimensions to it. There is the departure but also the cloud; the severance of fellowship and the reception by the Father; Jesus' consequent absence until his parousia, and his presence through the Holy Spirit whose sending followed the ascension; there is absence and presence. In short, it is a happening in this world that can be dated but it is also an event that occurs in the life of God and so has eternal significance.

b. The resurrection and the ascension

Was the ascension simply the last of Jesus' resurrection appearances, as is often claimed? It is true that there is an obvious connection. The interaction immediately before the ascension occurred during the last of the resurrection appearances. However, the ascension itself is qualitatively different both from the resurrection, the point at which Jesus emerged from death, and the later sightings of him recorded in the Gospels. In each of the preceding resurrection appearances Jesus eventually and suddenly disappears. Later, he reappears at another place. In this case, his departure is not a sudden vanishing but a concealment that takes place while the apostles watch, a diminishing into the distance. Moreover, it is confirmed by the angels as a continuous absence until his parousia. After the resurrection, he appears in fully recognizable form, albeit with enhanced powers; Mary Magdalene thinks he is a gardener, the disciples on the road to Emmaus talk with him as though he is simply another traveller. But after his ascension, on the two occasions he appears to Paul and John respectively (Acts 9:1–19; Rev. 1:9–20) he is transformed, so suffused with glory that the life is almost knocked out of them. If we think of the ascension as simply the ending of the last of a sequence of similar appearances and so having no significant difference from the resurrection itself, we miss the goal towards which Jesus is heading as man; the glory of God, the right hand of the Father. We miss too the connection with Pentecost and all that follows. We also sever the connection between us in our world and the new creation in Christ.

c. The ascension and reception by the Father

The ascension, then, is a definitive parting. It is for an indefinite and unspecified time, to be ended only at Jesus' return. As Farrow states, it is 'a real departure, the exchanging of a shared . . . history for an altogether distinct and unique one', a liturgical act (following the

199

Venerable Bede) which was the link between our fallen world and the new creation.[13] In this, the act of benediction – paradigmatic for all that follows – conveys divine blessing into our place.

Moreover, we must bear in mind the inseparable connection in all this with ourselves. All that Jesus did is not only for us but is done in union with us, his people. We were, and are, in him as he ascends to the right hand of the Father. As he disappears into the glory of God, so in union with him do all who believe. We too are ascended in Christ; our life is hid with Christ in God (Col. 3:1–4). We are seated with him in heavenly places (Eph. 2:6–7), in the closest union and communion with Christ, reigning with him even as we suffer and struggle in our present condition. This is a pledge of our ultimate salvation, a tonic in the face of dispiriting circumstances, a vast encouragement to faithfulness to Christ and to perseverance in adversity.

> He has raised our human nature
> In the clouds to God's right hand;
> There we sit in heavenly places,
> There with him in glory stand!
> Jesus reigns, adored by angels;
> Man with God is on the throne;
> Mighty Lord, in thine ascension
> We by faith behold our own.[14]

The ascension, then, relates particularly to Jesus as our Mediator and Saviour. As the Son of God he is eternally in indivisible union with the Father and the Holy Spirit, the three mutually indwelling each other. Here, in his ascension, he raises our human nature, our flesh, in the clouds to God's right hand.

4. The ascension and Christ as priest

Luke records Jesus' parting words and gesture at his ascension. There at Bethany *lifting up his hands he blessed them. And as he blessed them, he parted from them and was carried up into heaven* (24:50–51). His final act was the priestly act of benediction (cf. Num. 6:24–26). This priestly act is thus characteristic of his continuing ministry thereafter. In parting from them he blesses them. Being parted from them he blesses them and continues to do so. As the author of Hebrews states it, Jesus, the Son of God has 'passed

---

[13] Farrow, *Ascension and Ecclesia*, p. 39.
[14] 'See the Conqueror mounts in triumph', Christopher Wordsworth, *The Holy Year* (1865).

through the heavens' and so is able to send us grace and help in time of need.[15]

His continuing priestly ministry following his ascension is three-fold: intercession, benediction and communion. First, *it is important to understand what Christ's intercession* is *not*. He does not plead on our behalf before a reluctant Father: this would have, among other things, enormous consequences for the Trinity! Nor is it to be equated with the kinds of intercession we make here and now. When we pray for this or that person or circumstance, it is always with the caveat 'if it be your will'. There is an element of un-certainty; we ask God to heal x, but he may have determined that x die a slow and painful death. The ascended Christ's intercession is not like that. There are no caveats. It is more to be compared with the high priest in the OT, who entered the holy of holies once a year after sacrificing the sin offering. He wore the prescribed breastplate, containing twelve jewels representing the twelve tribes of Israel. In his representative capacity he was, so to speak, bringing the twelve tribes with him into the sanctuary of God. In an analogous way, Christ, having passed through the heavens, brings us his people with him into the presence of God, the right hand of the Father, and he does this since he himself not merely represents man but *is* man himself. In his incarnation he, the Son of God, permanently united to himself our nature, our flesh and blood, and so carries it before the Father on a permanent, everlasting basis. As *The Westminster Larger Catechism*, 55 puts it, his intercession is 'his appearing in our nature continually before the Father in heaven'. The ascended Christ's continuing intercession is his constant presence with the Father *as man*. Thus, in the words of Charitie Lees Bancroft,

> When Satan tempts me to despair,
> And tells me of the guilt within,
> Upward I look and see him there,
> Who made an end of all my sin.[16]

Secondly, the *benediction* characteristic of the ascended Jesus' continuing ministry should also clearly be distinguished from prayer. While intercessory prayer is the expression of a desire that this or that happen, if it be God's will, a benediction is a declaration of a state of affairs that actually exists and a bestowing of the reality of that state of affairs on those to whom it belongs. There is none of

---

[15] Heb. 4:14–16.
[16] 'Before the throne of God above', Charitie Lees Bancroft (1841–1923).

the hesitation or uncertainty that there is with our own intercessions. In the case of the ascending and ascended Christ, this uncertainty is entirely absent, for as king he has ascended far above all heavens, that he might fill all things. Christ's priestly benediction grants to his people all that they need for salvation both in this life and in what follows; in it he guards, protects, and nourishes his church, governs the world and brings his sovereign judgments to bear on its inhabitants, as depicted in the book of Revelation. This includes all that is entailed in the author of Hebrews' description of him as our forerunner (Heb. 6:19–20), foreshadowed in John (John 14:1–3). He has gone before, we follow. We follow because he has gone before; in going before he brings us there by the Holy Spirit who he has sent. Indeed, all that occurs consequent to the sending of the Spirit – his blessing of his church, his ministry to its members, his witness to the world – is implied in this.

Third, there is *union and communion*. We noted earlier how Jesus refers to his ascension immediately after the bread-of-life discourse, which has often been associated with the Eucharist (John 6:47–58; cf. 62). I have written elsewhere on the eucharistic nature of this discourse so I will not argue or press the point here.[17] From this, and from the fact of communion with Christ in the Lord's Supper – evident elsewhere in the NT than this one passage – it follows that the ascension and the Eucharist are closely linked. Calvin saw this clearly. Jesus is absent from us. Yet we feed on his body and drink his blood. How? Through the Holy Spirit (John 6:63) who lifts us up to heaven. Similarly, the author of Hebrews writes that we are no longer tied to the covenant made at Mount Sinai but we have come now to Mount Zion, to the city of the living God, to an innumerable company of angels, and to Jesus (Heb. 12:18–24). The bodily ascension of Jesus is the basis for our communion with him – according to both natures – through the Holy Spirit, who unites things separated by distance. The Eucharist is for the church until Christ's parousia. It is coterminous with his ascended ministry. So long as he intercedes for us and blesses his church, so we feed on him in the Eucharist. It points to our destiny, union with God in Christ; the ascended Christ has sent the Spirit to unite us to him and thus to the Father. It is the ascension that makes room for this to occur. As Jesus said, 'It is to your advantage that I go away'.[18]

---

[17] Robert Letham, *The Lord's Supper: Eternal Word in Broken Bread* (Phillipsburg: Presbyterian & Reformed, 2001), pp. 7–15.

[18] John 16:7.

5. The NT beyond Luke-Acts

It would be a serious mistake to assume that, in the NT, the ascension was a matter for the writings of Luke alone. That is very far from the case.

First, *the ascension crops up a number of times in John.* In John 3:13 Jesus links his incarnation with the ascension: 'no one has ascended into heaven except him who descended from heaven, the Son of Man'. Then, in John 6:62 Jesus asks the disciples, grumbling over the hard saying of the bread-of-life discourse, perplexed by Jesus' crude imagery of eating his flesh and drinking his blood, 'what if you were to see the Son of Man ascending to where he was before?' He makes the obvious point that it is more difficult for us to comprehend the ascension than even the imagery of the discourse. We will refer to this link with the Eucharist later. In John 14:2–3, Jesus reassures his disciples, disturbed by his announcement of his impending departure, with the fact that 'I go to prepare a place for you' and that 'I will come again and will take you to myself, that where I am you may be also'. From John 14:16 he gives a lengthy and detailed account of the coming of the Holy Spirit and his ministry subsequent to his departure (14:16 – 16:33). In particular, in John 16:5 he says he is going to the one who sent him – the Father. This he reiterates to Mary Magdalene in the garden after his resurrection (John 20:17).

Second, *Peter refers to the ascension in 1 Peter 3:18–22.* Leaving aside the enormous complexities of this passage, let us say that if – as to my mind seems most likely – verses 19–21 are a parenthesis, we have a progression in Peter's thought from the crucifixion ('put to death in the flesh', flesh in the redemptive historical Pauline sense of the old age) to the resurrection ('made alive in the Spirit', by the Spirit and in the new age of the Spirit) to the ascension ('who has gone into heaven and is at the right hand of God').[19]

Third, *Paul refers specifically to the ascension in Ephesians 4:8–10.*[20] Here, citing Psalm 68, he argues that the church is founded on the basis of Christ's ascension. The ascended Christ has given gifts to his church, gifts of *persons,* including the apostles, for particular strategic tasks. Again, in the hymnic citation in 1 Timothy 3:16, which refers to the incarnation, resurrection and the preaching of the apostles, comes the phrase 'taken up in glory'.

[19] See the literature but particularly William J. Dalton, *Christ's Proclamation to the Spirits: A Study of 1 Peter 3:18–4:6,* Analecta Biblica 23 (2nd ed., Rome: Editrice Pontificio Instituto Biblico, 1989).

[20] I have written on the authorship of Ephesians in Robert Letham, *The Holy Trinity: In Scripture, History, Theology, and Worship* (Phillipsburg: Presbyterian & Reformed, 2004), pp. 73–74; C. E. Arnold, 'Ephesians', in *DPL,* pp. 238–249.

Fourthly and finally, *the ascension is absolutely crucial for the author of Hebrews*. There are many implicit references to it but also a number which are clear and explicit. Jesus is our great high priest 'who has passed through the heavens',[21] and so is able to help us in our time of need, as well as able to sympathize with us due to his own experience of temptation as man; he is our forerunner who has entered into 'the inner place behind the curtain',[22] from where 'he is able to save to the uttermost those who draw near to God through him'.[23] He has entered 'once for all into the holy place',[24] 'into heaven itself, now to appear in the presence of God on our behalf'.[25] He has 'sat down at the right hand of God'.[26] All these passages trace the journey of Jesus from the cross to the right hand of God without reference to the resurrection as such but instead focusing on the ascension as portraying his passage into the holy of holies, the presence of God.

6. The ascension and Christ as king

We have already looked in some detail at how Luke regards the ascended Christ as our high priest, blessing his people in the act of departure. Now we will concentrate on the point that his ascension establishes the fact that Christ rules the universe. In it he publicly displays his conquest of his enemies, as in a triumphant victory procession. In Ephesians 4:8–10, citing Psalm 68:18, Paul teaches that the ascended Christ has pervasive authority. A victorious king would travel throughout his territory establishing and confirming his rule in every place throughout his domain.[27] So Christ's realm is the entire cosmos. He has ascended far above the heavens and now fills all things. He has passed through his territory and has won the authority throughout his realm. Athanasius wrote along these lines, as did Abraham Kuyper.[28]

We can take our earlier statement a stage further. All this he did in union with us, his people. By his ascension he establishes the

---

[21] Heb. 4:14–16.

[22] Heb. 6:19–20.

[23] Heb. 7:25.

[24] Heb. 9:11–12.

[25] Heb. 9:24.

[26] Heb. 10:12–13.

[27] Markus Barth, *Ephesians: Translation and Commentary on Chapters 4–6*, AB (New York: Doubleday, 1974), pp. 472–477; Charles Hodge, *A Commentary on the Epistle to the Ephesians* (London: Banner of Truth, 1964), pp. 212–219.

[28] Athanasius, *Orations against the Arians* 2:79 (*NPNF*², vol. 4); *PG* 26:314. Abraham Kuyper, 'Inaugural address, Free University of Amsterdam, 1880', cited in James D. Bratt (ed.), *Abraham Kuyper: A Centennial Reader* (Grand Rapids: Eerdmans, 1988), p. 488.

church, granting gifts to it for its preservation and advancement (Eph. 4:11–16). All that he did and does is not only for us, in our place, on our behalf but also in union with us. We were in him in his ascension. We too have ascended to the right hand of the Father in Christ. We too sit with him in heavenly places.

7. The ascension and Christ as prophet

Jesus Christ is more than a prophet, for he himself is the truth. A prophet spoke not in his own name but in the name of the Lord. His oracles were usually introduced by the saying, 'Thus says the Lord', or 'The word of the Lord came to me, saying . . .' He simply bore witness to the truth, for he himself was not the truth. In dramatic contrast, Jesus speaks in his own name and by his own authority. He sets himself in opposition to the traditional teachings of the rabbis where that diverged from the truth. In the Sermon on the Mount he says time after time 'You have heard that it was said . . . but I say to you . . .' He had no need to refer to a truth outside himself, for he *is* the truth (John 14:6), the everlasting Son of the Father (Heb 1:1–4), the Word who was in the beginning with God and who was God (John 1:1–2). This the ascension openly proclaims.

Jesus equates the presence and ministry of the Holy Spirit after Pentecost (and so post-ascension) with his own (John 14:16–19). The Spirit's indwelling of the disciples will be the permanent indwelling of all three persons of the Trinity (John 14:23). Earlier in John, Jesus refers to the gift of the Holy Spirit following his glorification (John 7:37–39). Those who believe in him will have rivers of living water flowing out of their inmost beings; this is a reference to the Holy Spirit. Moreover, the Spirit would lead the apostles into all truth (John 16:12–15), teaching them what Jesus was unable to teach at that time due to their inability to receive it. The Spirit was to enable the apostles to receive the truth and convey it to them. In this, Jesus refers to the teaching of the apostles recorded in the pages of the NT. Thus the NT is the gift of the ascended Christ via the Holy Spirit. Christ's prophetic ministry (insofar as it is legitimate to call it that since he so far transcends the prophetic) continues after his ascension through the apostles and their inspired writings. We have it recorded in the pages of the NT. The word of the apostles in the canonical writings is the word of the Holy Spirit and so also of the ascended Christ.

8. Christ's ascension and our present life

The ascension marks the boundary between two closely related pairs of contrasts.

First, *there is the redemptive-historical contrast of two ages*: the world in Adam, from the fall onwards, subject to sin, corruption and death, an age that is passing away; and the world in Christ, from the incarnation, resurrection and ascension onwards, which is being renewed, and is marked by life, which will last for eternity.

Second, *this contrast is also seen in relation to creation.* The creation, as made by God, was good, made in Christ,[29] but it was affected by human sin and is described by Paul as currently in bondage. On the other hand, there is the new creation, from the resurrection and ascension, renewed in Christ and ultimately destined for his eternal rule. These two pairs of contrasts intersect, distinct but inseparably related.

9. The relationship of Christ's ascension to aspects of current human existence

We face *hardship, suffering and a world of terror.* The book of Revelation addresses such a world, and unmasks the powers that claim the allegiance of its contemporaries. The book comes from the ascended Jesus to seven weak and beleaguered churches in Asia Minor, under threat from the rampant emperor worship of the Roman Empire. It portrays the horrific forces behind the scenes but demonstrates that Christ is sovereign over all, for he is the 'ruler of kings on earth'.[30]

In relation to *death* Christ's ascension points us to the sure and certain hope of the resurrection to life eternal.

As we consider Christ's ascension in relation to *everyday living*, Paul, in Colossians 3:1–4 directs us to set our minds where the ascended Christ is seated at the right hand of God, for that is where our life is located. The ascended Christ is to be the centre of our thought and the prime director of our motivations. Gerrit Dawson shows how this focus worked out in one context of practical ministry; far from leading to heavenly mindedness that was of no earthly use, it unleashed a flood of practical action and an extension of ministries that neither he nor anyone had contemplated.[31]

The ascension should affect *the way we treat people.* Today, the corporate world treats its employees as disposable commodities. Behaviourist principles govern the way it treats people; given certain stimuli they will respond in this or that particular way. The ascension highlights the point that human beings are not to be equated with

[29] Cf. Athanasius, *On the Incarnation*, 1, 3, 12, 14; *PG* 25:97–102, 115–122.
[30] Rev. 1:5.
[31] Gerrit Scott Dawson, *Jesus Ascended: The Meaning of Christ's Continuing Incarnation* (London: T&T Clark, 2004).

programmable animals. Those in Christ have ascended in him to the right hand of God. As Paul says, our life is hid with Christ in God (Col. 3:1–4).

Finally, we consider the ascension in relation to *the mandate of creation*. The task of subduing the earth to the glory of God is foundational to the whole of human life (Gen. 1:26–31). Here the two pairs of contrasts we mentioned before both come into play. From the standpoint of the ascension we have the task of bringing to bear the effects of the redemptive work of Christ in a world that is subject to death because of sin. We also have the privilege of participating in the ascended Christ's renewal of creation.

Grant, we beseech thee, Almighty God, that like as we do believe thy only-begotten Son our Lord Jesus Christ to have ascended into the heavens; so we may also in heart and mind thither ascend, and with him continually dwell, who liveth and reigneth with thee and the Holy Ghost, one God, world without end. Amen.[32]

---

[32] Collect for Ascension Day, *The Book of Common Prayer.*

Colossians 1:15–20
22. Lord of creation, head of the church

Paul expounds a similar theme to the author of Hebrews in Colossians 1:16–17, where he affirms that *all things were created in him, things in heaven and on earth, things visible and invisible, whether thrones and dominions, rulers and authorities, all things were created through him and to him. And he is before all things, and in him all things hold together.*[1]

The background to this letter is what is often called the Colossian heresy. There is some uncertainty as to what it was. It may have involved the veneration of angels. If so, this passage is a strong antidote. Paul is emphatic that Christ is not one of a range of beings between God and humanity, even if he be held to be of a higher status than any other. He is supreme. This appears to be a hymn, whether pre-Pauline or composed by the apostle himself is for our purposes neither here nor there. The subject of this hymn is the Son, into whose kingdom we have been transferred by the Father after having been in the grip of the kingdom of darkness (1:13–14). The purpose is to reinforce the church's faith in him and to divert it from any other focus.

1. Christ and creation (15–16)

a. The Son is the image of the invisible God

God is beyond human vision, being in light inapproachable. No one has ever seen him; indeed, it is not possible to look on him and live (Exod. 33:20). It is Jesus Christ, the Son, who makes him known. He is the *exact* representation of God, and the *visible* representation of

[1] Author's translation.

God.[2] The invisible God is made visible in Jesus Christ. As Jesus said to Philip, 'Have I been with you so long, and you still do not know me, Philip? Whoever has seen me has seen the Father.'[3] He makes God known in human history, on our own level. This entails pre-existence, his being before all things, and so transcends his life on earth. Mark traces Jesus' career back to his baptism, when his public ministry began. Matthew and Luke move it back before that to his conception, and trace his lineage to David and Abraham, and in Luke's case to Adam. However, John pushes it back even further, before the creation, for he is the creator. The fact that Christ is the true representation of God establishes right away his supremacy over the angels.

Many dispute whether pre-existence is in view here. Elsewhere I have commented on this position with reference to the similar passage, Philippians 2:5–11.[4] Typical of this consensus is James Dunn, who argues that a full view of Christ's personal pre-existence is not found in Paul but only in Hebrews and John, which he regards as significantly later documents. In particular, the *locus classicus*, Philippians 2:5–7, does not refer to the claimed pre-temporal existence of Christ at all, he argues, but contrasts Christ with Adam. Adam wanted to be like God and grasped the prize of the forbidden fruit. In contrast, Christ refused to act like this. Dunn concludes that since Paul compares Christ with the temporal Adam there is no need to seek any pre-temporal reference in the passage.[5] However, it is a logical fallacy to assume that even if Paul refers to Adam that pre-existence is thereby precluded. Moreover, the majority of scholars hold that pre-existence is in view, and the force of the language supports it.[6] I suggest that similar conclusions arise from this passage in Colossians. There is a definite reference to Adam, insofar as Adam was created in the image of God, which Paul identifies

---

[2] Murray J. Harris, *Colossians & Philemon* (Grand Rapids: Eerdmans, 1991), p. 43.

[3] John 14:9.

[4] Robert Letham, *The Holy Trinity: In Scripture, History, Theology, and Worship* (Phillipsburg: Presbyterian & Reformed, 2004), pp. 41–43.

[5] James D. G. Dunn, *Christology in the Making: A New Testament Inquiry Into the Origins of the Doctrine of the Incarnation* (2nd edition, London: SCM, 1989), pp. 114–121. On this passage he asserts that Paul was not affirming actual pre-existence of Christ prior to creation but that Christ is the climactic manifestation of the pre-existent divine wisdom by which the world was created (James D. G. Dunn, *The Epistles to the Colossians and Philemon: A Commentary on the Greek Text*, NIGTC [Grand Rapids: Eerdmans, 1996], p. 89). Kim opposes Dunn on this (Seyoon Kim, *The Origin of Paul's Gospel* [Grand Rapids: Eerdmans, 1982]), and considers that Paul is the originator of the teaching of Christ's pre-existence. Also opposed to Dunn are F. F. Bruce, *The Epistles to the Colossians, to Philemon, and to the Ephesians* (Grand Rapids: Eerdmans, 1984), pp. 60–61, and Ralph Martin, *Philippians*, NCBC (Grand Rapids: Eerdmans, 1980), pp. 94–96.

[6] L. W. Hurtado, 'Pre-Existence', in *DPL*, pp. 743–746.

here as Christ.[7] That of itself can hardly preclude pre-existence; indeed, in asserting Christ's priority to Adam, it demands it. The remarkable conclusion that follows is that, if this passage (like the one in Philippians) is an early Christian hymn in wide liturgical use, its teaching was widely, possibly universally, believed some considerable time before Paul wrote. Thus, belief in Christ's pre-existence came 'remarkably early' and was 'an uncontested and familiar view of Christ in Paul's churches'.[8] Together with the prologue to John and the introduction to Hebrews these passages reflect a belief present in the church from the very start. Paul was giving voice and clarity to what it already believed.

b. Christ is lord of creation

The *firstborn* in Israel had priority over all the other offspring. He inherited a double portion of the father's estate (Deut. 21:15–17). Paul is saying that Christ, the Son, is heir to the entire creation. It is his inheritance. He owns it. It is not that he is the chief part of creation; the following lines undermine any such notion. Rather, he is the lord and ruler of the universe. It is his by right.[9]

c. Christ is the creator (16)

The aorist tense here points to completed action. The universe was brought into existence at a particular point. Its creation is due to the Son. Christ created all things. The *all things* in view is comprehensive. It includes material and non-material elements, visible and invisible. These correspond in general to things on *earth* and things in *heaven*. In short, both those elements that we can observe, see, feel, touch and measure, and those that are not visible were all brought into being by Christ.[10] The invisible things include the angels that some at Colossae may have been tempted to worship. Paul lists four categories of angel, without explaining exactly what they are or whether they are some form of hierarchy: *thrones, dominions, rulers* and *authorities*.[11] We know from the book of Daniel that angels were at work behind the scenes of world history, grappling with the earthly powers (Dan. 10:10–14; 12:1). They are evidently exceedingly powerful – the angel of the Lord slaughtered 185,000 troops in one

---

[7] Peter T. O'Brien, *Colossians, Philemon*, WBC 44 (Waco: Word Publishing, 1982), p. 43.

[8] Ibid., p. 746.

[9] See O'Brien, *Colossians, Philemon*, p. 45.

[10] Harris, *Colossians & Philemon*, pp. 44–45.

[11] Bruce, *Colossians, Philemon, and Ephesians*, pp. 63–64.

go (Isa. 37:36). They travel at immense speed and can traverse the boundaries of the spiritual and material (Dan. 9:21; Luke 1:19, 26). However, they are merely creatures, brought into existence by Christ. He is to be worshipped, they are not. All things were created in him, in living dynamic relation to him; through him, as the agent of creation; and for him, as the goal of creation. The entire universe exists for the sake of Jesus Christ. The goal towards which it is heading is conformity to him. As Paul wrote to the Ephesians, all things will be under the headship of Christ for eternity (Eph. 1:10).

2. Christ and providence (17)

In line with the teaching of Hebrews 1, Paul asserts that all things are sustained by Christ. He provides the order in the universe. He is the lord of providence, of the ongoing government of the cosmos. It is clear that *all things* here in verse 17 can hardly be less comprehensive than the reference to *all things* in verse 16. So Christ governs all he has created, material and spiritual, directing them to the goal which he has for them. Murray Harris remarks, 'what Christ has created he maintains in permanent order, stability, and productivity'.[12] Physics has shown that the universe is not static but dynamic. It is Christ that empowers the creation in this regard.

C. S. Lewis stated that there can be no neutral territory in the universe.[13] The Dutch theologian and former prime minister, Abraham Kuyper famously declared 'There is not a square inch in the whole domain of our human existence over which Christ, who is Sovereign over all, does not cry: "Mine!"'[14] All things are his. Denial of this elemental truth constitutes rebellion against the living God. It follows that Christian education, properly understood, does not consist in simply tacking on some teaching from the Bible to a consideration of this subject or that from an apparently neutral perspective. The only education that deserves the name of Christian approaches each and every area of knowledge from the premise that Christ is the one who has authority over it, that all truth is his.[15]

[12] Harris, *Colossians & Philemon*, p. 47.

[13] Cited in N. T. Wright, *The Epistles of Paul to the Colossians and to Philemon* (Leicester: IVP, 1986), p. 79.

[14] 'Inaugural address, Free University of Amsterdam, 1880', cited in James D. Bratt (ed.), *Abraham Kuyper: A Centennial Reader* (Grand Rapids: Eerdmans, 1988), p. 488.

[15] This does not mean that a simplistic and literalistic application of the Bible to this or that branch of knowledge can qualify as Christian education either. God gave humanity the task of subduing the earth (Gen 1:26–31). Scientific investigation was an integral aspect of it (Gen. 2:19–20), as were the arts (Gen. 4:21). God revealed aspects of his nature in creation (Ps. 19:1–6; Rom. 1:19–20), thereby endowing it with the dignity required for humans to seek to understand it on its own terms.

3. Christ and the church (18)

The creator of the world is the *head of the . . . church*, 'he himself and no other'.[16] This is the effective point, due to the emphasis on the personal pronoun. In writing of Christ as the head of the church Paul has two related images in mind. As head, Christ has *authority* over the church. He governs it.[17] It is his church. He protects it against the attacks of the evil one, such that the gates of hell cannot prevail against it (Matt. 16:18). The book of Revelation makes this clear, while also stating in no uncertain terms that he can and does act in judgment over it (Rev. 2:4–5, 14–16, 20–24; 3:1–4, 15–20). In the second place, he is the *source* of its life.[18] The head animates the whole body, directing it in every way. So too Christ imparts life and power to his church by the Holy Spirit. The church is a living organism, its relation to Christ as close as it is possible to imagine. It is a living, dynamic, vital relationship. The church is not an ecclesiastical club, existing for the comfort of its privileged members.

Christ is head of the church as the one who rose from the dead, *the first-born from the dead*. The *risen* Christ is the head of the church.[19] Whereas he was and is always supreme over the universe, for he created it and governs it, he became the head of the church upon his resurrection, having completed the work of redemption. This is because he is the one who is incarnate, who has added human nature and lived amongst us as one of us. It was in the flesh that he died, and in the flesh that he was resurrected. This indicates graphically that salvation is a renewal of creation, for humanity is part of creation. Salvation goes beyond the forgiveness of our sins and everlasting life for ourselves, although that is a central and wonderful part of it. It reaches out to a vast scenario encompassing the whole universe renewed in righteousness.

4. Christ and God (19)

The incarnate Christ is the complete and perfect embodiment of God. In him the full and undiluted presence of God is to be found. Bruce comments that 'the totality of divine essence and power is resident in Christ' so that he is the one all-sufficient intermediary between God and the world of humanity.[20] We referred to Jesus'

[16] Cf. Harris, *Colossians & Philemon*, p. 47.

[17] Ibid., p. 48.

[18] Bruce, *Colossians, Philemon, and Ephesians*, p. 67.

[19] Bruce, *Colossians, Philemon, and Ephesians*, p. 71; O'Brien, *Colossians, Philemon*, p. 50.

[20] Bruce, *Colossians, Philemon, and Ephesians*, pp. 73–74.

statement to Philip earlier. He who has encountered Jesus Christ has encountered God, for he is – in his inmost being – God. This is the point at which God is reconciled to the human race, overcoming the estrangement due to human sin. At the point of his conception God the Son took into union humanity; from that moment there was no possible reversal. Human nature was now permanently united to the eternal Son of the Father![21] That this is so momentous is because of Jesus' personal identity as the Son.

The full deity of the Son is stated with the recognition that this is fully compatible with the oneness of God.[22] This is not peculiar to this letter. Paul's characteristic name for Jesus Christ is 'Lord' (*kyrios*).[23] This is the Greek word used to transliterate the tetragrammaton, YHWH, the covenant name of God in the OT. In applying it to Jesus Christ, not on an occasional or casual basis but pervasively, Paul shows he regards Jesus as having the status of God, fully and without the slightest abridgement. This is particularly clear in Philippians 2:9–11, but it so pervades his letters that the only conclusion possible is that he took it for granted. Moreover, he makes no attempt to explain or defend it. He uses it so unselfconsciously that, as Hurtado comments, it entails its being regular, everyday currency among the early Christians. Paul's letters are the earliest of the NT documents and so this title testifies to belief in the full deity of Jesus Christ from the very start of the Christian church, as its basic axiom not as a point of contention. It was assumed as given in Palestinian Christianity. This, Hurtado points out, is confirmed by the Aramaic acclamation Paul cites in 1 Corinthians 16:22: *marana tha* 'Lord, come!' He uses this in a Gentile context without any explanation or translation, where Jesus Christ is addressed in corporate, liturgical prayer, with the reverence shown to God. Moreover, the roots of this prayer are obviously Palestinian, widely familiar beyond its original source and so pre-dating Paul's use of it.[24] This fits well with the thesis of Seyoon Kim that the origins

---

[21] The verb denotes permanence; see O'Brien, *Colossians, Philemon*, p. 53.

[22] Wright, *Colossians and Philemon*, pp. 75–76.

[23] See Donald Guthrie, *New Testament Theology* (Leicester and Downers Grove: IVP, 1981), pp. 291–301; Arthur Wainwright, *The Trinity in the New Testament* (London: SPCK, 1963), pp. 757–792; Gerald O'Collins, SJ, *The Tripersonal God: Understanding and Interpreting the Trinity* (London: Geoffrey Chapman, 1999), pp. 54–59; Jules Lebreton, *History of the Dogma of the Trinity: From Its Origins to the Council of Nicea*, trans. Algar Thorold (8th ed., London: Burns Oates and Washbourne, 1939), pp. 267–280, 303–306; and from an Eastern perspective, Boris Bobrinskoy, *The Mystery of the Trinity: Trinitarian Experience and Vision in the Biblical and Patristic Tradition* (Crestwood: St Vladimir's Seminary Press, 1999), pp. 114ff.

[24] L.W. Hurtado, 'Lord', in *DPL*, pp. 560–569.

of Paul's gospel go back to the very earliest days of Christianity, a thesis Kim has recently defended strongly against his critics, particularly Dunn.[25] Hurtado produces a range of citations from Paul where he applies the tetragrammaton to Christ *via* the title *kyrios* 'without explanation or justification, suggesting that his readers were already familiar with the term and its connotation'.[26] In Witherington's words, referring to John, he 'is willing to predicate of Jesus what he predicates of the Lord God, because he sees them as on the same level'.[27] Hurtado argues that the development of this 'mutation or innovation' in early Christian Christ-devotion that included Christ as an object of worship began among Jewish Christian circles within the earliest years of the Christian movement, a development 'almost explosively rapid in the first few years'. Consequently 'elaborate theories of identifiable stages of Christological development leading up to a divine status accorded to Christ are refuted by the evidence'.[28] From its earliest days the church worshipped Christ, acknowledging him to be the Lord.

5. Christ and the future (20)

This reconciliation will embrace the entire universe. The *all things* that are reconciled can hardly be other than the *all things* Christ created or the *all things* he now governs. A renewed, revitalized and redeemed cosmos is in view. The mention of reconciliation entails the fact that disruption and enmity had entered the creation. Human sin had a devastating effect on the human race; it had a dire effect on the creation as well. Paul writes of the creation groaning in travail awaiting the revelation of the sons of God (Rom. 8:18–23). Salvation is the deliverance of humanity – the chief part of the creation – and in consequence the cosmos.

This Christ accomplished at the cross. The expression *the blood of his cross* refers to his life laid down in death as a sacrifice.[29] From Christ's atoning death and the resurrection and ascension that

---

[25] Kim, *Origin*; Seyoon Kim, *Paul and the New Perspective: Second Thoughts on the Origin of Paul's Gospel* (Grand Rapids: Eerdmans, 2002).

[26] Certainly in the following passages: Rom. 4:8 (Ps. 32:1–2); 9:28–29 (Isa. 28:22; 1:9); 10:16 (Isa. 53:1); 11:34 (Isa. 40:13); 15:11 (Ps. 117:1); 1 Cor. 3:20 (Ps. 94:11); 2 Cor. 6:17–18 (Isa. 52:11; 2 Sam. 7:14). Probably in the following: Rom. 10:13 (Joel 2:32); 1 Cor. 1:31 (Jer. 9:23–24); 10:26 (Ps. 24:1); 2 Cor. 10:17 (Jer. 9:23–24); and possibly in a range of others. See Hurtado, 'Lord', p. 563.

[27] B. Witherington III, 'Lord', in *DLNTD*, p. 672.

[28] L.W. Hurtado, 'Christology', in *DLNTD*, pp. 178–179.

[29] See A. M. Stibbs, *The Meaning of the Word 'Blood' in Scripture* (London: Tyndale Press, 1948).

followed emerges a 'new creation',[30] a heaven and earth 'in which righteousness dwells'.[31] There at the cross Christ dealt with human sin and, in doing so, with the effect it had on the material and spiritual world as a whole. Paul means neither that each and every person will be saved, nor that the fallen angels will be delivered. He does not address those matters. He is not talking of aggregations of individuals, or of some kind of mathematical or statistical balance between belief and unbelief. Rather, his concentration is on large categories; he is painting a picture with broad brush strokes. The consequence of what Christ – the everlasting Son of the Father – has done is to establish his kingdom into which we have been transferred, a kingdom that will stand and grow for ever in a glorious and renewed cosmos.

> Crown him the Lord of years,
> The Potentate of time;
> Creator of the rolling spheres,
> Ineffably sublime:
> All hail, Redeemer, hail!
> For thou hast died for me:
> Thy praise shall never, never fail
> Throughout eternity.[32]

[30] 2 Cor. 5:17.
[31] 2 Pet. 3:13.
[32] 'Crown him with many crowns', Matthew Bridges (1800–94).

Hebrews 2:5–9
23. Everlasting ruler of the renewed cosmos

The supremacy of Christ is arguably the central theme in the letter to the Hebrews.[1] The first chapter presents him as God's Son, the final word given for our salvation (Heb. 1:1–4). He is superior to the prophets (Heb. 1:1–2) and the angels (Heb. 1:4–14). In the same chapter the author refers to psalms where God addresses God ('ĕlōhîm, in Ps. 45) and Lord ('ădōnî, in Ps. 110), arguing that these refer to the Son by whom God has spoken in these last days. Therefore the readers – listeners to the letter as it was read to them – need to advance in their grasp of such a great salvation (Heb. 2:1–4). Interestingly, the Dead Sea Sect venerated angels, and in particular the Archangel Michael who they believed was to rule the eschatological kingdom. Possibly for reasons such as this the author stresses that Christ is superior to all angels, as many in the community to which the letter was written were tempted to revert to some form of Judaism. 'And to which of the angels has he ever said, "Sit at my right hand until I make your enemies a footstool for your feet"? Are they not all ministering spirits sent out to serve for the sake of those who are to inherit salvation?'[2]

1. Humanity's universal dominion (5–8a)

a. Angels do not have jurisdiction over the coming world (5)

In view of this exalted position accorded to angels in the Qumran sect, stemming from the interest in the angelic realm seen in the later

---

[1] See ch. 13. Philip Edgcumbe Hughes, *A Commentary on the Epistle to the Hebrews* (Grand Rapids: Eerdmans, 1977); P. E. Hughes, 'The Christology of Hebrews', *SWJT* 28 (1985), pp. 19–27.
[2] Heb. 1:13–14.

OT,[3] the writer is anxious to bring a corrective. The angels do not have charge over the future world. What is this *coming world* (*oikoumenē*)? It refers to the inhabited world, the world of culture and civilization, the world that is to come but is now present. In this sense, it is roughly equivalent to the kingdom of God, the order of the redeemed human race in which the 'great salvation' (2:3) is to be worked out and realized. It is 'coming' since, while it has already begun, it will not be fully made known until the future day when the cosmos itself will be renewed. But the church is already in contact with it, with the powers of the age to come, that are associated with the gospel (Heb. 6:5; 9:11; 10:1; 12:22). Vos describes it projecting into its life 'as a headland projects out into the ocean'.[4] Angels do not and will not be in control, they will not rule this great corporate order. Who then will rule it? The astounding answer the writer gives is that it is humanity who will direct and administer it. He goes on to cite Psalm 8, which reflects on the creation account in Genesis 1:26–28, in which the created order is subordinated to Adam and the race. However, before he can do that he must explain at length – using Psalm 8 as his basis – the relevant factors that shape these conclusions.

b. Humanity's inherent frailty (6)

It is obvious that human beings are weak and lowly in comparison with the universe and its unimaginable vastness. The bright lights of the city can obscure from our sight the immensity of the night sky but when we get the opportunity and look up at the stars, the constellations and the galaxies, remembering the stupendous distances they are from us, and that there are many, many more that are far beyond our vision, we can only be struck by how puny we seem in comparison. We are like a footnote in a vast cosmic library. I remember occasions in rural France or Vermont, far from civilization, where the night was black and clear and the stars without number and this reality, known theoretically of course, was brought home to me with immense power.

Yet God has committed this cosmos to our charge! Its future is not in the hands of angels but of the human race! It is akin to the last part of *The Lord of the Rings*[5] where Gandalf departs, leaving the scouring of the Shire to the care of the hobbits. This is a marvel of

---

[3] Dan. 10:1 – 12:13; Zech. 1:7 – 6:15.
[4] Geerhardus Vos, *The Teaching of the Epistle to the Hebrews* (Nutley: Presbyterian & Reformed, 1975), p. 51.
[5] The book, not the film.

grace. The verb 'to visit' is frequently used in the NT for displays of God's grace (Luke 1:68, 78; 7:16; Acts 7:23; 15:14).

c. Humanity's exalted status (7–8a)

This is the backcloth for the author's explanation of the position towards which we are heading. The psalmist says three things about humanity in this section of the psalm. First, *we were made a little lower than the angels*. We know very little about angels. We understand that they are creatures and not divine. They are spirits and not material, although they have the ability to take material form and, according to common interpretations of Genesis 6:1–4, to beget children by intercourse with human females.[6] As we saw in chapter 22,[7] they are extremely powerful and capable of incredibly swift movement. Yet, as created, humans were only a fraction short of the angels. The expression *brachy ti* can mean *a little while* and could thereby refer to the fact that man was destined to be lower than the angels for only a comparatively short time.[8]

Second, *humans were crowned with glory and honour*. Adam was made king over creation (Gen. 1:26–30), for a crown is the prerogative of a king. *Glory and honour* is frequently used as a paraphrase for the majesty of God. In short, Adam was created with a specific orientation towards God. This is denoted in his being created in the image and likeness of God, something never used for any other creature. He was in God's image, God's representative, God's appointed king over his creation.

Third, *all things were subjected to the human race*. Humans were put in charge of the world, over everything except God himself. This universal dominion and kingship is the theme the author develops in the commentary he provides on the psalm in the section that follows. This universal aspect is the focus of his argument. The point here is that this high privilege is not the end point of a protracted evolutionary struggle in which humanity proves itself superior or stronger than any other creature; neither is it achieved by force, but by the decree of God the creator. It is a lawful authority. It is not the result of humanity's being a lucky member of the ecosystem.

---

[6] Gordon J. Wenham, *Genesis 1–15*, WBC 1 (Waco: Word, 1987), pp. 135–141; Derek Kidner, *Genesis: An Introduction and Commentary*, TNTC (London: Tyndale Press, 1967), pp. 83–84.

[7] Pp. 210–211.

[8] Hughes, *Hebrews*, p. 85; F. F. Bruce, *Commentary on the Epistle to the Hebrews: The English Text with Introduction, Exposition and Notes* (London: Marshall, Morgan & Scott, 1964), p. 34.

2. Humanity's present failure (8c)

As we look around at the world today what a contrast there is with what Psalm 8 depicts! The author has a strong adversative here both in syntax and content: *we do not yet see (nyn de oupō horōmen) everything in subjection to him.* On the one hand, we have developed our abilities and control a great deal. Exploration of the planet and of space, the advance of technology and the progress of civilizations all demonstrate the point that the human race has been invested by God with supreme created gifts which in many ways reflect the glory of our creator.

However, we are also struck by the massive problems that exist, mostly of our own making. Between the lofty grandeur of Psalm 8 and the reality of our present state – with seemingly intractable environmental problems, discord at national and personal levels, terrorism, murder and hatred, to say nothing of gruesome diseases – there is a huge and seemingly unbridgeable gulf. We do not yet experience the fulfilment of our God-given destiny. We do not yet appear as the king of creation. Above all, we cannot control ourselves due to sin.

3. Jesus' triumphant achievement (9)

The situation seems dire. Yet in reality it is quite the reverse. *But we see . . . Jesus* who has fulfilled Psalm 8. The scene shifts from humanity-in-general to Jesus-in-particular. Our high calling, apparently frustrated due to sin, has been brought to realization.

At this point, in his commentary on the psalm, the author makes a chiasmus, a common literary device at the time. In this, the four clauses of Psalm 8:5–6, cited in verses 7–8, instead of being considered sequentially are arranged in a pattern in which the outer two clauses are related, and the inner two related. The flow of thought therefore runs as follows: 'We see Jesus, who for a little while was made lower than the angels so that by the grace of God he might taste death for everyone, because of the suffering of death crowned with glory and honour.'

He was made *for a little while lower than the angels: brachy ti* can mean a little while, in terms of time, or a little, in terms of status. A decision on this point is finely balanced. Since the idea of status is clearly in the picture in the context there is a case that 'a little lower' is correct. On the other hand temporal considerations cannot entirely be ruled out, as the author has a strong sense of redemptive history. The immediate focus here, however, is on status. What he means is that the Son was true man. He was not an angel but, being the Son with the status of God, he was also fully human. This he expounds in detail later in the chapter (Heb. 2:10–18).

So that by the grace of God he might taste death for everyone. Jesus' tasting death means more than that he sampled it, like finger foods handed round at a reception before the main meal, as if he had a short experience of what death entailed but did not actually die. It is a euphemism meaning that he died. He did so for everyone who is a citizen of *the coming world, of which we speak* (5). His death was not on his own account, but as our high priest, on behalf of his people who he represents.

Because of the sufferings of death crowned with glory and honour. Following his death on the cross, Jesus was exalted to the highest place, having 'sat down at the right hand of the Majesty on high'.[9] In this he fulfilled Psalm 8 as man, for *man* dies and *man* is raised from the dead. Behind Psalm 8 is Genesis 1:26–28; the first Adam failed to live up to his calling, but the last Adam has achieved the destiny appointed for humanity. He has been exalted to the place where the coming world is in subjection to him. He stepped down in his incarnation, born of a woman, living under the law. Now he is lifted up as man and crowned as king over the universe (cf. Eph. 1:19–22). What Adam was given and lost, the second Adam regained and has fulfilled. Even more, he has been raised to a position far greater than Adam ever had: 'in him the tribes of Adam boast more blessings than their father lost.'[10]

So we share – in union with him – in this rule, in Christ's kingship over the coming world. We do so now, as sharers in the great salvation he has won for us (2:1–4), and in the future in the renewed and restructured creation. Adam was created *in* the image of God; Christ, the second Adam, *is* the image of God (Heb. 1:1–2; 2 Cor. 4:4; Col. 1:15; John 1:14–18). In Christ we will share in the administration of the renewed cosmos! Our sense of worth as persons is to be found in Christ and nowhere else.

In the words used by Gustav Mahler with breath-taking effect in the vast final movement of his second symphony, sung by the contralto soloist, blending with the huge choir in excruciatingly exquisite modulation, and rising above the enormous orchestra:

Bereite dich zu leben! (Prepare yourself to live!)

---

[9] Heb. 1:3–4.
[10] 'Jesus shall reign where'er the sun', Isaac Watts, *The Psalms of David* (1719).

Revelation 1:9–20
24. The Living One

1. John shares the troubles of the seven churches

John had been sent into exile, probably because of his preaching (9), possibly to work in the quarries on the island of Patmos. He shares the sufferings of the churches, which are called into the kingdom of God (1:6) and so suffer and need to endure with patience the distresses of the present time. There was a penal settlement located on Patmos and it is likely that John was there.[1] The island itself is quite small, only about thirty square miles, crescent shaped and mountainous, so the sea is close to any point on the land. This shapes the imagery of the book.[2] John was *in the spirit on the Lord's day* (10), which implies he was engaged in worship, whether with a small group of other Christians or alone. Since it was on *the Lord's day*, we can assume – in the absence of countervailing evidence – that it was the first day of the week when he would customarily have met with the church, although there is no evidence that he was with others here.[3] Evidently, he was under the direction of the Holy Spirit at the time the events he records occurred. The expression also distinguishes him from all kinds of false prophets. It is at this point, on *the Lord's day*, in the Holy Spirit, that John hears *a loud voice like a trumpet* and so begins a chain of visions that eventually leads to the composition of this amazing book. This sound comes from

[1] Leon Morris, *The Revelation of St John: An Introduction and Commentary* (Grand Rapids: Eerdmans, 1969), p. 51; Philip Edgcumbe Hughes, *The Book of the Revelation: A Commentary* (Leicester: IVP, 1990), p. 24.

[2] Morris, *Revelation*, p. 51; Henry Barclay Swete, *The Apocalypse of St John: The Greek Text with Introduction, Notes and Indices* (London: Macmillan, 1906), p. 12.

[3] G. K. Beale, *The Book of Revelation: A Commentary on the Greek Text*, NIGTC (Grand Rapids: Eerdmans, 1999), p. 203; Morris, *Revelation*, pp. 51–52; Swete, *Apocalypse*, p. 13; Hughes, *Revelation*, pp. 24–25.

behind him and so takes him completely by surprise; it is not as if he was expecting these events or conjuring them up out of thin air. The identity of the voice is unclear. It could belong to an angel or be from Christ.[4] Moreover, he is said to turn to *see* the voice; the unusual nature of this expression denotes that what is to happen is to be extraordinary. Whatever the source, these visions were not given for John's benefit alone but for the churches to whom the book is addressed and, through them, to the church at large down the ages. In particular it is to the *seven churches* listed in Asia Minor that the contents of the book are directed (11) and in whose context the book should be interpreted. These churches were pitifully small, mostly fragile and facing persecution from both Jewish and Roman sources. Most of them were faced with pressure to compromise on their profession of Christ due to the imposition of pagan worship from the growing Caesar cult. This is the background against which the vision in the first chapter is set.

2. The vision of a son of man (12–16)

a. Among the lampstands (12–13a)

The first thing John notices after he is startled by the loud voice is not the voice but *seven golden lampstands*. As a Jew he would immediately have been reminded of the golden lampstand set in the tabernacle, which had seven branches (Exod. 25:31–40). In addition, in the post-exilic prophecy of Zechariah the seven-branched lampstand is connected directly with the Holy Spirit (Zech. 4:1–6). In this, the lampstand represents the temple and the temple indicates the people of God.[5] It is rich with covenantal significance: the Spirit of God was given to the people of God at Pentecost. Indeed, in verse 20 we are given the meaning of the lampstands. They represent the *seven churches* of Asia Minor to which the book was to be sent. Instead of one lampstand with seven branches, as in the tabernacle, this is a vision of seven lampstands. It indicates the greater glory of the new covenant and also demonstrates that there is but one church with seven branches.

Among these lampstands stands *one like a son of man* (13a), or, like a human being. The expression – son of man – is reminiscent of Daniel 7:13–14 where one like a son of man is given a kingdom that extends over all nations of the earth and is indestructible. It was also used in Ezekiel to refer to the prophet as a human being. Jesus used the term

---

[4] Beale, *Revelation*, pp. 203–205.
[5] Ibid., pp. 206–207.

as his most common designation of himself. So it could mean that this figure is human; that is evidently true as we proceed. However, on top of this it may also mean that the one John sees is the son of man predicted by Daniel and who is identified in the Gospels as Jesus Christ. The context following makes it clear that this is so; this is a human figure who is also the Son of Man.[6] 'The figure, beyond doubt, is Christ, the incarnate Son now resplendent in the glory that is now his.'[7] Here he appears in the midst of the churches. He is there as the world ruler, 'the ruler of kings on earth' (1:5). The churches are small and vulnerable, pitifully weak and fragile, but he is among them and so in the final analysis they are in safe hands. Moreover, while the following vision depicts Christ in his undiluted glory it is in our humanity, no less. He is present in and amongst his church, in our nature, ruling, guarding, protecting.

b. His appearance (13b–16)

The *son of man*'s garments denote a person of the highest status. The word for *robe* (*podērēs*) was used in the LXX for various priestly garments, such as the ephod and breastplate, although not exclusively for those connected with the priests. However, there is sufficiently close connection with the office of priest to indicate that the Son of Man, Jesus Christ, exercises a priestly ministry in the midst of the seven churches.[8] His *golden sash* points us back to Daniel 10:5 and is indicative of a king, a ruler.[9] The son of man in Daniel 7 was given a kingdom, a rule that could never be destroyed and which extended to all nations and languages. This priest who moves among the churches is also a world ruler who is able to act on behalf of his people because he possesses the power and authority to do so.

Christ's physical appearance is striking to say the least. Like the Ancient of Days in Daniel 7:9 *the hairs of his head were white like wool, as white as snow.* His appearance is akin to one who represents God. Some of the church Fathers understood the white hair to point to the eternal pre-existence of the Son. While his eternal pre-existence is of course true, it is doubtful if the phrase can be taken to refer specifically to it, as some of the Fathers thought, although Beale suggests it denotes his divine attributes.[10] As H. B. Swete points out,

---

[6] Beale, *Revelation*, pp. 208–209; Morris, *Revelation*, p. 53; Hughes, *Revelation*, pp. 25–26.

[7] Hughes, *Revelation*, p. 25.

[8] Beale, *Revelation*, p. 209; Swete, *Apocalypse*, p. 15.

[9] Morris does not consider the garments to be priestly and thinks the golden sash points simply to someone important (*Revelation*, p. 53).

[10] Beale, *Revelation*, p. 210; Hughes, *Revelation*, p. 26.

the author frequently attributes to the glorified Christ attributes and titles which belong to the Father.[11] His eyes are said to be *like a flame of fire* (14), indicating burning, penetrating vision, from which nothing can be hidden. His feet *were like burnished bronze* (15), literally meaning a mixture of metals similar to brass or bronze, a brilliant precious metal, aglow as in a crucible.[12] The impression here is of stability and great strength. In Daniel this stands in marked contrast to the feet of clay possessed by the fourth beast of Nebuchadnezzar's dream, which denoted a fragility that was eventually to lead to disintegration (Dan. 2:33, 41). The form, as Hughes remarks, is 'of indescribable beauty and strength' although it falls far short of the reality.[13]

Christ's voice *was like the roar of many waters* (15b). Here the language is from Ezekiel 43:2, the vision of the final fulfilment of the temple, the central place of the covenant between Yahweh and his people.[14] With the roar of the Aegean beating against the rocks of the shore ringing in John's ears at the time, we can appreciate how this image would impress on his mind the sheer beauty, power and splendour of Christ.[15]

Any one of these images is breath-taking but considered together they present a composite picture of the undiluted strength and majesty of the glorified Christ. Yet the reality far outstrips the sign. These are simply glimpses, given to John on a level he and we can grasp, of the transcendent splendour of the Christ who rules the universe, protects and strengthens his church, and who will reduce all his foes to servitude. All this is a picture of him in his humanity, as the Son of Man, the incarnate Son, now risen, ascended and endowed with glory and honour at the right hand of the Father. This is the one who is found among the seven struggling and beleaguered churches of Asia Minor in the first century.

c. His church (16)

In Christ's hands are *seven stars*. These are identified in verse 20 as *the angels of the seven churches*. These could be actual angels who have been given jurisdiction over particular churches. There is something to be said for this interpretation. Angels are said to be ministering spirits whose task is to serve the heirs of salvation (Heb. 1:14) and the churches are a peculiar part, a vital and central part, of

[11] Swete, *Apocalypse*, p. 16.
[12] Ibid., p. 17.
[13] Hughes, *Revelation*, p. 27.
[14] Beale, *Revelation*, p. 210.
[15] Swete, *Apocalypse*, pp. 17–18.

this great work. The primitive church believed that certain angels were given charge over particular members of the church (Matt. 18:10; Acts 12:15). Beale considers that these are angels who represent the seven churches and are in some way accountable for them.[16] Swete's proposal that 'the prevailing spirit' of each church is in view is hardly sustainable; for one thing, it is too abstract and furthermore it makes no sense that letters be written to a 'prevailing spirit'.[17] However, the word *angelos* can also mean 'messenger' and in this sense could refer to the bishop or minister of each congregation.[18] This may be the more likely meaning – despite the overwhelming use of the word elsewhere in this book to refer to spirits – for it is hard to see how a human author could write a letter to angels, as John is asked to do in chapter 2.[19] Either way the fact is clear that Christ has complete charge of his church. After all, it is *his* church. Its leaders are in his hands. Whatever awaits them he will ensure that the gates of hell do not prevail.

In addition, *from his mouth came a sharp two-edged sword.* The word of God is likened in the NT to a sharp sword with two edges (Heb. 4:12–13; Eph. 6:17). In both of these passages, and in this instance, John would have been reminded of the language of Isaiah 11:4 where it is said of the Christ that 'he shall strike the earth with the rod of his mouth, and with the breath of his lips he will slay the wicked'. In these passages the theme of judgment is to the fore. By the two-edgedness of the sword may be indicated the point that the word of Christ cuts two ways, in blessing to his church and in judgment on the wicked. It never fails to bring either salvation or condemnation (cf. 2 Cor. 2:14–16). The church will be protected; its adversaries will be overthrown. In all this John would surely have remembered the transfiguration of Jesus; how could he forget?

3. Reaction and reassurance (17-19)

a. Collapse (17a)

The overwhelming impact of John's meeting the glorified Christ knocks all strength out of him. He falls down as if he were dead. Such is the experience of all who were given a minute refracted

---

[16] Beale, *Revelation*, pp. 217–219.

[17] Swete, *Apocalypse*, pp. 21–22.

[18] Morris considers this possibility but rejects it (*Revelation*, pp. 56–57) as does Swete (*Apocalypse*, p. 21).

[19] See Rev. 2:1, 8, 12, 18; 3:1, 7, 14. Hughes is in agreement on this point (*Revelation*, pp. 30–31).

glimpse of the glory of Christ. It was true of Isaiah (Isa. 6:5), Ezekiel (Ezek. 1:28), Daniel (Dan. 8:17; 10:9, 11) and Paul (Acts 9:3–9). God dwells in inapproachable light; we cannot see his glory in this fallen condition and live (1 Tim. 1:17; 6:16; Exod. 33:18–20). Such a revelation had a physical and emotional impact on John.[20]

b. Restoration (17b)

John needed special grace to sustain him. Christ gives it. First, he places *his right hand* on him, a symbol of his power.[21] Second, he speaks words of reassurance: *Do not fear*. Those in Christ have no need to be terrified of their Saviour and Lord. His words immediately after his resurrection – 'peace be to you' – underline that point. When he returns and we see him as he is, we ourselves will be like him and will continue to be so as we appear before his judgment seat (1 John 3:1–3; 2 Cor. 5:10). The hand that sustains the universe and holds the churches raises individual lives.

c. Revelation (17c-18)

Christ adds further reassurance as he discloses to John more of who he is and what he sovereignly does. He says, *I am the first and the last*. This is a merism, an expression that refers merely to the end parts of a sequence.[22] In this case, Christ affirms that he is the beginning and the end and every point between. This is a clear statement of his deity. It was a title of the God of Israel (Isa. 44:6; 48:12).[23]

He adds *I am . . . the living one*, again an OT title for God, who is the living God in contrast to the idols of paganism.[24] He lives eternally since he is life itself. As such, he is the creator of all contingent life, the governor of the cosmos.

Yet in an astonishing contrast he *became dead*. He who says *do not fear*, himself experienced the reality of human fear and death itself. *This* is the stupendous miracle. The eternal Son of God subjected himself to the experience of human death so that no circumstance on our part, however dire, is beyond his knowledge. As Swete comments, he experienced not the semblance of death but its reality.[25]

---

[20] Morris, *Revelation*, p. 54.
[21] Hughes, *Revelation*, p. 28.
[22] Beale, *Revelation*, p. 213.
[23] Hughes, *Revelation*, p. 28; Morris, *Revelation*, p. 55; Swete, *Apocalypse*, p. 19.
[24] Swete, *Apocalypse*, p. 19.
[25] Ibid., p. 20.

That of course is not the full story. As Christ goes on to say, *See, I am alive unto the ages of the ages [for evermore].* He rose from the dead. He lives a resurrection life as human. His post-resurrection life is now 'coterminous with his divine life'.[26]

So consequently he adds, *I have the keys of Death and Hades.* He has total authority over the grave, the place of the dead.[27] Through his death and burial and by virtue of his victory over death in his resurrection, all is under his charge as our mediator and saviour. He invaded death and Hades in our humanity. He destroyed its power. He has brought in new life in the power of the Spirit.

d. Therefore – write! (19)

John is given a series of astonishing visions to communicate to the seven churches of Asia Minor. In these visions, Christ presents himself as governing the process of world history, protecting and ruling his church. In the midst of the sufferings and vulnerability of the faithful, they are to know that Christ reigns and is bringing history to its intended goal. Part of the challenge they faced was the temptation to submit to the growing cult of Caesar, in which the Emperor was accorded divine status and offerings made accordingly. In some cases, trade guilds required worship at the imperially sanctioned shrines as a condition of doing business. In the face of this acute challenge the followers of Christ were to remain faithful, if necessary unto death. As an encouragement to this end, this book was given.

To all who read the book of Revelation, although separated from the original recipients by so many centuries, the same challenge applies. In our own varied circumstances, whether under persecution or at ease, whether in good health or ill, the same principles are at work. We have seen how from the start of the human experience, with its fall into sin, God the creator had planned that his Son take our nature, restore us to God and prepare us for an unimaginably glorious eternal future. As time went on he revealed more and more of the identity of the deliverer until, when the event at last took place, he was clearly and precisely identified. Instead of our attempting somehow to reach out to the divine by human thought or action, God himself acted, made himself known, and provided access to himself. That revelation, that deliverance and that access is found nowhere else than in Jesus Christ, who is God from eternity, who for us and our salvation took our humanity into

[26] Ibid.
[27] Hades means the place of the dead.

union. This calls, on our part, for a response of faith and obedience, of joyful anticipation of knowing, loving and serving Christ as long as life shall last, and beyond into the endless vistas of the renewed universe.

Thanks be to God!

Appendix
Did the church get it wrong? *Who* is Jesus Christ? From Nicaea (AD 325) to Constantinople II (AD 553)

The Trinitarian crisis of the fourth century: the Son and the Father

Is Christ an intermediary between God and man? The church answered no

Early in the fourth century the church was forced to consider how Jesus Christ was related to God. A number of problems were ticking like time-bombs, destined sooner or later to explode. The chief of these was how to reconcile the unity of the one God with the status of Christ. For those determined to maintain the unity of God and resist anything savouring of dual or threefold gods – the monarchians – there was a danger of regarding the Son and the Holy Spirit as identical to the Father, as differing appearances of the one God at different times for our salvation. This blurred any distinctions between the three, for they were at root not three but one. This was *modalism*. A prominent exponent, Sabellius, held that the only God, Father in the OT, had become Son in the NT and sanctified the church as Holy Spirit after Pentecost. The three were merely successive modes of the unipersonal God. In this Christ was merely an appearance of the one God but did not have any distinct personal identity of his own.[1] With modalism, God's revelation in human history as the Father, the Son and the Holy Spirit does not reveal

---

[1] Bertrand de Margerie, SJ, *The Christian Trinity in History*, trans. Edmund J. Fortman (Petersham: St Bede's Publications, 1982), pp. 85–87; Boris Bobrinskoy, *The Mystery of the Trinity: Trinitarian Experience and Vision in the Biblical and Patristic Tradition*, trans. Anthony P. Gythiel (Crestwood: St Vladimir's Seminary Press, 1999), pp. 217–220.

who he is eternally and so Christ gives us no true knowledge of God. Moreover, the net effect is to undermine God's faithfulness, for we could not rely on him if what he disclosed of himself in Jesus Christ did not truly reflect who he eternally is.

On the other side of the spectrum were those who, recognizing the distinctions of the three, accorded a lower status to the Son and the Spirit. They held that God was a hierarchical being, maintaining the unity of God with the Father imparting deity to the Son and Spirit. This was *subordinationism*. It was an endemic attitude at this time, for the conceptual and linguistic resources did not exist to distinguish between the way God is one and the way he is three. This tendency was generally held within bounds by placing the relations of the three firmly within God, as opposed to the creature.

However, this was an unstable, explosive situation. Modalism was suppressed at the Council of Antioch in 268, but the subordinationist question was unresolved. Suddenly, bursting on the scene came an Alexandrian cleric called *Arius*, whose claims came to light around 318. He maintained that the Son was not co-eternal with the Father, came into existence out of nothing, and was in fact a creature. If true, these teachings would fatally undermine the Christian faith. Jesus Christ could not then be the revelation of the one true God. Moreover, Arius was an effective propagandist. He attracted a large following, drawn by a range of choruses he composed. The dangers for the church were great.[2]

Arius' claims can be summarized as follows:

1. God is solitary, the Father unique. (*This shows Arius' concern to maintain the unity of the one God.*)
2. The Son had an origin, *ex nihilo* (out of nothing). There was a time when he did not exist. He was created, existing by the will of God. Before he was created he did not exist. (*The logic here is that since everything created came into being out of non-existence, and the Word of God is a creature, so the Word of God also came into being out of non-existence. Thus God was not always Father, for before he created the Son he was solitary.*)
3. God made a person (Word, Spirit, Son) when he wanted to create. In short, he created by an intermediary.
4. The Word has a changeable nature and remains good by freewill only so long as he chooses.
5. The *ousiai* (substances or beings) of the Father, the Son and the Spirit are divided and differ from one another. The Father is the Son's origin, and the Son's God. There are two wisdoms,

---

[2] In many ways, Arius was a precursor of the modern Jehovah's Witnesses.

one that existed eternally with God, the other the Son who was brought into existence in this wisdom. Thus there is another Word of God besides the Son, and it is because the Son shares in this that he is called, by grace, Word and Son.[3]

The text where Jesus says 'I and the Father are one',[4] in the hands of Arius and his sympathizers, was taken to mean a unity in harmonious agreement of will, not identity of being. Thus for Arius will is primary rather than essence (being). The Son was an underworker, an assistant to the Father, operating under orders. Thus the monarchy of God (his single rule) was preserved, since the Son was and is not true God.[5]

From his opponents' perspective, Arius' strong attempt to identify the Son with human beings severed his connection with God. They were alarmed at his idea that the Son came into existence from nonexistence. This clearly taught that the Son was a creature. After ecclesiastical manoeuvrings Arius' views were outlawed by the Council of Nicaea in 325.

After Nicaea, the situation was confused. Detailed consideration of the differences (theological, political, personal, ecclesiastical) is enough to make one's head spin. Nor was the controversy created by the supposed intrusion of Greek thought into the domain of biblical faith, although Greek ideas were used. It arose out of questions basic to the Christian gospel – belief in one God together with the recognition that Jesus Christ is divine. 'The theologians of the Christian Church were slowly driven to a realization that the deepest questions which face Christianity cannot be answered in purely biblical language, because the questions are about the meaning of biblical language itself.'[6]

Later in the century Eunomius of Cyzicus, a far more able figure than Arius, appeared on the scene. He and his followers – the

[3] Athanasius, *Of Synods*, 16, for Arius' *Profession of Faith* (*NPNF*[2], vol. 4).
[4] John. 10:30.
[5] Robert C. Gregg and Dennis E. Groh, *Early Arianism: A Way of Salvation* (Philadelphia: Fortress Press, 1981), pp. 1–129.
[6] R. C. P. Hanson, *The Search for a Christian Doctrine of God: The Arian Controversy 318–381* (Edinburgh, T&T Clark, 1988), p. xxi. On the conflict, see also the following works: de Margerie, *Christian Trinity*, pp. 87–91; J. N. D. Kelly, *Early Christian Doctrines* (London: Adam & Charles Black, 1968), pp. 226–231; Bobrinskoy, *Mystery*, 220–221; Basil Studer, *Trinity and Incarnation: The Faith of the Early Church*, trans. Matthias Westerhoff, ed. Andrew Louth (Collegeville: Liturgical Press, 1993), pp. 103–105; Gregg and Groh, *Early Arianism*, pp. 1–129; Charles Kannengiesser, *Arius and Athanasius: Two Alexandrian Theologians* (Aldershot: Variorum, 1991); Rowan Williams, *Arius: Heresy and Tradition* (London: Darton, Longman, and Todd, 1987); Lewis Ayres, *Nicaea and Its Legacy: An Approach to Fourth-Century Trinitarian Theology* (Oxford: Clarendon Press, 2004).

Eunomians – were rationalists, confident in the extensive capacities of human logic. By logic, they maintained, we are able to comprehend God. They assumed there to be a correspondence between the minds of God and man such that meaning is identical for both. For them, the Son is absolutely unlike the Father. Because of the identity between the mind of God and human reasoning, the Son's generation from the Father is to be understood in terms of human generation. Since eternal generation is inconceivable, the generation of the Son must have had a beginning. There was a time when the Son did not exist. The Son is the first to be created and is the instrument by which God created the world.

Eunomius' views were therefore much as Arius'. Opponents described him as 'the leader of Arius' theatrical dancing-floor'.[7] His rationalism is evident in that 'God does not know anything more about his own essence than we do, nor is that essence better known to him and less to us; rather, what we ourselves know about it is exactly what he knows, and, conversely, that which he knows is what you will find without change in us'.[8] The creed he cited at the start of his *Apology* is the creed Arius presented to Alexander.[9] God is one, and has sole supremacy. He is unbegotten being. God is prior to the Son and so the Son is subordinate to the Father, a creature, subject to the Father in essence and will. He was made. He came into existence, with a beginning[10] begotten by the will of God, so the Father is the cause of his existence. So the Son and God (the Father) are different beings.[11]

For the Eunomians and others in the Arian tradition, the line between God and all other beings came between the Father and the Son, with the Son on the side of the creature. The supporters of Nicaea, on the other hand, placed it between the triad (the Father, the Son, and the Holy Spirit) and all other beings.[12] However, Eunomius did not think the Son was a creature like all others, for he

[7] Richard Paul Vaggione, text and introduction, *Eunomius: The Extant Works* (Oxford: Clarendon Press, 1987), Fragment iii, 179.

[8] Ibid., Fragment ii, 179; Graham A. Keith, 'Our Knowledge of God: The Relevance of the Debate Between Eunomius and the Cappadocians', *Tyndale Bulletin* 41 (1988), pp. 60–88.

[9] Eunomius, *Apology*, 4–5; Vaggione, *Eunomius*, pp. 38–39.

[10] Eunomius, *The Fragments*, i; Eunomius, *Apology*, 7–15, 17, 20–23, 26–27; Eunomius, *An Apology for the Apology*, 1.ii.b., 2.v., 3.ii-iii, vi-vii, xi; Eunomius, *The Confession of Faith*, 2–3; Vaggione, *Eunomius*, pp. 40–55, 60–63, 70–71, 102–103, 112, 116–118, 122, 126, 150–153, 177.

[11] Eunomius, *Apology*, 15–27; Eunomius, *An Apology for the Apology*, 3.iii–vii; Eunomius, *Confession*, 3–4; Eunomius, *Fragments*, i; Vaggione, *Eunomius*, 52–71, 117–122, 152–157, 177.

[12] Richard Paul Vaggione, *Eunomius of Cyzicus and the Nicene Revolution* (Oxford: Oxford University Press, 2000), pp. 123–124.

created all others.[13] In short, Arians of all shapes froze the triad into a hierarchy, the one God who became the Father, plus two different, subordinate and non-eternal beings.

The Council of Constantinople (381)

The resolution came largely through the work of the group of bishops and theologians known as the Cappadocians because they came from Cappadocia. The leader of this group was Basil the Great, bishop, monastic founder and organizer. His brother, Gregory of Nyssa and his friend Gregory of Nazianzus also made huge contributions.[14]

A number of factors lay behind this resolution. Firstly, the Cappadocians used terms, hitherto bedevilled by confusing philosophical baggage, in a non-technical way so as to give voice to the reality they were attempting to describe. This brought about a simplification of the discussion. Basil in particular made it a rule to use particular words for the way God is one and the way he is three. Second, it was widely recognized that the Son is one identical being with the Father and that this was integral to the gospel itself. So the Council of Constantinople unequivocally rejected the claim that the Son is simply an intermediary between God and man. Such an idea would have destroyed the gospel. Jesus Christ would not have given us true knowledge of God as he would not have been one with God from eternity. As such he could not have saved us.[15]

The Nestorian crisis and the Council of Ephesus (431)

Is the incarnation a conjunction between the Son and humanity?
The church answered no

In the early fifth century a major crisis erupted over the identity of Jesus Christ. Since he was and is the eternal Son of God, how does this relate to the fact (obvious from the Gospels) that he is also human? How are his deity and humanity related? How do these things affect what we read in the Gospels? Flowing from this, what is the significance for our salvation? These questions were thrust into the foreground in the year 428 by Nestorius, the Bishop of Constantinople.[16] He began to attack the term *theotokos* (God-bearer), a popular

---

[13] Ibid., pp. 124–126.
[14] See Robert Letham, *The Holy Trinity: In Scripture, History, Theology, and Worship* (Phillipsburg: Presbyterian & Reformed, 2004), pp. 146–166.
[15] See Letham, *Holy Trinity*, pp. 167–183.
[16] On Nestorius see G. Prestige, *Fathers and Heretics* (London: SPCK, 1940), pp. 120–149; Kelly, *Doctrines*, pp. 310–317.

liturgical title for Mary. Since he distinguished sharply between the deity of Christ and his humanity,[17] he held that Mary could only strictly be called mother of *the man* Jesus. She could be termed *christotokos* (Christ-bearer) with no qualms, since in this there was no danger of confusing deity and humanity. Talk of Mary as *theotokos* conjured up in his mind the spectre of Arianism. Arius and Eunomius had reduced the Son's deity to creaturehood. Nestorius feared that use of *theotokos* would lead to a blurring of the creator-creature distinction. He wanted to avoid any notion of a mixture of deity and humanity, and so his aim was to preserve the integrity of the human nature.

Nestorius was also alert to the danger of *Apollinarianism*. Apollinaris (*c.* 315–before 392), a strong supporter of the Council of Nicaea, had wandered into heresy in his old age by teaching that the Logos – the Son – took the place of a human soul in the incarnate Christ. The Word assumed flesh – a body – only. He was condemned by Constantinople I (381). The problem with Apollinaris' teaching, in Gregory Nazianzen's words, was that 'whatever is not assumed cannot be healed'. If the Son did not assume into union a full humanity, including a soul, there was no incarnation. We could not then be saved, since Christ would have been less than man, since a human being minus a soul is not human. Nestorius' correct concern was to affirm the full integrity of Christ's human nature. His problem was that, while he had a firm grasp of the distinctiveness of Christ's divinity and humanity, he was less sure of the unity of his person. So he spoke of a 'conjunction' of the divinity and humanity rather than a 'union'. This conjunction resulted in a *prosōpon* of union, a single object of appearance, which was identical with neither of the two natures. The *prosōpon* of union, not the Logos or Word, was the subject of the incarnate Christ.

Nestorius was vehemently opposed by Cyril of Alexandria, who began from the premise of Christ's unity.[18] For Cyril, Nestorius threatened not only the unity of Christ's person but also the incarnation itself, for his teaching effectively denied that there was a real participation by the Son of God in our humanity. The two natures, so it seemed, were more like two pieces of board held together by glue. Cyril stressed that salvation was a work of God, that the man

[17] See D. Wallace-Hadrill, *Christian Antioch: A Study of Early Christian Thought in the East* (Cambridge: Cambridge University Press, 1982).

[18] For Cyril see St Cyril of Alexandria, *On the Unity of Christ*, trans. J. A. McGuckin (Crestwood: St Vladimir's Seminary Press, 1995); J. A. McGuckin, *St Cyril of Alexandria and the Christological Controversy: Its History, Theology, and Texts* (Crestwood: St Vladimir's Seminary Press, 2004); Prestige, *Fathers*, pp. 150–179; Kelly, *Doctrines*, pp. 317–323; N. Russell, *Cyril of Alexandria* (London: Routledge, 2000).

Jesus could not defeat sin and death by his human nature alone. To do this, the eternal Logos assumed into *union* the human nature of Christ.[19]

In his *Second Letter to Nestorius* Cyril starts with the unity of Christ's person. The Word 'united to himself . . . flesh enlivened by a rational soul, and in this way became a human being'. There is an 'unspeakable and unutterable convergence into unity, one Christ and one Son out of two'. To reject this personal union is to fall into the error of positing two sons. 'We do not worship a human being in conjunction with the Logos, lest the appearance of a division creep in . . . No, we worship one and the same, because the body of the Logos is not alien to him but accompanies him even as he is enthroned with the Father.' The Word did not unite himself to a human person. The Virgin Mary is *theotokos* since it is *the Word* that united himself to this human body and soul.[20] In short, for Cyril, Nestorius' stress on the integrity and distinctiveness of Christ's humanity had jeopardized his unity.

In his *Third Letter to Nestorius*, Cyril again stresses the personal union of the Word with the flesh. All expressions in the Gospels refer to the one incarnate person of the Word. Mary is *theotokos* since she 'gave birth after the flesh to God who was united by *hypostasis* with flesh', man ensouled with a rational soul.[21] Cyril adds twelve anathemas to this letter. In these, he declares that 'if anyone will not confess that the Emmanuel is very God, and that therefore the Holy Virgin is the Mother of God (*theotokos*), inasmuch as in the flesh she bore the Word of God made flesh . . .; let him be anathema'. He insists, *inter alia*, that it is the Word who suffered, was crucified, and died *according to the flesh*.[22] For Cyril, the Word who existed before the incarnation is the same person after the incarnation, now enfleshed. This union excludes division but does not eliminate difference.

The council called to Ephesus to resolve the matter expelled Nestorius from the episcopal office and the priesthood.[23] The council

[19] See J. Meyendorff, *Christ in Eastern Christian Thought* (Crestwood: St Vladimir's Seminary Press, 1975), pp. 18–19.

[20] L. D. Davis, *The First Seven Ecumenical Councils (325–787)* (Collegeville: The Liturgical Press, 1990), pp. 149–150; R. A. Norris Jr, *The Christological Controversy* (Philadelphia: Fortress Press, 1980), pp. 131–135, esp 133.

[21] E. R. Hardy (ed.), *Christology of the Later Fathers*, The Library of Christian Classics (Philadelphia: Westminster Press, 1954), pp. 349–354, esp. 352–353.

[22] Hardy, *Later Fathers*, p. 354; Davis, *Councils*, pp. 150–151; H. R. Percival (ed.), *The Seven Ecumenical Councils of the Undivided Church: Their Canons and Dogmatic Decrees*, A Select Library of Nicene and Post-Nicene Fathers of the Christian Church: Second Series (Edinburgh: T&T Clark, 1997 reprint), p. 206.

[23] Davis, *Councils*, p. 160.

declared that Christ's humanity, wholly human, was appropriated by the Word as his own, and so forms the basis for our own salvation.[24] A conjunction between deity and humanity – existing side by side – is not incarnation and could not save us.

Eutyches and the Council of Chalcedon (451)[25]

Is the humanity of Christ absorbed into the divine? The church answered no

Before long a fresh crisis arose, generated by Eutyches from Alexandria, who Kelly calls an 'aged and muddle-headed archimandrite'.[26] Eutyches was an extreme exponent of Cyrilline Christology, without Cyril's theological sophistication. For Eutyches, before the incarnation Christ was of two natures but after it he is one nature, one Christ, one Son, in one *hypostasis* and one *prosōpon*. Christ's flesh was not identical with ordinary human flesh, since Eutyches thought this would entail the Word assuming an individual man, thus destroying the union. Behind this, he understood nature to mean concrete existence – so Christ could not have two natures or he would have two concrete existences and so be divided.[27] Thus, he had an overpowering emphasis on the unity of Christ's person, exactly the opposite of Nestorius. Where Nestorius had sought to uphold the distinctness of the two natures and so threatened the unity of Christ, Eutyches so underlined Christ's unity that he blurred the distinctness of the two natures, his humanity swamped by his deity, although to be fair he did insist on the full and complete humanity. His ideas raised similar problems to those of Apollinaris, for our salvation depends on the reality of the incarnation, of a real assumption of unabbreviated humanity by the Son of God. If Christ was not truly and fully man we could not be saved, for only a second Adam could undo the damage caused by the first.

Eventually Marcian, the Emperor, called a council to be held at Nicaea in 451, to which Pope Leo sent three legates.[28] However,

[24] Meyendorff, *Christ*, p. 21.

[25] See A. Grillmeier, *Christ in Christian Tradition: Volume One: From the Apostolic Age to Chalcedon (451)*, trans. J. Bowden (rev. 2nd ed., Atlanta: John Knox Press, 1975), pp. 520–557; J. Pelikan, *The Christian Tradition 1: The Emergence of the Catholic Tradition (100–600)* (Chicago: University of Chicago Press, 1971), pp. 263–266.

[26] Kelly, *Doctrines*, p. 331.

[27] See Kelly, *Doctrines*, pp. 330–334; Davis, *Councils*, p. 171.

[28] For the Council of Chalcedon, see R. Sellers, *The Council of Chalcedon: A Historical and Doctrinal Survey* (London: SPCK, 1953), pp. 209ff; Kelly, *Doctrines*, pp. 338–343; Davis, *Councils*, pp. 180–182; Percival, *Seven Ecumenical Councils*, pp. 243–295.

due to invasions by the Huns, the Emperor ordered the council to move to Chalcedon, across the Bosphorus. The bishops reaffirmed Cyril's *Second Letter to Nestorius* and Pope Leo's *Tome*, addressed to the Council.[29] A commission was appointed to draw up a doctrinal statement. In composing the Definition, the bishops drew on a variety of sources; Leo's *Tome* was the single most decisive contributor, even though there were more quotations from Cyril.[30] The Definition clearly distinguishes between one person and two natures.

> Therefore, following the holy Fathers, we all with one accord teach men to acknowledge one and the same Son, our Lord Jesus Christ, at once complete in Godhead and complete in manhood, truly God and truly man, consisting also of a reasonable soul and body; of one substance with the Father as regards his Godhead, and at the same time of one substance with us as regards his manhood; like us in all respects, apart from sin; as regards his Godhead, begotten of the Father before the ages, but yet as regards his manhood begotten, for us and for our salvation, of Mary the Virgin, the God-bearer; one and the same Christ, Son, Lord, Only-begotten, recognized in two natures, without confusion, without change, without division, without separation; the distinction of natures being in no way annulled by the union, but rather the characteristics of each nature being preserved and coming together to form one person and subsistence, not as parted or separated into two persons, but one and the same Son and only-begotten God, the Word, Lord Jesus Christ; even as the prophets from earliest times spoke of him, and our Lord Jesus Christ himself taught us, and the creed of the Fathers has handed down to us.

That Christ subsists in two natures is a decisive rejection of Eutyches. The Definition rejects any notion of the union that might erode or threaten the differences of the natures. At the same time, it also insists that Christ is not divided or separated into two persons, as the Nestorian heresy implied.

The anti-Nestorian stance is evident in a number of ways. The repetition of the phrase 'the same', and the reaffirmation of the Virgin Mary as *theotokos* are two obvious points. Again, towards the end,

---

[29] After Leo's *Tome* was read, at the second session of the council, 'the most reverend bishops cried out: This is the faith of the fathers, this is the faith of the apostles. So we all believe, thus the orthodox believe. Anathema to him who does not thus believe. Peter has spoken thus through Leo. So taught the apostles' (Percival, *Seven Ecumenical Councils*, p. 259).

[30] Pelikan, *The Christian Tradition 1*, pp. 263–264; Sellers, *Chalcedon*, pp. 209–210.

the Definition denies that Christ is parted or separated into two persons, but rather asserts that the two natures 'come together to form one person and subsistence', echoing Cyril's *Second Letter to Nestorius*. In all these it clearly affirms the unity of the person of Christ. On the other hand, the Definition equally repudiates the Eutychian heresy, which had occasioned the Council in the first place. Christ is 'complete in manhood', so much so that he is 'of one substance with us'. The distinction of natures is in no way annulled by the union. There are also clear restatements of opposition both to Apollinarianism, in the point that Christ has 'a reasonable soul and body', and also to Arianism in that Christ is 'of one substance with the Father'.

Above all, the famous four privative adverbs together form the central hinge of the Definition.[31] The incarnate Christ is *'in two natures, without confusion, without change'*. Here is an explicit rejection of Eutyches. The union neither changes Christ's humanity into anything else, nor absorbs it into the divinity. The humanity remains fully humanity. On the other side of the spectrum, the natures are *'without division, without separation'*. By this it is declared impermissible so to focus on either nature of Christ that the personal union is undermined in the manner Nestorius had done. These four adverbs outlaw both Nestorianism and Eutychianism.

The Council also anathematizes those who talk of two natures of the Lord before the union but only one afterwards. This is directed at Eutyches, probably at the behest of Pope Leo and the Papal legates.[32] It was to cause problems later, for the monophysites were accustomed to think of 'nature' as synonymous with what we would now call 'person' and so considered Chalcedon a capitulation to Nestorius by apparently positing two persons. However, the problem was more a lack of knowledge of Greek by the Latins, who had pressed this point. Taking *physis* (Greek) to mean *natura* (Latin), it seemed to Leo and his legates that the Alexandrian mantra of one incarnate nature (*physis*) of the Logos was a heretical belief in only one *natura*, thus ascribing only one nature to Christ and so jeopardizing his humanity. It failed to appreciate that the Greeks used *physis* and *hypostasis* interchangeably, and so were simply defending the unity of Christ's person, using *physis* to mean the same thing as the Westerners meant by *hypostasis* (person). Confused? So were they! Another century passed before Emperor Justinian I brought a clear distinction between these two terms. In reality, the real objection in this anathema is, as Sellers observes, to Eutyches' false interpretation

---

[31] The words in question are adverbs in Greek.
[32] Sellers, *Chalcedon*, pp. 224–226.

of the formula, not to Cyril's position, which was not in view at the time.[33] It was, then, in defence of the gospel that the Council rejected any idea that Christ's humanity was truncated or absorbed by deity; if that had been so we could not be saved.

Assessment of Chalcedon

Chalcedon failed to do justice to some real concerns of the Cyrillians. The point that 'the distinction of natures being in no way annulled by the union but rather the characteristics of each nature being preserved and coming together' could be taken to mean that human attributes must be predicated only of the human nature, and the divine of the divine. This sounded Nestorian to these people. It gave the impression that Christ was some form of schizoid, for whom some things could be related only to one part of him and other things to another part. Their strong concern for the unity of Christ seemed to have been given short shrift. It seemed as though the idea that salvation begun by the union of the human nature of Christ with the divine was under attack. Chalcedon certainly allows the deity and humanity to be seen as two each in its 'ownness'.[34]

Moreover, Chalcedon left the concept of the personal union unclear. For instance, it did not specify *who* exactly it was who had suffered and been crucified. Nor did it say – a vital theme for Cyril's supporters – that the deification of man began in the union of Christ's humanity with his divinity. It also appeared that the two natures were seen as prior to the person, for they were said to come together to form the person. The monophysites later thought that Chalcedon was soft on Nestorianism by asserting 'two natures after the union', precisely because it made no mention of the hypostatic (personal) union, refusing to include the confession 'out of two'. Chalcedon satisfied the West but not the East.[35]

Furthermore, two passages in Leo's *Tome*, effectively canonized by Chalcedon, were held by the monophysites to be indisputably Nestorian, where 'Leo so separates, and personalizes, what is divine and what is human in Christ that the hypostatic union is dissolved'.[36] Leo states that the properties of both natures are kept intact so that 'one and the same mediator between God and human beings, the human being who is Jesus Christ, can at one and the same time die in virtue of the one nature and, in virtue of the other, be incapable of

---

[33] Sellers, *Chalcedon*, p. 226.

[34] Ibid., p. 224.

[35] Sellers, *Chalcedon*, pp. 256–260; Davis, *Councils*, p. 187; Meyendorff, *Christ*, p. 28; Pelikan, *The Christian Tradition 1*, pp. 265–266.

[36] Sellers, *Chalcedon*, p. 266.

death'.[37] In the absence of mention of the hypostatic union, followers of Cyril were loath to accept Chalcedon. Moreover, they strongly held to the personal identity of the incarnate Christ with the pre-existent Son, and this the Council did not affirm,[38] although the repeated phrase 'one and the same' must be borne in mind in response to this claim.

Chalcedon was never intended to be the final definitive verdict on Christology. As Sellers points out, 'it allows deductions to be made from its dogmatic decisions, and, in effect, encourages enquiry into the mystery'.[39] 'It is intended to explain just one definite question of the church's Christology, indeed the most important one. It does not lay claim to having said all that may be said about Christ.' It was far from innovative but, rather, was in line with the preceding tradition. 'Few councils have been so rooted in tradition as the Council of Chalcedon. The dogma of Chalcedon is ancient tradition in a formula corresponding to the needs of the hour. So we cannot say that the Chalcedonian Definition marks a great turning point in the Christological belief of the early church.'[40] At the same time, it left a good deal of unfinished business on the table.

The monophysites and Constantinople II (553)[41]

How is Christ to be understood as one indivisible person? The church answered that the person of the Son takes a human nature into union as his own

Having rejected the idea that the Son absorbs the humanity, how was the union of the two natures of Christ to be understood and proclaimed? Did it happen by metamorphosis? Was it akin to ingredients in soup? English pancakes are made of flour, milk and eggs beaten and mixed together, and then fried in a frying pan. Each ingredient is a necessary part of the finished product; without them

[37] Norris, *Controversy*, p. 148.

[38] Davis, *Councils*, pp. 196–197.

[39] Sellers, *Chalcedon*, p. 350.

[40] Grillmeier, *Christ in Christian Tradition 1*, p. 550.

[41] A. Grillmeier, SJ, *Christ in Christian Tradition: Volume Two: From the Council of Chalcedon (451) to Gregory the Great (590–604): Part Two: The Church of Constantinople in the Sixth Century*, trans. T. Hainthaler and J. Cawte (London: Mowbray, 1995), pp. 438–475, 503–513; Sellers, *Chalcedon*, pp. 254–350; H. M. Relton, *A Study in Christology: The Problem of the Relation of the Two Natures in the Person of Christ* (London: SPCK, 1917); T. Ware, *The Orthodox Church* (London: Penguin Books, 1969), p. 37; J. Pelikan, *The Christian Tradition 2: The Spirit of Eastern Christendom* (Chicago: University of Chicago Press, 1974), pp. 49–61; Pelikan, *The Christian Tradition 1*, pp. 277, 337–341; W. Frend, *The Rise of the Monophysite Movement* (Cambridge: Cambridge University Press, 1972); Meyendorff, *Christ*.

one does not have an English pancake. Yet none of the ingredients on its own makes a pancake. They must be added together and mixed. Put the eggs, flour and milk side by side in separate containers and there is no pancake. Moreover, the pancake differs from each of the ingredients; it is something other than any one, or all, of the items with which it is composed. So is the person of Christ like that? Is Christ composed of deity and humanity but not to be identified with either but instead a third thing, a mixture? The answer is clearly no. This would not be incarnation; neither the deity nor the humanity would be preserved and so we could not be saved.

Following Chalcedon, sections of the church went into a schism that still continues. This breakup occurred over whether the Chalcedonian formula, by its stress on the integrity of the two natures and the appropriate attributions to be made to either one, actually left the door open to a Nestorian interpretation that undermined the unity of Christ's person. Many were disconcerted that not nearly enough emphasis was laid on Christ's unity and on his personal identity with the eternal, pre-existent Logos. These people, known as *monophysites* (those who held to 'one nature') took as their lodestar Cyril's phrase 'the one incarnate nature of the Word made flesh'.

The foundational point of disagreement between the monophysites and the Chalcedonians surrounded the unity of Christ and the place accorded to his human nature. The monophysites insisted on the absolute unity of the person of Christ and his continuity with the pre-incarnate Logos. The Chalcedonians, on the other hand, were fearful of minimizing the humanity of Christ.

Leontius of Byzantium[42]

Leontius shared the Alexandrian stress on Christ's unity but he was also concerned to preserve the true humanity.[43] He came up with the idea of Christ's humanity as *enhypostatos* (existing in a *hypostasis* – roughly 'person' – of another nature). Thus, the human nature in Christ is both *anhypostatos*, having no independent existence,[44] and also *enhypostatos*, subsisting *in* a *hypostasis* of another nature, the

[42] Grillmeier, *Christ in Christian Tradition*, 2:2, pp. 181–229; Relton, *A Study in Christology*, pp. 69–83; B. Daley, 'Leontius of Byzantium: A Critical Edition of His Works, with Prolegomena', D.Phil. dissertation, Oxford University, 1978.

[43] Davis, *Councils*, p. 221.

[44] This is often rather unhelpfully called 'the impersonal humanity'. Of course it is impossible to contemplate humanity that does not have personhood. What this idea attests is that the assumed humanity of Christ exists only as the humanity of the Son of God. In turn, *enhypostasia* underlines the point that this humanity *is* that of the eternal Son of the Father.

single *hypostasis* (person) of Christ, the eternal Word in whom are two natures, divine and human. All operations of both natures are attributed to the *hypostasis* (person) of the divine Word.[45]

Grillmeier considers this the work of Leontius of Jerusalem, further developed by Emperor Justinian. Both Relton and Sellers take the older view that Leontius of Byzantium propounded *enhypostasia*.[46] For Leontius of Byzantium, we have translated extracts from *Three Books against the Nestorians and Eutychians* (his chief work).[47]

Leontius of Jerusalem[48]

The other Leontius, whose contribution to the debate occurred between 532-36, was emphatic that the one subject in Christ is clearly the *hypostasis* (person) of the Logos.[49] Grillmeier comments that there is thus complete identity of the person before and after the incarnation. The pre-existent Logos himself is the subject of the incarnation. He assumes a human nature and so is the subject of both divine and human natures.[50]

Thus, for Leontius, the assumed humanity becomes the source of divine life, since it is the Word's own flesh. Because Christ's humanity has divine life since it is the humanity of the eternal Son, we can – in union with Christ – receive divine life by grace and participation.[51] Later, Calvin affirmed that since Christ's human nature is the human nature of the eternal Son of God, it is suffused by the divine qualities of the Son, *while remaining human*.[52] The biblical evidence for this,

---

[45] Davis, *Councils*, p. 234; Meyendorff, *Christ*, pp. 61–68.

[46] Sellers, *Chalcedon*, pp. 308–320, esp. 316–319; Relton, *A Study in Christology*, pp. 69–83.

[47] Hardy, *Later Fathers*, pp. 375–377.

[48] Grillmeier, *Christ in Christian Tradition 2*, pp. 276–312.

[49] Ibid., p. 277.

[50] Ibid., p. 279.

[51] Meyendorff, *Christ*, pp. 78–79; Leontius of Jerusalem, *Contra Nestorius*, 1:49 in *PG* 86:1512b. But see comments by Andrew Louth, *John Damascene: Tradition and Originality in Byzantine Theology* (Oxford: Oxford University Press, 2002), pp. 160–161.

[52] This statement is based on my reading of the patristic source. Bill Evans has pointed out to me the penetrating observations of Bruce McCormack to the effect that for Reformed theology the Holy Spirit, not the hypostatic union, preserves the incarnate Christ from the taint of sin. This is indeed so, as I have myself affirmed elsewhere (R. Letham, *The Work of Christ* [Leicester: IVP, 1993], pp. 114–115; Letham, *The Holy Trinity*, pp. 56–57). However, the work of the Holy Spirit and the personalization of the incarnate one by the eternal Son are not at loggerheads as if they were from disparate sources. The Son and the Spirit act distinctly, yet harmoniously and indivisibly in all the ways and works of God. Both are involved, with this distinction – the assumed humanity is in *personal union* not with the Holy Spirit but with the eternal Son. See B. L. McCormack, *For Us and Our Salvation: Incarnation and*

among other places, is evident in the words of the angel in Luke 1:35 that the Holy Spirit in overshadowing Mary and bringing about the new creation in the conception of Jesus, would also effect the result that he would be called 'the holy Son of God'.

Justinian I

The third contributor to the resolution of the post-Chalcedon Christological problem was the Emperor Justinian I (483-565, emperor from 527). In many ways, he is the principal architect of the resolution of the crisis at Constantinople II. His interest in theology propelled him on to the stage as a force to be reckoned with theologically as well as politically. He was no mere dilettante. He was a man 'orthodox and deeply pious with a taste for theological discussion'. He intervened forcefully in ecclesiastical matters more than any emperor before. He recognized that the formula of the Scythian monks, 'one of the trinity suffered for us' (designed to smoke out any with Nestorian sympathies), was true to Chalcedon and at the same time likely to win over Cyril's supporters among the monophysites. Moreover, the Pope approved it, effectively providing the backing of the Western church.[53]

Between 532-36, Leontius of Jerusalem insisted on identifying the incarnate Christ with the pre-existent person of the Word. Christ's manhood had no pre-existence for 'the *hypostasis* of Christ is the Divine Logos, One of the Holy Trinity'.[54] Jesus *is* the second person of the Trinity, incarnate.[55] Thus *hypostasis* (person), not nature, is the foundation of being, entailing a *personal* foundation of reality and that God is primarily love.[56] It also means that the single *hypostasis* in Christ was the *hypostasis* of *both* the divine *and* human natures. Christ's humanity had no separate *hypostasis* of its own. This clarified Chalcedon (the union of two natures in one *hypostasis*) by identifying the *hypostasis* of Christ as the pre-existent *hypostasis* of the divine Word.[57] In short, the person of Jesus Christ *is* the eternal Son of God, now incarnate.

Atonement in the Reformed Tradition, Studies in Reformed Theology and History (Princeton: Princeton Theological Seminary, 1993), pp. 17–22. Evans discusses this question himself in W. B. Evans, *Imputation and Impartation: Union with Christ in American Reformed Theology* (Eugene: Wipf & Stock, 2008), pp. 167–168.

[53] Davis, *Councils*, pp. 225–229.

[54] K. P. Wesche, *On the Person of Christ: The Christology of Emperor Justinian* (Crestwood: St Vladimir's Seminary Press, 1991), p. 12.

[55] Wesche, *Christology of Justinian*, p. 31, from Justinian's 'Letter to the monks of Alexandria against the Monophysites'.

[56] Ibid., pp. 13–14.

[57] Davis, *Councils*, p. 232.

The Edict of Justinian 'The Edict on the True Faith' (551)

In this edict, the emperor set forth the orthodox doctrine, stating that 'we confess that our Lord Jesus Christ is one and the same Divine Logos of God who was incarnate and became man'.[58] He enlarges on this by saying that 'the *hypostatic* union means that the Divine Logos, that is to say one *hypostasis* of the three divine *hypostases*, is not united to a man who has his own *hypostasis* before [the union], but that in the womb of the Holy Virgin the Divine Logos made for himself, in his own *hypostasis*, flesh that was taken from her and that was endowed with a reasonable and intellectual soul, i.e. human nature'.[59]

So the one hypostasis of the Logos was incarnate and is recognized in both natures.[60] So 'we never refer to the human nature of Christ by itself, nor did it ever possess its own *hypostasis* or *prosopon*, but it began to exist in the *hypostasis* of the Logos'.[61]

Grillmeier remarks that Justinian had 'a commendable understanding of the problems of incarnational theology' and that 'in Justinian we find for the first time the sketch of a complete interpretation of Christ's person and its union of divine and human nature in the one divine *hypostasis* of the Logos'.[62] While he bases his edict on Chalcedon, he has a stronger grasp of the union, due to the presence of Cyrilline elements and the model provided by Leontius of Jerusalem.

The Second Council of Constantinople (553)

Justinian called the Council, explaining its purpose in a letter read at its first session as 'to unite the churches again, and to bring the Synod of Chalcedon, together with the three earlier, to universal acceptance'.[63] A series of anathemas stressed the unity of Christ, and another series defended the distinction (but not separation or division) of the natures.[64]

Canon II ascribes two births to the God-Logos, the one from eternity from the Father, without time and without body, and the other his being made flesh of the holy and glorious Mary, Mother

[58] Wesche, *Christology of Justinian*, p. 165.
[59] Ibid., p. 166.
[60] Ibid., p. 178.
[61] Ibid., p. 179.
[62] Grillmeier, *Christ in Christian Tradition 2*, p. 438.
[63] Percival, *Seven Ecumenical Councils*, p. 302.
[64] Davis, *Councils*, pp. 244–246; Sellers, *Chalcedon*, p. 330; Hardy, *Later Fathers*, pp. 378–381.

of God. The next three Canons are all strongly anti-Nestorian. Canon III says that the God-Logos who works miracles and the Christ who suffered should not be separated, for it is one and the same Jesus Christ our Lord, the Word, who became flesh and a human being.[65] Behind this is the fact that Christ's unity is a true union, not a mingling or division. Canon V asserts that there is only one subsistence or person. The incarnation is to be seen solely from the hypostasis of the Son who is one of the Trinity. Thus 'one of the trinity has been made man'. Canon VIII, on the other hand guards against monophysitism, pronouncing that both natures remain what they were: 'For in teaching that the only-begotten Word was united hypostatically [to humanity] we do not mean to say that there was made a mutual confusion of natures, but rather each [nature] remaining what it was, we understand that the Word was united to flesh.'[66] Canon IX declares that the worshipping of Christ in two natures is in fact one act of worship directed to the incarnate God-Logos with his flesh.[67] Grillmeier concludes that Constantinople II is 'not a weakening of Chalcedonian terminology, but its logical clarification ... Nevertheless the use and application of the main concepts were clearer and more unambiguous than at Chalcedon'.[68]

Summary of the Christological crisis

In summary, the church's mature reflection, tempered by long years of conflict and sometimes misunderstanding, was that in the incarnation the Son took into personal union a human nature which from the moment of conception was his own. That humanity has no independent existence by itself; it was and always is the humanity of the Son of God. Therefore we cannot divide the person of Christ.

On the other hand, his humanity remains humanity and must not be confused with his deity even while it exists solely as the humanity of God the Son. Underlying all this is *both* the creator-creature distinction, which is inviolate, *and also* the compatibility of God and man, both features that exist in the creation of man in the image of God.

Moreover, by being solely the humanity of the eternal Son of God, Christ's flesh and soul are permeated with the glorious qualities of

---

[65] Grillmeier, *Christ in Christian Tradition 2*, p. 446; Percival, *Seven Ecumenical Councils*, p. 312.

[66] Percival, *Seven Ecumenical Councils*, p. 313.

[67] Percival, *Seven Ecumenical Councils*, pp. 314–316; Grillmeier, *Christ in Christian Tradition*, 2:2, pp. 447–453.

[68] Grillmeier, *Christ in Christian Tradition 2*, p. 456.

the Son, accommodated to human compass. It is obvious that this in no way was ever held to jeopardize their integrity as *human* nature. The compatibility of man as created with God underlies this.

These conclusions were reached in response to ideas that threatened the gospel. The church recognized that for us and our salvation a genuine incarnation had to take place. Contrary to overwhelming pressures from the ancient religious and philosophical environment to think of God as too high to get involved with the mire and mess of human life, the church affirmed that the Son – one with the Father from eternity – came among us as man, lived a fully human life and remains so forever. In contrast to the notion that the divine and creaturely are mixed into one – as eggs, flour and milk are merged and become pancakes – the church affirmed that the humanity of Christ remains human and is not absorbed or merged into something else, for if that were so we could not be saved, as our humanity would not then remain. In all these struggles, the church never saw itself as innovating but rather as confessing the faith delivered by Christ through the apostles and recorded in the pages of the New Testament.

Study Guide

HOW TO USE THIS STUDY GUIDE

The aim of this study guide is to help you get to the heart of what Robert Letham has written and challenge you to apply what you learn to your own life. The questions have been designed for use by individuals or by small groups of Christians meeting, perhaps for an hour or two each week, to study, discuss and pray together. When used by a group with limited time, the leader should decide beforehand which questions are most appropriate for the group to discuss during the meeting and which should perhaps be left for group members to work through by themselves or in smaller groups during the week.

PREVIEW. Use the guide and the contents pages as a map to become familiar with what you are about to read, your 'journey' through the book.

READ. Look up the Bible passages as well as the text.

ANSWER. As you read look for the answers to the questions in the guide.

DISCUSS. Even if you are studying on your own try to find another person to share your thoughts with.

REVIEW. Use the guide as a tool to remind you what you have learned. The best way of retaining what you learn is to write it down in a notebook or journal.

APPLY. Translate what you have learned into your attitudes and actions, considering your relationship with God, your personal life, your family life, your working life, your church life, your role as a citizen and your world-view.

Introduction (pp. 21–23)

1. What is (and is not) the purpose of this book (pp. 21–22)?
2. Why does the author describe the writing of the book 'simultaneously the best of times and the worst of times' (pp. 22–23)?

Introduction and Prologue (pp. 25–33)
Genesis 1:26–28; 3:13

1 How has the plurality in God in Genesis 1:26–27 been interpreted and how does it shape our understanding of Adam as the image of God (pp. 25–27)?
2 What stylistic feature in Genesis 1 draws attention to the creation of humanity (p. 27)?
3 Where is the creation of humans in the image of God highlighted in the New Testament and what implications can be drawn from it (pp. 28–29)?
4 What do John 1, Colossians 1, Ephesians 1 and Revelation 5 add to our understanding of Christ as Creator (pp. 29–30)?
5 How did God communicate with Adam before the fall (pp. 30–31)?
6 Why should we understand Adam's state in Genesis 2 in terms of covenant (pp. 31–32)?
7 Why is Genesis 3 a 'sorry tale' (pp. 32–33)?

PART 1. CHRIST PROMISED

Genesis 3:15
1. The offspring of the woman (pp. 37–40)

1 How should we interpret 'the serpent' and what is intended by the references to 'offspring' and 'bruising' in this verse (pp. 37–39)?

'The name "Satan" means adversary, opponent. Satan opposes the human race largely by promoting discord and conflict. Daniel 10 – 11 provides a glimpse behind the scenes of world history, vast angelic powers in constant combat impacting the course of international politics, the rise and fall of kingdoms and empires' (p. 38).

---

2 In what ways was Christ's victory to compare and contrast with Adam's defeat (pp. 39–40)?

Genesis 12:1–3
2. The seed of Abraham (pp. 41–46)

1 What evidence is there that Abram's call was entirely from the side of God (pp. 41–43)?
2 What promises did God make to Abram and why did they call for faith (pp. 43–44)?

3 How are God's promises to Abram brought into both broader and narrower focus as scripture unfolds (pp. 44–45)?

4 Is Paul justified in identifying Christ with the promised offspring (pp. 45–46)?

2 Samuel 7; Psalm 110
3. The son of David (pp. 47–51)

1 While the logic of King David and Nathan the prophet was faultless, why was Nathan's response countermanded by God (pp. 47–48)?

2 How can the oracle from Yahweh be divided and what evidence is there of a covenant theme (pp. 48–49)?

3 What does Psalm 110 add to the parameters of Davidic kingship (pp. 49–51)?

Isaiah 7:14–17; 9:6–7; 11:15; Micah 5:25
4. The great king (pp. 52–62)

1 What is the historical setting of Isaiah 7:14–17 (p. 52)?

2 Was Ahaz sincere in his refusal to accept the sign offered by Yahweh (pp. 52–53)?

3 What features highlight the unusual nature of the promise (pp. 53–54)?

4 How do the names ascribed to the promised child add to our understanding (pp. 55–57)?

'No, Yahweh was not going to leave matters in the hands of wicked King Ahaz, or Assyria, or Babylon, or anyone else for that matter. He was to give his people his true King, born of a woman, born in Judah, born of David's line, who would receive his kingdom, a rule that would increase "till all his creatures own his sway"' (p. 57).

---

5 Why does Isaiah refer to 'the stump of Jesse' rather than 'the house of David' (p. 58)?

6 How is the 'amazing change' in the stump of Jesse developed (pp. 59–61)?

7 In what two ways does Micah's prophey narrow the focus on the coming ruler (pp. 77–79)?

8 How significant is the image of a shepherd and his flock (pp. 61–62)?

Isaiah 41 – 50
5. The Servant of the Lord (1) (pp. 63–68)

1 What different possibilities for the identity of the Servant are suggested by these chapters (p. 63)?
2 In what ways might Isaiah 42:1–9 be interpreted with reference to (a) Cyrus, (b) Jesus (pp. 63–64)?
3 What evidence is there that Isaiah 49:1–6 refers to Isaiah himself and what elements indicate a larger trajectory (pp. 64–66)?
4 What possible interpretations of Isaiah 50:4–9 can be ruled out (pp. 66–67)?
5 How did Jesus fulfil the constituent parts of this prophecy (pp. 67–68)?

Isaiah 52:13 – 53:12
6. The Servant of the Lord (pp. 69–78)

1 Why is Isaiah 52:13 – 53:12 best applied to Jesus and on what grounds might that interpretation be dismissed (p. 69)?
2 What contrast is presented in Isaiah 52:13–15 (p. 70)?
3 How does the response of Israel differ from that of the Gentiles and why (pp. 70–71)?
4 On what grounds was Jesus rejected by the good and the great and how is it anticipated in Isaiah 53:3 (pp. 71–72)?
5 How should we understand the relationship between sin and suffering and how is the death of the Servant related in verse 7 (pp. 72–74)?
6 In what way is sheep imagery in verse 7 used differently of the Servant compared to its use in verse 6 (p. 74)?

'He was innocent and so deserved no punishment at all. It is clear that the Servant could not be Israel, whose guilt is placarded across virtually every page of the OT. Nor could it even be Isaiah, who had confessed that he was a man of unclean lips (Isa. 6:5). As for the alleged 'Deutero-Isaiah', where on earth was such a person, other than in the imaginations of a coterie of OT scholars carried away with their own hypotheses? This servant cannot be found, even from the most diligent search of the OT or other ancient literature. His identity is only established in the record we have of the life and death of Jesus Christ' (p. 75).

---

7 In what ways are the trial and burial of Jesus prefigured in verses 8–9 (pp. 74–75)?

8 What ultimately was (and was not) the purpose behind the Servant's death (pp. 75–76)?

9 What is implicit in the Servant's seeing his offspring, verse 11, and what will be the results (pp. 76–77)?

10 How is the metaphor of the *spoil* in verse 12 to be understood (pp. 77–78)?

PART 2. CHRIST INCARNATE

Luke 1:26–38
7. Birth announcement (pp. 81–88)

1 Why is the announcement of Christ's birth linked to the future task and identity of John (p. 81)?

2 What contrast is presented by the mission and message of Gabriel (p. 82)?

3 How should we understand Mary's relationship to the grace of God (pp. 82–83)?

4 What features of Gabriel's announcement underline the surpassing greatness of Jesus (pp. 83–84)?

5 What was the motive for Mary's question in verse 34 (pp. 84–85)?

6 Why was the angel's answer in verse 35 expressed in poetic terms and how does it relate to the creation account in Genesis 1 (pp. 85–86)?

7 What reassurance was given to Mary and what can we learn from her response (pp. 86–88)?

Luke 2:41–52
8. Growth and development (pp. 89–95)

1 What was the significance of the *bar-mitzvah* (p. 89)?

2 How could Jesus not have been missed by his parents and how could his action have been misinterpreted (pp. 89–90)?

3 What was (and was not) Jesus' attitude in his dialogue with the rabbis (p. 91)?

4 Where do we see the impact of the Holy Spirit at this stage of Jesus' life and what was unique about his consciousness of sonship (pp. 92–93)?

5 In what ways did Jesus develop as a human being and what conclusions can we draw from these facts (pp. 93–95)?

Matthew 3:13–17
9. Baptism (pp. 96–101)

1 Is there any significance in Jesus' arriving from Galilee (p. 96)?
2 Why was John reluctant to baptize Jesus and why did Jesus insist on being baptized (pp. 96–97)?
3 Why did Jesus say his baptism ws 'fitting to fulfil all righteousness' (pp. 97–98)?

'The Spirit's descent seals the fact that Jesus' public ministry is to be a new creation. Moreover, while the Spirit of God in the OT was sometimes associated with the fire of judgment, here he is seen in the form of a harmless dove, possibly denoting the fact that Jesus had come to save, to deliver the poor and afflicted' (pp. 99–100).

---

4 What were the four sequels to Jesus' baptism and what lessons can we draw from them (pp. 98–101)?
5 What is the relationship between baptism in water and baptism in the Spirit and how does the baptism of Jesus help us to define it (pp. 99–100)?
6 What light is thrown on the identity of Jesus by the voice from heaven (p. 100)?
7 How does this incident help us in our understanding of the Trinity (p. 101)?

Hebrews 2:10–18
10. Human experience (pp. 102–110)

1 What is an *archēgos* and what analogy can help us to understand it (p. 102)?
2 How does the writer to the Hebrews understand salvation and sanctification (pp. 103–104)?
3 What light does Psalm 22 throw on the author's argument at this point (p. 104)?
4 Why does the author of Hebrews cite passages from Isaiah and how do they contribute to his argument (pp. 104–105)?
5 In what ways were the temptations of Jesus different from ours and in what way were they the same (pp. 106–107)?

'Indeed, no one faced temptation like he did since no one resisted it as he did. Like walking into the force of a gale, the wind's power is more strongly felt than if one simply goes with the flow. Jesus'

persistent, complete and comprehensive faithfulness to the Father meant that he experienced the force of temptation more graphically and urgently than any of us could ever do' (p. 107).

6 What evidence is there that Jesus' sufferings were not restricted to the cross (p. 107)?
7 To what extent was the death of Jesus the same kind as ours and how was it different (p. 108)?
8 Why might the death of Jesus seem a contradiction of what was said earlier about him and what made it effective (pp. 108–109)?
9 What does it mean (and not mean) that Jesus was *made perfect through suffering* (pp. 109–110)?
10 What is the relationship between our sonship and Christ's (p. 110)?

John 1:1–5
11. The deity of Christ (pp. 111–117)

1 How does the beginning of John's Gospel compare with that of Matthew, Mark and Luke (p. 111)?
2 Which Old Testament passage is reflected in the opening of John's Gospel and how do verb tenses help us to understand that context (pp. 111–112)?
3 What does John mean by *the Word* and why does he use this term (p. 112)?
4 Does the grammar of John 1:1 allow the interpretation put forward by the Jehovah's Witnesses (pp. 113–114)?
5 Which Old Testament and New Testament passages confirm John's assertion that the Word made the universe (pp. 114–115)?
6 What is implied by the statement, 'In him is life' (pp. 115–116)?
7 How should we understand the metaphor of light in this context (p. 116)?
8 Did Jesus himself confirm this high view of his deity (pp. 116–117)?

John 1:14–18
12. The Word became flesh (pp. 118–123)

1 Why is the use of the verb *became* in verse 14 remarkable and how does it differ from its use earlier in the chapter (pp. 118–119)?
2 What should we understand by the Word becoming flesh (pp. 119–120)?
3 Who are the witnesses to Christ's glory (pp. 167–169)?

4 In what way is Christ's glory different than might have been expected (pp. 121–122)?

5 Which reading has greater textual support, 'only begotten of God' or 'only begotten Son' (p. 122)?

Hebrews 1:1–14
13. The supremacy of the Son (pp. 124–130)

1 Who wrote the letter to the Hebrews and why was it written (p. 124)?

2 What evidence is there that Old Testament revelation was piecemeal and incomplete (p. 125)?

3 In what senses was Jesus a prophet and yet more than a prophet (pp. 125–126)?

4 How does the Son of God radiate the Father's glory and represent his being (p. 127)?

5 What impact does Christ's role in creation have on the relationship between Christianity and science (pp. 127–128)?

6 What 'scene shift' takes place within Hebrews 1:3 (p. 128)?

'As the Son, he is perfectly equipped to be our mediator and deliverer. He is the chief and the final prophet, greater than a prophet since he is one with God the Father. He is the great high priest who has made atoning sacrifice for sin once for all and so cleansed his people from the guilt and defilement that this had brought. As our high priest and mediator he is also king, seated at the right hand of the Father, the creator and sustainer of the universe' (p. 129).

---

7 What indications are there that salvation is a finished work and how does that contrast with the Old Testament (pp. 128–129)?

8 What influence contemporary with the original readers may the author be countering and in what way (pp. 129–130)?

Philippians 2:6–8
14. Suffering servant (pp. 131–137)

1 What problem was Paul addressing in his letter to the Philippians and how did he respond to it (pp. 131–132)?

2 Why would a crucified Christ be so unacceptable to a citizen of Philippi (p. 132)?

3 How should we interpret the phrase *in the form of God* (p. 133)?

4 What are the three main interpretations of *harpagmos* and which appeals most to you (pp. 134–135)?
5 In what sense did Christ empty himself and where should we look for the background to this self-emptying (pp. 135–136)?
6 What point is Paul driving home in developing the concept of Christ's self-emptying (pp. 136–137)?

PART 3. CHRIST CRUCIFIED

Matthew 26:57 – 27:44
15. Jesus rejected and crucified (pp. 141–151)

1 What were the main factors influencing the Sanhedrin when they met to try Jesus (pp. 141–142)?
2 Why was the claim of the false witnesses considered to be so serious (p. 142)?
3 How did Jesus and Caiaphas differ in their view of the title *Christ the Son of God* (pp. 142–143)?
4 Why did the Sanhedrin send Jesus to the Roman authorities for trial and on what grounds (pp. 143–145)?
5 Why was the release of Barabbas and the condemnation of Jesus such an injustice (pp. 145–146)?
6 In what senses do the trial and suffering of Jesus represent both justice and injustice (pp. 146–148)?
7 What indications are given that Jesus was exhausted to the point of collapse and why did he refuse the sedative (pp. 148–149)?
8 How did those who witnessed Christ's crucifixion react and how significant were those reactions (pp. 150–151)?

Matthew 27:45–56
16. The death of Jesus (pp. 152–158)

1 What Old Testament backgrounds are suggested by the supernatural darkness that occurred at the crucifixion (pp. 152–153)?
2 What possible interpretations have been suggested for the offering of wine vinegar to Jesus and which seems more likely to you (pp. 153–154)?
3 What are the 'two astounding actions' in verse 50 (pp. 154–155)?
4 Why is the tearing of the temple curtain significant (pp. 155–156)?
5 What should we conclude from the phenomena in the natural world (p. 156)?

6 What five conclusions can be drawn from the resurrection appearances described in verses 52–53 (pp. 156–157)?

7 Why is the focus on the soldiers and the women noteworthy (pp. 157–158)?

Matthew 27:57–66
17. The burial of Jesus (pp. 159–163)

1 What do we learn about Joseph from Matthew's account of him and his actions (pp. 159–160)?

'In all this, where were the disciples, the eleven whom Jesus had chosen? Nowhere to be seen! Everything was too much for them. They proved unreliable and fickle; it would take a supernatural effusion of the Holy Spirit to put this right. At root, however, it was necessary that they should fail like that. Jesus had to suffer alone, to die alone, to be buried in obscurity. There could be no inkling of any other person sharing in these events, for this was the work of the Son of God and only he could put right the consequences of human sin' (p. 161).

---

2 What do the details recorded by Matthew indicate about Jesus' burial (pp. 160–161)?

3 Why did the Jewish authorities request such tight security on the tomb (pp. 161–162)?

4 In what ways was the burial of Jesus of significance (pp. 162–163)?

PART 4. Christ risen

Matthew 28:1–15
18. The empty tomb (pp. 167–173)

1 'We never see the bomb explode.' What does the writer mean by this (p. 167)?

2 Where does the emphasis lie in the accounts of the resurrection (pp. 167–168)?

3 Who were the first to visit Jesus' tomb and why did they not go immediately (p. 168)?

4 What is the significance of the earthquake and the appearance of the angel (pp. 169–170)?

5 The angel gave five encouragements followed by instructions. What were they (pp. 170–171)?

6 How did the women react to the angel's message (pp. 171–172)?

7 Is there a conflict between the accounts of Matthew and John (p. 172)?

8 What is striking about Jesus' appearance to the women in Matthew and how does it contrast with their encounter with the angel (pp. 172–173)?

Luke 24:13–49
19. The resurrection appearances (pp. 174–180)

1 What misunderstanding clouded the minds of the two disciples (pp. 174–175)?

2 Where did Jesus direct them to correct this misunderstanding (pp. 174–175)?

3 'The terminology [Luke] uses is sacramental.' What does this mean and what parallels can we find in the New Testament (p. 176)?

4 What factors contributed to the revealing of Christ's true identity (pp. 177–178)?

'While the Bible is capable of being studied academically, it has been given by God to the church not to the university. To approach the Scriptures – and particularly the OT – without reference to Christ is to misunderstand them and ultimately to abuse them. It is a blind alley that leads nowhere and the result is the blind – be they ever so clever and learned – leading the blind' (p. 179).

---

5 What elements of Christ's appearance to the disciples in Jerusalem indicate (a) continuity and (b) discontinuity with his pre-resurrection presence (pp. 178–179)?

6 'Both the text and the interpreter need the illumination of the Holy Spirit.' How is this illustrated in Luke 24 (pp. 179–180)?

1 Corinthians 15
20. Paul on Christ's resurrection (pp. 181–190)

1 What does Paul insist upon as the fundamentals of Christian faith and life (pp. 181–182)?

2 Why did resurrection pose a problem for many at Corinth and how did Paul underline its importance (pp. 182–183)?

3 Who were the witnesses to the resurrection cited by Paul and why were they significant (pp. 183–185)?

4 What further reason does Paul give in verses 12–19 for the importance of Christ's resurrection (p. 185)?

5 How is the concept of Christ's resurrection as *first fruits* developed (pp. 185–187)?

6 What analogies does Paul draw on in explaining the nature of the resurrection body (pp. 187–188)?

7 Why is Adam introduced into the argument (pp. 188–190)?

8 What transformation will take place at the Christian's resurrection (p. 190)?

PART 5. Christ ascended

Luke 25:50–53; Acts 1:6–11
21. The ascension (pp. 193–207)

1 Which sections of the Old Testament form the background to the ascension and what conclusion can we draw from them (pp. 195–196)?

2 What are the three salient features of the ascension as described in Luke's Gospel and what do they teach us (p. 195)?

3 Why is the mention of the cloud 'more than merely a weather report' (pp. 196–197)?

4 How was the experience of Elisha paralleled in that of the disciples (pp. 197–198)?

5 What are the opposite dangers in our interpretation of the ascension (pp. 198–199)?

6 Should we think of the ascension as the final resurrection appearance of Jesus (p. 199)?

'We are seated with him in heavenly places (Eph. 2:6–7), in the closest union and communion with Christ, reigning with him even as we suffer and struggle in our present condition. This is a pledge of our ultimate salvation, a tonic in the face of dispiriting circumstances, a vast encouragement to faithfulness to Christ and to perseverance in adversity' (p. 200).

---

7 How is Christ's ascension connected with us (pp. 199–200)?

8 What are the elements of Christ's three-fold priestly ministry and what is distinctive about them (pp. 200–202)?

9 Where do we find references to the ascension in the writings of John, Peter, Paul and the author of Hebrews (pp. 203–204)?

10 Why is the ascension crucial to Christ's reign as king (pp. 204–205)?

11 How far is it appropriate to describe Christ as a prophet and how does the ascension relate to his prophetic ministry (p. 205)?

12 What impact does the ascension have on our present life (pp. 205–207)?

Colossians 1:15–20
22. Lord of creation, head of the church (pp. 208–215)

1 What are the arguments for and against the concept of pre-existence in this passage and which is more convincing to you (pp. 208–210)?

2 How should we interpret the term *firstborn* in this context (p. 210)?

3 What elements of creation are included in Christ's creative work (pp. 210–211)?

4 What is the extent of Christ's role in providence and how should it impact our lives (p. 211)?

5 What are the implications of Christ's headship over the church and why is his resurrection so key to it (p. 211)?

6 What does the title *Lord* confirm about Christ's identity (pp. 213–214)?

7 Why was reconciliation necessary and how was it accomplished (pp. 214–215)?

Hebrews 2:5–9
23. Everlasting ruler of the renewed cosmos (pp. 216–220)

1 Why did the author of Hebrews need to stress the supremacy of Christ (p. 216)?

2 In what sense is the world to come already present and why is it not fully present (p. 217)?

3 What is 'astounding' about the rule of the future world (p. 217)?

4 In what three ways is humanity described by the psalmist (p. 218)?

'Between the lofty grandeur of Psalm 8 and the reality of our present state – with seemingly intractable environmental problems, discord at national and personal levels, terrorism, murder and hatred, to say nothing of gruesome diseases – there is a huge and seemingly unbridgeable gulf. We do not yet experience the fulfilment of our God-given destiny. We do not yet appear as the king of creation. Above all, we cannot control ourselves due to sin' (p. 219).

---

5 What scene-shift is brought into focus in verses 8 and 9 (p. 219)?
6 What is a chiasmus and how is it used and developed in this passage (pp. 219–220)?
7 In what way has Christ fulfilled human destiny (pp. 219–220)?

Revelation 1:9–20
24. The Living One (pp. 221–228)

1 What distinguishes John from all kinds of false prophets (p. 221)?
2 Where in the Old Testament do we find the background to John's vision of Christ and how does that influence our interpretation of it (pp. 222–223)?
3 What do the different elements of the description of Christ signify (pp. 222–224)?
4 Who are the angels of the seven churches (pp. 224–225)?
5 Why are Christ's words described in terms of 'a sharp two-edged sword' (p. 225)?
6 How did John react to the vision and where in scripture do we find similar reactions (pp. 225–226)?
7 What reassurances did John receive (pp. 226–227)?
8 What is the enduring challenge of the book of Revelation (pp. 227–228)?

Appendix
Did the church get it wrong? *Who* is Jesus Christ?
From Nicaea (AD 325) to Constantinople II (AD 553) (pp. 229–246)

1 What is *modalism* and what danger does it present (pp. 229–230)?

'*Early in the fourth century the church was forced to consider how Jesus Christ was related to God. A number of problems were ticking like time-bombs, destined sooner or later to explode. The chief of these was how to reconcile the unity of the one God with the status of Christ.*' (p. 229).

---

2 What is *subordinationism* and why was it so influential in the early centuries of the church (p. 230)?
3 What views were promoted by Arius and which Council outlawed them (pp. 230–231)?

4 What influence did Eunomius of Cyzicus have and how did his opponents respond (pp. 231–233)?

5 Who were the Cappadocians and what was their contribution to the debate (p. 233)?

6 What did Nestorius teach and how was it countered by Cyril of Alexandria (pp. 233–236)?

7 What was wrong with the position adopted by Eutyches and how was it dealt with by the Council of Chalcedon (pp. 236–239)?

8 How should we assess the legacy of the Council of Chalcedon (pp. 239–240)?

9 How far is the analogy of a baking recipe helpful in understanding the Christological debates of the early church (pp. 240–241)?

10 What contributions to resolving the post-Chalcedon Christological problem were made by Leontius of Byzantium, Leontius of Jerusalem and Justinian I (pp. 241–244)?

11 What affirmations were made by the second Council of Constantinople (pp. 244–245)?

12 What are the pitfalls in defining the person of Christ and how can they best be avoided (pp. 245–246)?

The Bible Speaks Today: Old Testament series

The Message of Genesis 1 – 11
The dawn of creation
David Atkinson

The Message of Genesis 12 – 50
From Abraham to Joseph
Joyce G. Baldwin

The Message of Exodus
The days of our pilgrimage
Alec Motyer

The Message of Leviticus
Free to be holy
Derek Tidball

The Message of Numbers
Journey to the promised land
Raymond Brown

The Message of Deuteronomy
Not by bread alone
Raymond Brown

The Message of Judges
Grace abounding
Michael Wilcock

The Message of Ruth
The wings of refuge
David Atkinson

The Message of Samuel
*Personalities, potential, politics
and power*
Mary Evans

The Message of Kings
God is present
John W. Olley

The Message of Chronicles
One church, one faith, one Lord
Michael Wilcock

**The Message of Ezra and
Haggai**
Building for God
Robert Fyall

The Message of Nehemiah
God's servant in a time of change
Raymond Brown

The Message of Esther
God present but unseen
David G. Firth

The Message of Job
Suffering and grace
David Atkinson

**The Message of Psalms
1 – 72**
Songs for the people of God
Michael Wilcock

**The Message of Psalms
73 – 150**
Songs for the people of God
Michael Wilcock

The Message of Proverbs
Wisdom for life
David Atkinson

The Message of Ecclesiastes
*A time to mourn, and a time to
dance*
Derek Kidner

**The Message of the Song of
Songs**
The lyrics of love
Tom Gledhill

The Message of Isaiah
On eagles' wings
Barry Webb

The Bible Speaks Today: New Testament series

The Message of the Sermon on the Mount (Matthew 5– 7)
Christian counter-culture
John Stott

The Message of Matthew
The kingdom of heaven
Michael Green

The Message of Mark
The mystery of faith
Donald English

The Message of Luke
The Saviour of the world
Michael Wilcock

The Message of John
Here is your King!
Bruce Milne

The Message of Acts
To the ends of the earth
John Stott

The Message of Romans
God's good news for the world
John Stott

The Message of 1 Corinthians
Life in the local church
David Prior

The Message of 2 Corinthians
Power in weakness
Paul Barnett

The Message of Galatians
Only one way
John Stott

The Message of Ephesians
God's new society
John Stott

The Message of Philippians
Jesus our Joy
Alec Motyer

The Message of Colossians and Philemon
Fullness and freedom
Dick Lucas

The Message of Thessalonians
Preparing for the coming King
John Stott

The Message of 1 Timothy and Titus
The life of the local church
John Stott

The Message of 2 Timothy
Guard the gospel
John Stott

The Message of Hebrews
Christ above all
Raymond Brown

The Message of James
The tests of faith
Alec Motyer

The Message of 1 Peter
The way of the cross
Edmund Clowney

The Message of 2 Peter and Jude
The promise of his coming
Dick Lucas and Christopher Green

The Message of John's Letters
Living in the love of God
David Jackman

The Message of Revelation
I saw heaven opened
Michael Wilcock